THIS BRIEFCASE IS NOT GOING TO EXPLODE

A GREAT BRITISH KERFUFFLE

ASIF RANA

ALIKSIR PRESS

To my dear parents, who sacrificed and endured much.

I wish I'd concocted a good number of anecdotes in this book. But alas, no. I've had to tweak a few names, dates, and places for obvious reasons. Frankly, life is too short for all the paperwork, and you know who you are.

Those who know me, may raise an eyebrow, or two, at some of the industrial language used within this book. Alas, again, it's not possible to faithfully narrate the story without repeating a (very) small sample.

O mankind! We created you from a male and female, and have made you into nations and tribes that you may know one another. Truly, the noblest of you, in the sight of God, is the one best in conduct.

— [QUR'AN 49:13]

CONTENTS

Preface   ix

1. In the Beginning   1
2. Teenage Training   31
3. A Few Academic Matters   55
4. Road to Exit   81
5. Eastward Migration   117
6. Back to Blighty   148
7. Workplace Gymnastics   183
8. Cultural and Religious Nuance   208
9. The Algorithm of Chaos   247
10. Back Home   264

Notes   277
Acknowledgments   281
About the Author   285

PREFACE

The year is 1993, and the month September, the start of my first
year at Manchester University. I bid a crisp farewell to my elder
brother as I clamber onto a rickety brown coach at Burnley Bus
Station. I'm carrying a small brown suitcase and two Head sports
bags crammed with clothes, books, toiletries and plastic containers
with a few days' supply of oily chicken curry. As I settle into my
seat, I'm overcome with a sense of tremendous excitement, anxiety
and relief. Excitement at the adventure ahead at university (though
perhaps not the studying pure mathematics for three years bit).
Anxiety at the possibility the containers in my sports bag crack
open and splatter *ghee* all over my t-shirts (*ghee* is notoriously tricky
to remove from clothes). And finally, relief, an overwhelming,
palpable relief that the hard, abusive and racist days growing up in
Burnley were well behind me. I push back into the coach seat and
recline my head. Yes, pristine skies and calm waters lay ahead for
me. My life was about to get a whole lot easier. I lean forward again
and remove the fresh chewing gum strands from the back of my
coat.

Growing up in Burnley in the 70s and 80s (more the 80s for
me, thankfully) wasn't for the faint of heart. Actually, sub 30

beats/min Tour de France cyclists would probably have struggled, even with a little creative medical assistance. Burnley and the surrounding towns in the north offered an unforgiving blend of poverty, derelict housing, poor schooling, anti-social behaviour and hooliganism, with a general lack of opportunities thrown in for good measure. If that wasn't sufficient, any off-white hue provided a tincture of additional excitement. It was raw, often violent, and terrifyingly racist.

We endured chants of black bastard, sambo, jigaboo, paki, coon, nigger, golly and/or wog, with Ali Baba a personal favourite. Curiously, I remember collecting badges from Robertson's jam, but thought the Golly character a little gratuitous even back then. Jigaboo now sounds like a Teletubbies character before they existed. Though, on the positive side, you couldn't fault the creativity and richness of abuse. My well-thumbed and dishevelled Pocket Midland Bank Griffin Saver dictionary testified to the variety.

I learnt the old-fashioned way that most of the lads (and lasses) hurling abuse weren't interested in debating linguistic or geographical minutiae when I highlighted my Indian/Pakistani ancestry. Specific hues didn't matter much. We weren't white; that's all that mattered during those days. I suppose things were simpler. Sure, as nominal Muslims, we had mosques, we ate halal meat, Muslim women covered their hair, and we had our Friday prayers. But these practices and religious credal differences were merely a curiosity for most. Our specific, non-Caucasian, foreign ethnicity made us targets.

A tangible, positive change occurred by the time I'd navigated through Manchester University, and later Imperial College, during the mid to late 90s, certainly within the academic bubble. With large numbers of overseas students, it wasn't exactly the environment to openly chant the KKK manifesto or hurl abuse at foreigners. A few years later, though, on 11th September 2001, a cataclysmic bolt struck from the skies, and the world changed. There was a new game in town. My own sunny skies forecast was about to crumble like Harold Camping's 'End of the World' prediction back in '94. This inflectional event, followed by the two wars in Iraq and Afghanistan, a myriad of the most heinous atrocities and terrorist attacks, the seemingly never-ending problems in the Middle East, and the so-called 'Arab Spring', and suddenly you couldn't keep Muslims out of the news. The constant activity, negative media coverage, imagery and stereotypes all created a chasm of distrust between Muslims and the rest of the populace.

On the 10th of September 2001, I could happily fiddle with my shoe heel (or underwear) on an aeroplane, buy a heavy-duty rucksack and wander around the streets of London without let or hindrance, browse flight simulator games at my local computer store, give my phone battery a jolly good rub on a train, and shout 'Allahu Akbar' in a crowded place, all, without anyone batting an eyelid.

Though the backlash against Muslims, particularly in the West post 9/11, comprised more than raised eyebrows browsing the latest *Microsoft Flight Simulator* game at *PC World*, and more than a whole new genre of bad guys in Hollywood movies. State surveillance, stop and search, vigilante attacks and harassment against Muslims increased exponentially in Europe and America. George's 'War on Terror' felt a little like 'War on all things Islamic'. Even those who looked a bit like Muslims suffered, as the Sikh community found out. Muslims had gone from an oddball but benign community to front and centre Public Enemy Number 1. The word Muslim became a 'pejorative term', so quipped one of my work colleagues. He wasn't joking.

Fast forward another few years, and in the raw aftermath of 7/7, I knew students who swapped their university rucksacks for clear polystyrene bags while making exaggerated 'I'm really not a threat' movements on public transport (not that it helped much).

The plastic bags weren't great for the environment or for carrying books, but anyone could see you'd need a planet-sized brain to hide anything dangerous inside. Muslims shaved their beards, as though participating in sheep shearing contests, sending Gillette shaving gel sales rocketing. Women removed their hijabs and niqabs for fear of random attack. Muhammads became Mos, Bilals Billies, Jameels Jimmies, and Khans Caans (I know a Billy Caan), all attempting to lower their profile.

Now, on the Venn diagram of 'let's beat this one with a cosh', I'm only surrounded by a couple of circles, unlike my black, Muslim, hijab-wearing sister (try drawing that). Thankfully, I've also got thick skin and a strong back. Growing up on the streets of Burnley will do that to a boy. I'm not the vulnerable lady in hijab smashed with a baseball bat by a thug on her way home from work, or the old man stabbed through the chest on his way to the mosque for morning prayers. Thuggery, suspicion, and surveillance on one side, and the general possibility of being caught up in an attack along with everyone else on the other; yes, the nail bomb doesn't discriminate.

And so, to this book. What's it like growing up as a non-Caucasian chap of Pakistani heritage in modern-day Britain, before and after 9/11 and 7/7? What are some of the specific oddities and challenges faced? When do we practice the deft touch, the shimmy, the feint pass? How has living here changed over the years? How do we navigate the pitfalls of modern life while adhering to our faith? This book isn't an encyclopaedia documenting every unpleasant incident I've ever experienced in Britain. That'd be boring, and I'm pretty sure I'd lose in a game of 'Tough Times Top Trumps'. It's not intended to generate sympathy, either. We don't want the victim label.

Though, I do hope this book gives the reader a glimpse behind the media headlines, a knowledge of 'the other', an insight into the life and experiences of a second-generation immigrant, a brown, practising Muslim living in the UK. Challenges and experiences most likely oblivious to the average, non-Muslim white reader in particular. There's an astonishing amount taken for granted. Some of the incidents and experiences described are bizarre, some humorous, and others just downright depressing.

I've shared many of these anecdotes with colleagues over the years, often greeted with shrieks of laughter and incredulity at how people can mistakenly interpret seemingly innocuous and harmless actions. Particularly, if the protagonist happens to be a sizeable 'person of colour' with a long beard.

So, as the Queen said, 'Off with his head...' Actually, no, as the King said, 'Let's begin at the beginning...'

1. IN THE BEGINNING

Help ægðer ge cuðum ge uncuþum þær þu mæge.
'Help both friends and strangers wherever you can.'

— OLD ENGLISH DICTS OF CATO

In 1962, as part of the ongoing post-war Commonwealth immigration drive, my father landed on this green and sceptred isle equipped with rudimentary English skills, a brown suitcase, and two tattered plastic carrier bags bulging with clothes. His first time away from Pakistan, a stranger in a foreign land, he was ready for whatever challenges lay ahead, no matter how unsavoury: manual labour, cotton mill work, refuse collection, sewage cleaning. In short, the morass of jobs nobody else fancied.

Britain welcomed the first waves of immigrants, though admittedly without children waving flags and singing in the streets. However, the welcome and niceties didn't last long. Fast forward a few years, and community tension, along with resentment to migrant numbers (miniscule by today's standards) entering the country was increasing. Six years later, Enoch Powell stood in the

Birmingham Conservative Political Centre, in full fiery flow, delivering his infamous *Rivers of Blood* speech:

> 'In 15- or 20-years' time, the black man will have the whip hand over the white man... As I look ahead, I am filled with foreboding. Like the Roman, I seem to see the River Tiber foaming with much blood.'

The Times declared it 'an evil speech', stating, 'This is the first time that a serious British politician has appealed to racial hatred in this direct way in our post-war history.'

Enoch, clearly detached from that great sage[1], apparently skipped history lessons at school, too. Nonetheless, his reference to the Aeneid[2] achieved its objective. Powell's emotive and incendiary language roused passions, and craftily tuned to the frequency of fear and insecurity amongst a proportion of the British populace. The speech successfully laid the foundations. A sharp upturn in race crimes followed, along with a new lexicon (including Paki-bashing). His speech also provided the lubricant for government change a few years later, despite his own expulsion from the Conservative Party.

As Enoch delivered his speech to a captivated audience on that April day in 1968, some 5000 miles eastward, my mother could barely contain her own excitement. She was packing her suitcases, ready to board a PIA plane and begin her new life in Britain.

What great timing.

1.1 VILLAGE 247

Let's rewind a little. My father was born in a tiny village within the city of Lyallpur (now Faisalabad), pre-partition India, circa June 1942. Well, we think it was around that time; we're not sure. As in most of the country during that period, records of births, deaths and marriages were not kept, and certainly not for the common folk.

The village, *Chak Tho-So Santhali* (Punjabi: Village 247), nestles in the heart of the city, the naming convention surreptitiously clever, if not a little sterile, a postal code and town name rolled into one. Similar to other numbered villages in the region, life in Village 247 offered a prescriptive, simple existence, as I found when we visited some years later. A dash of blue paint adorned the clay constructed houses. A single school and small white mosque lay in the centre of the village while a maze of muddy tracks connected one end to the other, where cattle would roam and defecate freely (much to our bemusement and delight). However, best of all, guava, orange and banana plantations encompassed the village. As we discovered, few things could trump wandering into the orchards and wolfing two or three ripe oranges, while sitting in the shade. However, one had to be careful of snakes when plucking bananas.

Unsurprisingly, farming and trading were popular professions in the village. Parents would send the odd child showing a tincture of academic prowess to colleges in nearby towns. However, the hand to mouth existence for most meant this was rare. Families needed boys to work in the fields, and girls, while mostly considered an inconvenience, to prepare for motherhood and homemaker roles (though many worked the fields, too). Despite my grandfather's encouragement and strict disciplinarian standards, my father wasn't particularly interested in academic pursuits, often choosing to skip school and play marbles in the sand with his friends. Once he'd reached his mid-teens, my father joined his father in the fields and continued labouring for the next few years.

By contrast, my mother, born some ten years later, was raised in the much more cosmopolitan city of Lahore. Her father had served several years with the British Indian Army in the Burmese theatre of World War II. He proudly showed us his uniform and medals when we visited, which he kept with immaculacy in a small brown trunk with silver clasps. The family, despite modest means, all received a decent level of education due to his regimented and industrious approach to life. My mother completed all her early education in English. Quite a privilege. However, times were tough, and even in Lahore, girls were generally considered burdensome. As soon as they reached eligible age, it was customary to source suitable husbands.

1.2 MIGRATION & MARRIAGE

In 1961, my father's brother-in-law had just returned to the village with exotic tales of Pakistanis travelling westward for work, to Germany, Spain, Italy and the UK. Bizarrely, the local populations welcomed immigrants into these countries, with jobs in plentiful supply. More importantly, the workers were sending sackfuls of converted rupees back home, with large *kotiyah* (Punjabi: villas) sprouting in nearby villages as a result. My grandfather didn't need much further persuasion, truly a 'where do I sign?' moment. After a few months of borrowing, scraping together enough money and collecting paperwork from various government departments, my father and his brother-in-law were on their way, the whole process proving surprisingly simple.

The pair arrived in England and headed for Preston, a popular destination in the North West. Together with half a dozen other Pakistanis, they found a small, terraced house. Not long after, searching for employment, they found themselves working for a local chemical company, spending 12 hours a day mixing noxious, bubbling liquids for £9 and 4 shillings a week. They would wake at 05:00, ready for work at 06:00. The lack of any protective equipment resulted in daily burns and respiratory problems, long before the days of Health & Safety inspectors. They needed to save and send money home, their raison d'être in Britain. Though, at this rate, mixing potions, they weren't going to see out the month. They needed to find alternative employment.

While discussing their predicament over some homemade chicken (they both quickly became proficient cooks), word from the other housemates and the migrant community advised they should head east. Several international manufacturing businesses had opened sites in the area, enticing immigrants towards Burnley, a small town to the east of Preston.

At the turn of the 20th century, Burnley was one of the most affluent places in the world (I still repeat this to anyone who'll listen) and a powerhouse of the booming textile economy at the time. At one point, the number of power looms in the town exceeded its population. Alas, the First World War heralded the collapse of the textile industry, with the Second World War sealing its fate. However, with the post-war industrial boom, many other industries sprouted across the country, including in Burnley.

With the promise of safer, manual type work, the two packed their few belongings and jumped on the rickety coach. It wasn't long before they found a small house to share and employment at the (French) Michelin Tyre Company. It appeared they'd found their eutopia; a stable job earning more than enough for their costs, a small savings pot, and remittance back home. They'd also settled in with new English colleagues who found their work ethic refreshing and language skills amusing. My father had everything, almost. Detailed in the blue *par avion* letters from 'back home', pressure to find a suitable wife mounted. Several years had now passed, and my grandmother was keen that my father returned home to look for a wife. She wasn't enamoured with the prospect of a potential English daughter-in-law. So, in the summer of '66, my father returned home for the search, missing the World Cup Finals as a result.

In anticipation, my father's parents had selected a string of potential girls around the village. But with his new international, cosmopolitan vista, my father had developed exacting standards, and none satisfied his specification. The search needed widening to bordering villages and towns. A strapping, handsome 25-year-old from England certainly wasn't short of suitors. Women came and left disappointed over the course of many months. Word filtered across the extended family, and by chance, my mother's father got wind of the proposal, so arranged a meeting. He immediately spotted the lucrative proposition, particularly with the prospect of migration. The initial gathering between the two fathers and my father went well. In a successive meeting, my father also had the opportunity to meet my mother, with all parties seemingly happy. That left one final interview, the most important. At the tender age of 15, my mother had to make the perilous journey to Village 247.

After a three-hour journey on a dirt track, my mother and her parents arrived, dusty and dishevelled, at the village just after noon. A cabal of local women had gathered in the family home, ready for the interview process. For the next two hours, they prodded, poked and stared at my mother from excruciatingly close distance (eyes and complexion being all-important). It seemed these village women must be ophthalmologists and dermatologists, too. An intimidating experience for my mother, but one she knew she'd have to endure. Once they'd established her aesthetic and domestic suitability, matters turned to finance. How much dowry would my mother's family give? Would she be willing to travel to England? The meeting concluded late into the evening with all parties satisfied, and a marriage date agreed.

So, after a selection process worthy of the next Michelin CEO, nearly two full years after his return from England, my mother and father were finally married in February 1968. Unfortunately for my mother, she had to relocate to the village under the supervision of her new mother-in-law during the interim period. Her young age, combined with a lack of domestic experience, resulted in a torrid few months. To compound problems, my mother's family hadn't met dowry expectations, which became an ongoing source of jibes and attacks, alas sometimes physical. While my mother grappled with the stove, dusted the yard and tried to make herself useful, my father was busy collecting the necessary immigration paperwork. Thankfully for my mother, the immigration process operated more efficiently back in the 60s, and just a few months later, they were on their way to *Blighty*³ ready for a new life.

MY FATHER FELT a noticeable climate change arriving back in Britain post Enoch's speech. An uneasiness and tension between communities had developed, with increased skirmishes and violent demonstrations throughout the country. He'd experienced racism previously in Preston and Burnley, but the temperature had undeniably risen a few degrees. Even previous friendly *goray* (Punjabi: white folk) work colleagues now appeared aloof and curt.

For the first few years, my parents stayed with my father's sister and brother-in-law, who were also back in the country. They'd managed to buy a small, terraced house for a few hundred pounds. Pockets of immigrant communities started sprouting in Burnley, leading to an interesting dynamic between the two cultures. Finding housing, suitable or otherwise, became a significant challenge, with the common but pernicious view that 'Pakis would lower the value of house prices' so 'we don't want your lot round here'. Renting, too, became difficult, with landlords worried about 'smelly Pakis⁴ not washing', apparently 'happy to live in filth', disinterested in house maintenance and exhibiting 'unusual toilet habits' (more on that later).

Differences in culture and language, and general distrust, along with the objectional smell of freshly made curry wafting through the streets, all contributed to the uneasy dynamic. It'd take several more years before acceptance of the novel cuisine.

Among the drama and cooking, my father was busy saving. He eventually scraped £250 to buy a one-bedroomed terraced house within the neighbourhood. My mother felt overjoyed – finally, the Queen of her own home in England.

1.3 BURNLEY WOOD

In 1974, beneath the shadows of disbanded cotton mills and blackened monolithic chimneys, close to the serpentine Leeds-Liverpool canal, my parents took me home from the maternity ward to our single bedroomed, terraced house to join my sister, Tasneem, and brothers, Amjad and Sajad. Times were still tough. My father worked shifts at Michelin, so would sometimes wake at 04:00 to reach work for 06:00, accounting for the 2-mile walk. We couldn't afford a car. After a full day shifting heavy rubber tyres in the sweltering basement, he'd have the reciprocal journey home, dressed in thick, heavy overalls and black boots. Arriving home exhausted, he would eat and sleep almost immediately. The labour, while physically taxing, wasn't overly hazardous, as with the noxious chemicals, or at least that's what he thought.

In total, my father spent around 25 years working as a labourer for Michelin. The nature of the work eventually led to all manner of physical problems later in his life, mostly back and arthritis related. Though in the early 70s, at the height of his physical powers, he was 6'3" and weighed around 15 stones. He wasn't the type to be crossed, inside or outside work. His workmates quickly nicknamed him Cassius. He set the record for most tyres shifted in a single day, which stood until the factory closed in the early 2000s.

With my father busy working, my mother was left alone for most of the day to entertain four boisterous young children aged between one and five. The housework, along with cooking, became a welcome distraction in-between our napping. Given the paucity of opportunities, my mother seldom left the house, but described trips to the laundrette as a particular highlight. There she would meet other local women, who welcomed her into the washing club. The women found my mother a genuine curiosity due to her ethnicity, young age and gregarious personality. She always found it very easy to make friends with people from different races, a quality that remains today. Her willingness to speak broken English and her distinctive phraseology probably helped her cause.

We stayed in the same house for a few years before moving across town to a slightly grander place, though still in the general area. We now had the luxury of two bedrooms. My father slept in one room, while my mother and the four kids slept in the other, with my father arguing he needed a good night's sleep before work. He won the argument.

1.4 RUNNING THE MOSQUE GAUNTLET

In our youth, the weekday routine was worthy of first-year cadets at Sandhurst. Awake at 07:30, breakfast, ready for school, a half-mile walk, and in the school playground by 08:45. At midday, we'd walk back home for lunch. School finished at 15:00. My mother would ensure piping hot tea and biscuits (usually Jammie Dodgers or Custard Creams) or jam toast were on the table before we got home. We'd then be out the door by 15:45 for the trek to the mosque, where we'd spend a full two hours sitting cross-legged aside a wooden bench, before leaving for home at 18:00. I'd be on the sofa watching *Knight Rider* at 19:00. Rain or hail, snow or wind, summer or winter, this routine *never* deviated. Moreover, the mosque was more than a mile away. As a 5-year-old, the journey felt like trekking across the Gobi. It's a shame we didn't have step or calorie counters.

The mosque experience itself proved a thoroughly fascinating experiment in the 70s and 80s, as first-generation immigrants searched for a method to educate their children in cultural and religious practices. The mosques attempted to teach kids the Arabic script and Qur'an reading, including memorisation.

Within the mosque, the teacher sat in the middle of the room against one wall. Three long benches completed a circle ahead of him, where children sat and learnt portions of the Qur'an, usually cramming last minute revision. One by one, each child walked to the teacher and either recited the Qur'an from book or memory. Despite being only ten or fifteen feet, the distance often felt like walking across no man's land in lead boots, particularly if the student hadn't completed the requisite homework.

The mosque demanded military-grade discipline, too. Any reading or memorisation mistakes were rewarded with either a forceful slap across the face or, more usually, a rap across the knuckles or palm with a short wooden stick (bamboo often the wood of choice). I preferred the palms. The bamboo left a disturbingly sharp and lingering sting, along with white streaks. To avoid whips and slaps, I developed a sneaky method of transliterating Arabic words into English without the teacher realising, sometimes scribbling on my hands or the page.

On one occasion, I arrived to see the teacher manoeuvring a piece of long flexible plastic piping into the mosque (I assumed due to house renovations or similar). The extended tubing opened the possibilities of 10+ feet remote strikes. A genius move, I thought. Well, until I received a stinging *thack* on the top of my head. Regularly, the teacher felt like stretching his legs, and made a couple of room circuits with the compact bamboo in hand. That usually helped raise recital decibel levels and keep kids focussed.

More serious offences, such as habitual recital errors or excessive chatter, resulted in dispatching the individual (boy or girl – mosques practised strict gender equality) into the dreaded *Murga* position (Urdu: hen/chicken). The stress position was a popular method of softening and generally embarrassing kids. The *Murga* arrived on these shores from the Indian subcontinent, along with poppadoms, lamb rogan josh and Kabaddi. The stance had a few variations, but the most prevalent involved squatting with arms threaded through the legs so your fingers could touch your ears. It's rather difficult to describe, but I encourage the reader to search for a picture and replicate. The spectacle was held in the centre of the room for maximum embarrassment. It quickly became an endurance test. After a few seconds, lactic acid would build in the thighs. After a minute, the pain became severe, resulting in trembling flesh. If the teacher felt particularly aggrieved, he'd force the position for more than 5 minutes. The torture usually ended with a thunderous crack on the buttocks with either hand or stick, although the discomfiture of the ordeal far eclipsed any physical pain, with a room full of giggling children staring and pointing at the unfortunate victim. Red-faced, sore, the poor child then returned to the cross-legged position on the floor.

I'm unsure how much the authorities knew about the happenings inside mosques or whether anyone cared. Ironically, in those days, it seemed to be a case of 'whatever happens in the mosque stays in the mosque', markedly different to the current position. Some undercover YouTube footage wouldn't have been a bad thing (quite a money generator, too).

Suffice to say, we didn't learn much at the mosque, except perhaps reflex and evasive manoeuvres from a would-be assailant brandishing a cosh. Yes, learning outcomes were poor, with kids emerging with more scars, bruises and general trauma than Arabic or Qur'anic reading proficiency. I often wondered why our parents continued to send us, paying for the service, too. Remarkably, in the five or so years trekking back and forth, we only played truant once. We spent the entire two hours in a local park, quite bored. Perhaps we preferred the alternative excitement. Whatever the case, the mosque experience helped build identity, character, and stoicism.

1.5 TELEVISION OF COLOUR

In June 1980, my father decided it was high time we joined the colour television revolution. At this point, colour broadcasting had been operational for more than a decade, so the technology well tried and tested. Our 14" portable black and white TV had served the family with distinction, but had become increasingly unreliable at the most inopportune moments, often requiring a swift right hand to remedy.

I recall returning home from school one lunchtime to see this magnificent 20" Philips Colour TV sitting within its own wooden stand in the middle of the living room. I switched it on and sat back in astonishment at the moving colour pictures, total sensory overload for a young child. Bungle, Zippy and George looked remarkably vivid and lifelike, as though present in the same room. Even Geoffrey appeared a man transformed by this wondrous technology.

Later that same year arrived the first sporting event I remember watching on the new television, though the 14" may have served better for the purpose. Unfortunately, the event was more memorable for the wrong reasons – the painful and systematic dismantling of Muhammad Ali at the hands of Larry Holmes in his 'Last Hurrah'[5].

Lazy Sunday mornings provided the ideal opportunity for the entire family to watch *The Waltons*. We then graduated to *The Little House on the Prairie*. Laura and Mary's use of Ma and Pa remained with us, even to the present day.

EACH WEEKDAY, the 21:00 BBC News theme tune heralded the first trigger to prepare for bed. Anyone brave enough to linger downstairs received a specific look a few minutes later, which provided further motivation. On one occasion, I had been quite ill. As the theme started and my brothers and sister fled, I stayed, feeling confident I could use my illness pass. The headline story featured a violent confrontation in London between the National Front, a prominent far-right group founded in the late 60s, an Anti-NF group and the black community. 'Send them back, send them back,' came the chants. The waves of NF supporters looked as menacing as ever, with the police caught in the middle. Too terrified, I didn't ask my father why they were fighting, but sat in silence. The abuse and hostilities were far too lifelike on the colossal colour television. Couldn't we reinstate the black and white TV?

Amongst the ditties chanted, one stuck with me, even though I didn't quite understand the lyrics at the time:

> *There ain't no black in the Union Jack...doo dah*
> *There ain't no black in the Union Jack...doo dah*
> *So, send the black twats back*

I glanced towards my father. I could tell he was worried. He remained silent, with eyes glued to the screen. The violence and threats seemed to be growing each day. The *goray* wanted us out.

1.6 LOCAL CHIPPY

The local fish and chip shop in Burnley Wood served many tasty and memorable feasts, often the culinary highlight of our week – *Chippy Tea* (Lancastrian: evening meal, comprising chips, usually with mushy peas, and, if lucky, battered fish). Only a stone's throw away from our house, I'd often accompany my mother on the walk down the street. The chippy offered a mesmeric experience for a young child, waiting in line, imbibing the delightful sights, sizzling sounds, and aroma of frying battered fish.

With the handful of coins she'd have in her purse, my mother would place our order. Jim, the proprietor, sported a tremendous white handlebar moustache and sideburns. He would grin whenever we entered, and always ensured we received large portions of chips and the fattest fish. I'd splash copious amounts of salt and vinegar on the feast before he'd immaculately wrap the meal in newspaper.

We'd carry the warm catch home with as much delight and pride as if we'd just hooked it from the local river. My mother would share the chips and fish between four ravenous children, often sufficing with only a few chips and a sliver of fish for herself. It was never enough, and we often grumbled, particularly Sajad, who remained perpetually hungry. But every morsel of those meals was full of joy – all the more delightful while watching the latest episode of *Knight Rider* or *The A-Team*.

1.7 BUZZ IN BURTON'S

In the early 80s, we had a hierarchy of racist and hostile individuals within the town. The apex predators, the kingpins, were the infamous Burnley Suicide Squad (BSS), an unsavoury group forged in the cauldron of football rivalry. Their standard uniform included long black Dr Marten's boots, tight jeans and a freshly shorn skinhead. The longer the boots, the more unpleasant, it seemed. Even now, some 35 years later, there's a queasy feeling in my stomach when I see a pair of Dr Marten's.

BSS misdemeanours would often spill out of the terraces into the local streets and town centre. As a general rule, when Burnley played home matches, we wouldn't venture outside. Curfew times typically ranged from 14:00 to 18:00 to avoid any chance encounter with football supporters. The town centre was a particular hot spot for trouble in the early-mid 80s. Fortunately, our house at the time lay far from the stadium and safely away from supporter paths. though we could hear the Turf Moor crowd roar on the odd chance Burnley scored.

On one Saturday afternoon, I happened to be in the town centre with my mother, blissfully unaware Burnley were playing that afternoon. As we looked at new school shirts and trousers, a mob of 50 or so football supporters (I didn't know if they were Burnley supporters or not) passed by the shop looking for trouble. A quick-thinking assistant locked the front entrance in time. The drunken mob banged on the windows in unison, chanting 'NF! NF! NF! Niggers out!' Many were draped in the Union Jack and George's Cross, words and symbols I didn't understand at the time. I stood back away from the windows and looked in horror, with my mother equally petrified. The rage continued for several minutes before police on horseback dispersed them with batons. A few more minutes, and I'm sure the windows would have shattered. The animated advertisement campaign in the 80s boasted, 'You get bags more buzz at Burton's'. But this was taking things a little far. We decided to stay in the shop to browse for a good while longer, until safe to make a beeline home.

The BSS set the general drumbeat and blueprint for the rest of the hierarchy. The hostility filtered down to all age groups, with their aggressive, racist posture and language repeated everywhere: playgrounds, streets, schools and homes. One moment you could find yourself with a group of friends, and the next moment, you'd be the centre of abuse, with friends joining in, or at least staring in tacit silence. Young children weaned on hate and racism were confident abusing other kids, and even adults, feeling secure there would be no retaliation or repercussions for their behaviour. And for a long time, it seemed they were right.

1.8 BURNLEY WOOD SCHOOL

After a carefree year at Rockwood Nursery, I spent the years 1979-84 at Burnley Wood Primary School, the experience only curtailed by arrival of council inspectors who deemed the building too hazardous to occupy. Yes, alas, our beloved school building was disintegrating, brick by brick and tile by tile, while we sat reading Roald Dahl and Enid Blyton.

Not unlike the surrounding area, our school was a modest and humble affair. No majestic architecture. No sprawling greenery housing cricket pitches and rugger fields. No library. No history of successful alumni displayed proudly in the central hall. There wasn't much of a canteen, either. If Ofsted Reports existed back then, we'd probably have been lucky to land in the positive integer range.

On the backfoot dodging bouncers from the beginning, the school was located in one of the most deprived parts of Burnley. Abuse, truancy and general child delinquency were rife, with the cane and *pump* (English: trainer) the main deterrents – at least for the years above me. As I progressed through the years, it became increasingly taboo to assault children with foreign objects, thankfully. However, hands and feet were still ok. Yet, despite all this, I thoroughly enjoyed my primary school experience, perhaps due to my relationship with my teachers and general enthusiasm for learning.

The school hall had high arching purple plaster columns leading to a glass square pyramid roof. Some particularly adventurous kids would try and scale the roof. One poor lad managed to fall right through. I never quite understood how he climbed up there in the first place, or how he survived the forty feet fall. Seven classrooms led off the hall like tiny burrows. We also had two small playgrounds, one with quite an impressive sloped rocky area that caused several bloody injuries each week.

Each morning, the entire school would gather to sit cross-legged in neat rows within the school hall. We'd always start by raising our hands and chant the traditional ecumenical Lord's Prayer in unison. 'Our Father, who are in Heaven...' I found this a little odd. I knew I wasn't a Christian, for a start. Second, I recall searching for the word 'trespass', which I struggled to place in context. Though, perhaps more curiously, why were we talking about bread every day? We always had our white, sliced Sunblest bread from Kwik Save. Perhaps the children may have benefited from a line-by-line exegesis of the prayer. After the headmaster's (Mr Brennan) short topical or motivational speech, we'd proceed to hymns from the book 'Come and Praise'. I found *Autumn Days* lively, *Morning Has Broken* tedious, and *Kumbaya, My Lord* baffling.

The munificent school hall hosted many sports, including quick cricket. On one occasion, I performed rather well, with the head-master unable to dislodge my wicket. After hitting a record 50 runs (which proved to be the finest cricket innings of my career), he called time, and we changed before heading back into the class-room for the next lesson, English.

We boisterously entered the classroom, with Mr Brennan already writing on the blackboard in pristine cursive handwriting, like a fine craftsman at work. I noticed that about him. Every painting, every piece of writing, every drawing appeared immaculate, a characteristic I tried to consciously adopt from him.

'Master Rana was at the crease and in full flow, like a young Vivian Richards...' the opening line read. He then proceeded to fill the entire blackboard with a description of my batting exploits, in embarrassingly eulogistic style.

I enjoyed a great relationship with Mr Brennan. Being a keen cricketer certainly helped, but enjoying school and working hard helped more. Whenever he required help within school (which came with the bonus of missing regular lessons) or out of school hours, he'd call my name along with the gang. Startingly, I can't remember any specific racist attitudes or behaviours from the teachers towards the Asian pupils. On the contrary, their behaviour towards everyone appeared scrupulously even-handed and fair. I recall being selected class monitor on many occasions, and I was always chosen for class reading. I constantly received more gold stars than anyone else, resulting in chocolate prizes at the end of term. On one occasion, the headmaster remarked, 'Asif, I would testify to your character in court.' Years later, I did later wonder which of the two interpretations he had in mind.

EACH DAY, around 30 minutes before home time, all the children would move from their tiny desks to the reading corner and sit cross-legged in front of the teacher. She would perch in a high chair with the latest reading book. Well, at least she sat in comfort. Enid Blyton was an admired author during my primary school years. We devoured most of her books outside the classroom: *The Secret Seven*, *Famous Five* and The *Adventure* Series. Tasneem, a great Blyton aficionado, read every title before her teenage years.

Noddy, that lovable character, came next on the reading list in class. Who couldn't adore Noddy with his bubbly friends Big Ears, Mr Plod, Bumpy Dog? And, of course, Mr Golly from Golly Town, a helpful chap, fixing Noddy's car on countless occasions. I don't think he ever charged Noddy, either. Each time the teacher read his name, or mentioned one of the 'rude, thieving golliwogs', a ripple of sniggers flowed from the class with surreptitious looks in my general direction. An uncomfortable experience. Thank goodness we had at least one decent non-white character, though – there weren't many of us around.

1.9 SCHOOL HOLIDAY

During my primary school years, my parents decided we should all visit my father's home village in Pakistan. We managed to swing a four-month sabbatical from school with little resistance. The conversation with the school was quite terse.

'We're going away for a while, around four months, I think,' I announced, one December morning. 'But don't worry, I'm sure we'll be back.'

'Oh, ok... In that case, why don't you take some extra reading books with you? That'll keep you busy,' my teacher suggested.

'Good idea; I'll take the next few in the series.' I was seven years old at the time, though admittedly, school and social services were slightly more malleable in the early 80s.

A few days later, my siblings and I are sitting on tufts of grass surrounded by green trees bursting with ripe oranges and guavas, the gelatinous aroma as intoxicating as the taste. We watch the final moments of the setting sun radiating a soothing red glow across the orchard, into the nearby fields and beyond, the crickets chirping nearby, and the distant grunting of cattle provide the only accompanying soundtrack.

A few minutes later, the *muadhin* (Arabic: caller) starts the call to prayer. We listen attentively to his melodic voice while continuing to munch our fruit. After swallowing my final orange segment, I spring to my feet, grab a long, hooked pole, and deftly manoeuvre it towards a bulging guava on a nearby tree. I yank the pole hook around the fruit with one swift move, and it falls to the ground with a satisfying thud. Sajad dives for it, but I manage to snatch it first, and quickly slice a strip with my pocket penknife. 'Enid was right – food always tastes much better outside,' Tasneem quips with a broad grin. We roar with laughter and joke about the poor pupils slaving back at school; the country gripped in a glacial winter.

1.10 ACCOSTED BY WOOLIES

To ensure kids didn't languish too long in bed and generally keep them out of mischief, mosque sessions also ran on weekends and holidays from 10:00 to 12:00. The weekend sessions focussed on Urdu (rather than Arabic), to safeguard their Pakistani heritage and mother tongue. Regrettably, though, the ruthless teaching style was much the same.

One freezing Saturday, returning from a morning mosque session, my brothers had walked some distance ahead of me. As I blew into my hands, trying to inject some life, an older, bigger boy suddenly appeared ahead and altered his path walking directly towards me. I tried to manoeuvre out of his way, but he again moved into my path. I tried again with the same outcome. He abruptly stopped ahead, and whispered, 'You fuckin' little Paki,' with menacing hate in his eyes. He gripped me around the neck and dragged me away from the main road into a side street.

Like a boy possessed, he unleashed his full fury, as though his blood had become transfused with distilled evil. Several punches to my stomach, and I was coughing and writhing on the ground. He pounced on top and pummelled me, with each blow cursing, 'Nigger... black bastard... get out of our country, you little Paki... we're gonna kick you out! Just wait!'

Squirming underneath, I tried punching him, but he was too heavy. He then grabbed my hair to lift my head before spitting in my face. Moments later, he leapt to his feet and sprinted away. I lay writhing on the ground, coughing and spluttering drops of blood on the grubby tarmac below. I could see the feet of shoppers as they walked on into Woolies. No one helped. No one even stopped. A few minutes later, my two brothers arrived, having realised I wasn't behind them. Fortunately for the boy, he'd scarpered. They helped me back to my feet and straightened my clothes. We solemnly continued the journey home.

At the age of nine, that was my first taste of hands-on racism. I'd heard the abusive names before, but hadn't understood what they meant or whether they were directed towards me. This time there was no ambiguity. Why did the boy tell me to 'get out of our country'? I thought this was my country.

When I got home, I sprinted upstairs and grabbed Tasneem's dictionary. I looked up the word 'nigger'. The definition left me confused. I closed it quickly and joined my brothers downstairs for lunch. We didn't mention the incident to our parents. They had enough concerns.

1.11 NATIVITY PLAY

The school run-up to Christmas was an exciting time, primarily due to fewer lessons and additional extra-curricular activities, including colouring. The top colourers in the class were selected to colour the largest and most complex festive pictures. Only the finest images adorned the school hallways. We also had the Christmas Nativity Play and associated rehearsals. My singing capabilities were limited at best, as my music teacher would often highlight with disturbing glee. She likened my singing voice to a frog (ironic, given my surname). I also showed little or no aptitude for musical instruments, although I did try my hand with the drums and my lips with the flute, a short-lived experiment. In any case, the combination of my croaky voice and instrument ineptitude excluded me from a good number of nativity roles. I thought I'd be a cert for one of the three wise men, who had a darker complexion, according to some accounts. Nope, not even my BAME status helped.

One year, the music teacher announced, 'Asif, we have the perfect role for you!' *Aha*, I thought, *they've finally recognised my thespian talents!*

'What's the role?' I asked impatiently.

'King Herod! It's a speaking part, so you learn the lines and show some hatred towards Baby Jesus. There's no singing or instruments involved. There are quite a lot of lines, though I'm sure you'll be ok.' She handed me a page with 20 or so handwritten lines.

My Herod wielded power and authority, which I enjoyed, perhaps a little too much. They'd even created an elaborate golden coloured throne for the position. I performed with passion and fervour and ventured off-piste for a while, but returned once I caught the music teacher glaring at me. The line, 'Kill them! Kill them all!' accompanied with a slamming fist that nearly broke the set drew gasps from the audience. Maybe I'd tried a little too hard that night. I wasn't invited back to reprise the role in subsequent years. Only years later did I understand the irony of my Herod role.

Meanwhile, my relationship with Mr Brennan continued to blossom. He realised my interests lay outside of music and drama, and allowed me to skip rehearsals and take extra computing lessons. We had two computers at school, a Link 480Z Research Machine and a Sinclair Spectrum. Our computer studies teacher, Mr Broadbent, was conjured straight from a Roald Dahl novel; diminutive, with a thick brown moustache, and an enormous gut bulging over a silver-buckled tight belt that magnetically drew the eye. His belly wobbled as he walked down the corridor in his pointed black shoes, though his enthusiasm for all things computing was genuinely infectious. Aside from playing *Haunted House*, *Manic Miner* and *Plunder* when he wasn't looking, I spent a good deal of time programming on the Spectrum. Those programming skills proved helpful in later life. Once I had mastered these two lines of code, everything else seemed easy:

```
10 PRINT "Spectrums rule!"
20 GOTO 10
```

1.12 PUNJABI NIGHTMARE

The official language of Pakistan is Urdu, an impossibly sweet and polite language, the language of literature and poets. Several regional languages also exist, including Punjabi[6] (spoken mainly in Punjab) and Pashto (spoken in the northern areas). Given my parents were born in Lahore and Faisalabad, they mostly spoke Punjabi, and reverted to Urdu only when absolutely required.

Punjabi is a peculiar language. At least within Pakistan, most people don't write Punjabi. There are no great works of literature, no books of grammar, no great poetry, not much of anything. It seems no one bothered, given the voluminous material available in Arabic and Urdu. Even Google can't be bothered with the translations.

Though the language excels in a few very particular areas. Areas wherein it has no equal. It's the Maradona, the Ronnie O'Sullivan of languages. The Punjabi language has an *enormous* range of crude, abusive and rude terms that roll off the tongue with no effort at all. It appears impossible to say anything polite. Everything sounds sarcastic, acerbic. Yes, Pakistan has the yin and yang of languages: Urdu and Punjabi.

We spoke Punjabi growing up. Or rather we tried to speak Punjabi with our parents. Amongst ourselves, we exclusively spoke English. Consequently, our English skills flourished, whereas our Punjabi skills festered. Lacking basic vocabulary, we'd often swap English words whenever convenient, much to our parents' annoyance. Conversations with people outside of the family always landed us in bother, particularly on the phone. Either we couldn't fully understand the message, or we'd fail to respond intelligibly. We'd often receive negative feedback. 'Are your children illiterate, or something?' or, 'Your children are *buddu!*' (Punjabi: simpleton). We'd also falter with formal and informal pronouns, adding to the general condemnation. Rather than improving our Punjabi skills, we developed sophisticated evasive techniques to avoid answering the house phone.

Buddu, an oft-repeated word in our house, also implied a level of docility and naivety. It seemed British life had moulded us that way. Our parents would often comment on our lack of cunning and guile, essential attributes for a successful life in Pakistan. They'd often wonder and fret how we'd survive in Pakistan once the skinheads and deportation boats took us back.

Our impotence with ethnic languages didn't prevent kids at school from trying to poke fun, imitating the accent, complete with head shake (think Apu in *The Simpsons*). One little ditty stuck out, coined by a girl in my class:

> *I'm a dilly dilly man and I come from Pakistan and*
> *my name is Asif Rana,*
> *If I go back where I belong, I can end this little song,*
> *dilly dilly dilly banana.*

I think Jeannine has her own YouTube channel now. I always knew she would go far.

1.13 SHOWER BEFORE SCHOOL

One of my most vivid memories from childhood is unsurprisingly also one of the most unpleasant; an encounter that took place on a blustery, grey October morning while on my way to school.

I grabbed my school bag and slammed the front door behind me. The metal door knocker rattled several times before settling. It was chilly outside. A few droplets of rain landed gently on my new brown sweater my mother had knitted. I pulled the bag's leather strap around my neck and raced past the first row of tiny, terraced houses, then the second, over the road and pushed open the door of the corner sweet shop.

Inside, the doorbell gave its usual comforting ringing sound. Still panting, I navigated my way around stacks of tins and packages on the floor. I edged towards the counter and gazed at the assortment of sweet jars on display – black, brown, yellow, red, green. In the background, a small orange electric heater gave a soothing warm glow. Wafts of heat fused with the sweet aromas and hung like thick stew in the air. The small wall clock ticked precisely to 08:50.

The shopkeeper momentarily looked up and then continued arranging newspapers on the counter. 'One moment lad, will be with you soon.' I stared at the chubby man in his pristine white apron. His fleshy pale hands moved slowly and deliberately over the reams of papers.

'LONDON RIOTS CONTINUE FOR FOURTH NIGHT' read the newspaper headline. The shopkeeper caught me peering at the paper.

'Bloody fools... Always causing trouble... Got nothing better to do.'

'Uh, um, yes,' I nodded my head.

'Right, how can I help you, son?'

My eyes twitched agonisingly between the jars again. I pushed my hand inside my trouser pocket. Thankfully, it was still there: a single silver ridged coin I'd been saving for a few days. 'Er, two ounces of midget ... er, choc ... er, sherbet lemons, please.'

'Are you sure, son? Two ounces... Right... These will soon warm you up. It's bloody chilly out there.' The man grabbed the jar, unscrewed the lid, and poured a few yellow balls into the silver measuring tray. Each clattered as it struck the polished dish. He tore a crisp white paper bag and tipped in the sweets. 'There you go, son.'

'Is that 10 pence?'

'*Bob on.*' (Lancastrian: Spot on). Satisfied, I grabbed the bag and stuffed it into my trouser pocket. Another glance at the clock; less than ten minutes to reach school.

I raced across the winding streets and arrived at the recreation ground adjacent to the school. My skinny frame allowed me to squeeze through the black, rusting railings. Pulling my bag, I jumped and landed painfully on the tarmac below. Dazed, I sluggishly rose to my feet and looked ahead. *Drat, there they are again.* I was about to run the gauntlet of abuse.

'Look, lads, we have a little coon coming!' the lanky mob chieftain announced.   I tried lowering my gaze, glancing upwards every few paces. The boy paused for a few moments before a ravenous smile crept across his face, causing a row of freshly sewn stitches on his upper cheek to bulge. Suddenly all eyes of the rabble were looking directly towards me. They needed no further encouragement.

'Paki, Paki, Paki!' they screamed. With ever decreasing step lengths, I continued edging towards the gang. I could feel my legs becoming increasingly heavy and sticky, as though wading through a marshy swamp. I scanned the area on my left and then right. A gaggle of scruffy teens lined both sides of the graffiti-strewn steps down from the park. *Could I make a run for it?* I thought. *Unlikely, at least not without a dozen feral youths in pursuit.* No, it was too late to turn back now. I had to continue the trek down the steps towards the school.

As I drew closer, the taunts became louder and more aggressive. 'What's that smell? Is that you, little Paki? You need to wash more often!' shrieked one of the girls, while pushing a large brown glass bottle to her lips.

At that moment, I could feel the temperature drop. The chilly wind gnawed at my bones as drops of rain started to fall.   I glanced up and saw dark clouds hovering against a steely grey sky, an eerie portent from the heavens.   My heart began to race faster and   faster   as   I   walked   through   the   wrought   iron gate frame and gulped. As though in some squalid narcotics den, a nauseating stench of alcohol, nicotine and urine filled my nostrils.

I approached the first step, still desperately trying to avoid the gaze of the rabble, only twelve steps to negotiate before my escape. In the corner of my eye, I caught a glimpse of a menacing black dog with a white stripe across its front. It seemed to have joined its master in the same stare.

'Be careful– watch you don't fall down the stairs!'

'Don't worry, all these niggers will be out as soon the NF get in!'

'NF! NF! NF!' the rage continued.

One step... two... three... suddenly, I felt a solid fist to the back. It didn't take much force to send me hurtling down the remaining steps. I landed on the hard, black tarmac floor amongst an assortment of broken beer bottles, cigarette ends and crisp packets. My school bag split open, and now my books were scattered over the ground. My sherbet lemons bounced from my pocket to join the litter.

I lifted my pounding head, still severely disorientated. *What just happened? Why did these people hate us so much? What had we done to them?*

'Ah, leave him alone now. He can't help it if he's black!' wailed another of the young girls. I was panting hard, and sat momentarily amongst the filth, still dazed. As I remained motionless, a warm liquid forcefully splattered on my head, dripping onto the ground.

'Don't worry. This will clean the little Paki up!'

'No, no, stop,' I lashed out, flapping my arms, trying to divert the stream away from my face. 'Stop... stop...'

The group had formed a circle at the bottom of the stairs. As the last bottle remnants dripped over my head, the ringleader announced, 'He looks cleaner now!'

'What do you mean?' howled one of the girls, 'He still looks too black.'

'Haha, let's get to school. It's past 9.'

Satisfied with their morning's work, the group dispersed. As their laughter grew less audible, I looked around. My schoolbooks, now strewn amongst the broken glass and crisp packets, were a soggy, filthy mess. I wearily put them back into my leather satchel. The sherbet lemons, alas, were unsalvageable. I kicked them away and trudged towards school.

1.14 PIRACY ON THE HIGH SCHOOL

Of course, the argument 'it will help with our schoolwork' finally swung the debate in our favour; my father capitulated and bought our first computer in 1984, after months of cajoling and general tantrums. The machine was a second-hand silver and black Texas TI994A with cartridge slot. From the time it entered our house, we became collectively enamoured, spending every spare (and busy) moment on the machine, connecting it to our new large screen colour TV. It generated a lifelong interest in computing.

The computer arrived with only two games, which we played incessantly. New TI994A games were costly (around £5) and not readily available in the major outlets, certainly not in Burnley. Consequently, we resorted to programming listings from computer magazines. Though, given the many hundreds of lines of code, errors invariably riddled our attempts. Thankfully, Sajad's friend's father patiently debugged the code, symbol by symbol, line by line. The effort would often take him hours, but we mostly returned home with a new, working game.

Saturday afternoons were a genuine treat. Either with my brothers or friends, we'd wander to the local Woolworths or Boots to see the latest computer games on show. A row of newer comput-ers, including the Commodore 64, Sinclair Spectrum 48K and

Amstrad CPC 464, would be neatly arranged on counters. Kids would go and play the games or show off their computer programming prowess, some churning out hundreds of lines. A distinctive, intoxicating, electronic aroma hung in the area, generated by the whirring machines and power supplies. It became *the* place to hang out and discuss all things computer related, much to the irritation of the store's assistants. It wouldn't be so bad if the kids bought the games, but these were even more expensive (typically between £5 and £10). Quite a few of the demo games would go 'missing', ironically producing a comical, real-life game involving the kids and assistants. I still distinctly remember the pasty-faced, wiry Boots manager. He must have been overjoyed when we moved away.

Computer piracy, the dubious alternative to buying software, was particularly rife, with the playground providing the ideal trading theatre. Copying computer games in those days involved a cassette player and a separate recorder (or a dual system, if you were particularly affluent), with a simple lead connecting the two – the process quite straightforward, if not a little laborious. My brothers and I used the cassette copying method with photocopied front covers to sell games to friends. We made quite a lot of money, too, which helped finance later machines. We argued games were far too expensive, and ultimately our exploits aided the software industry by popularising amongst a broader audience. A few years later, I wrote a compelling argumentative essay for my GCSE English assignment. Well, my English teacher and I were convinced, at least.

1.15 OILY TREATS

A slightly musty smelling chipboard cabinet stretched the length of our living room in Burnley. How we acquired or managed to squash it through the front door remains a mystery. Multi-purpose, too, and large enough to accommodate clothes, cereal packets, books, and cutlery. My father exclusively reserved the far right cupboard, placing essential documents and stuff inside. I loathed opening the door, and not due to the inevitable clip round the earhole. Just a slight peep inside would release a biting odour.

The offending item? A 500ml Seven Seas Cod Liver Oil bottle. No fancy flavours. Just pure distilled fish oil. Each day after dinner, we'd await my father's call, and line, single file, with dread, Tasneem first. He'd then administer a full tablespoon to each of us. Theatrical shrieking, gagging, vomiting motions, and Olympic sprints to the toilet invariably followed.

Throughout the years, I can't remember my father replacing the musty bottle, despite our daily dose. Somehow, the oil level never seemed to drop, either. Perhaps he secretly replenished the bottle each night from another stash. Whatever the case, my father, like many of his generation, had worked out the benefits of the oil ahead of the curve. Tasneem also found a cunning and potent retaliatory technique against her cohort of annoying brothers by lacing our favourite food and drink with minute droplets. Simple, but *highly* effective.

2. TEENAGE TRAINING

'What is learned in youth is carved in stone.'

— ARAB PROVERB

The Spartans, those legendary warriors, had a creatively unusual method of educating their youth called the *agōgē* (Greek: guidance or rearing). This extreme training programme covered a range of valuable skills, including military combat, hunting, survival techniques, singing, and even enduring whipping. Singing no doubt proved helpful on the battlefield. The programme prepared Spartan youth for life, future employment and the harshness of war, while cultivating loyalty to Mother Sparta. Enduring public whipping was seen as a test of fortitude and stoicism.

Unbeknown to me, our unstructured programme in Burnley had many parallels with the Spartan regime (minus any mayoral loyalty). The robust experiences in our formative years, on the streets, at school, and in the mosque, prepared us for future trials, lasting well into adulthood. We matured quickly. We became increasingly streetwise, learnt evasive techniques, communication skills, and the art of negotiation.

Moving into my teenage years, I developed a much greater understanding of my immediate surroundings, and the socio-political complexities therein. Much of the confusion and, alas, innocence, from my childhood had dissipated. Some people existed who didn't like us, before they even got to know us. They didn't want us in 'their country'.

We were different: culturally, colourfully, and religiously different.

2.1 MUSCULAR MARTIAL ARTS

The skirmishes and violent incidents during our early years all highlighted missing arrows within our quiver. We needed to learn the art of defence (or fighting), and hit the gym. We'd already developed a fascination with Eastern Martial Arts, regularly read *Combat* magazine, and played a host of fighting games on our computer. Somehow, we'd even acquired a couple of shuriken stars which we threw with remarkable liberty in the park. So, frankly, we were halfway on the path to Shaolin Mastery.

To our delight, we heard about jujitsu lessons at a local club. Sajad and I immediately enquired, and convinced our parents to let us join. The first few lessons were a painful revelation, learning striking and defensive manoeuvres, and rolling around on the blue matted floor with (supposed) grace and control. The discipline and rigour added to the intrigue. We were the only children in the class, let alone the only non-white faces. But the Sensei and the rest cheerfully welcomed us into the group, which mainly comprised seasoned practitioners.

Just as lessons were progressing and our enthusiasm rocketing, my mother announced the two of us could no longer continue together. The 50p sessions, twice weekly, multiped by two practitioners, were a drain on family resources. One of us had to drop. Unsurprisingly, Sajad decided he would continue, leaving me little say in the matter. A disappointing day for me personally, but at least one could benefit from the Sensei.

That stalled my martial arts training for a few years, but importantly the experience had planted a seed in fertile soil.

AFTER MONTHS OF SAVING, and rabbinically studying the Argos catalogue each day after school just after mosque, we'd finally decided which dumbbell set to buy: a beautifully engineered grey vinyl Weider suite, comprising eight 2kg discs, complete with plastic handles. Surely this piece of equipment would turn us into musclebound monsters that nobody would dare abuse. Well, that's what the pictures suggested.

Amjad carefully counted the £22 in single pound notes, silver and copper coins, before handing them to Sajad. 'Don't lose this money! And don't show anyone until you get to Argos!'

'Aren't you coming?' I asked.

'No, I've got football this morning, you two can go and collect.'

'Ok, I'm sure we'll manage. Let's go!' exclaimed Sajad.

'Yes! Let's go!' I echoed.

The Argos store, over a mile from our house, lay in the heart of Burnley town centre. We covered the distance effortlessly, given the downhill route, sprinting first, and resting every few minutes. We arrived at the store, panting with excitement. Once inside, we knew the procedure well. Sajad grabbed the blue biro and wrote down the product code, which we both chanted from memory. After handing the slip and the two handfuls of money, we patiently awaited the prize.

'Right lads, where do you want this?' the counter lady asked.

'Er, here?' *Where on earth would we want it?*

'Where is your parent's car?' she continued.

'Uh, er, they aren't here,' replied Sajad.

I shook my head to confirm. 'No, it's just us,' I smiled with a broad grin.

'Right... are you going to be ok carrying this? It's quite heavy.'

Two strapping Argos-hands hoisted the dumbbell box and slammed it on the counter. I looked at Sajad as he glared at the box. The enormity of our predicament now became apparent. We certainly hadn't budgeted for a taxi ride home. But, surely we could carry the 16kg dumbbell set back?

'Right, grab hold of the other side...' Sajad ordered.

Between us, we shuffled the box off the counter.

'Did we order the right set? Feels a lot heavier than 16kg,' I remarked.

Sajad grimaced. 'Let's get home.'

Clutching either side, we first manoeuvred out of the shop and down the back alley through town. The sight of two young Pakistani boys carrying a large box through the centre attracted attention from passers-by.

'What's in the box? Chapatis?' one shouted.

I'd take the chapatis round about now, I thought.

'Where've you robbed that, lads?' screamed another.

Every twenty yards or so, we'd put the box down (sometimes gravity simply took over) to regain composure and bring life back into our bony frames. Fifteen minutes later, after surviving several busy roads and irate beeping drivers hurling abuse, we reached the foot of the final incline.

'Just look down and focus on the next few steps,' he yelled. The sweat now poured from our brows.

I sighed. 'Right, ok.'

The resting distance had now reduced to around five yards. Next, past second-hand shop row, round the grassy knoll, beyond the sewage works entrance. The nauseous stench filled our nostrils, providing just the right motivation to keep soldiering forward.

'My arms feel like they're going to drop off!' I wailed.

'Come on, nearly there... Keep going, keep going, just look down.'

Nearly there?! We were still several hundred meters away, but it was a good tactic. Slowly and painfully, we crept the remaining distance, up the final few winding streets and finally, we could see our green door.

Two hours from our exit, I feebly lifted the metal door knocker.

Amjad opened with a beaming smile. 'Did you get it?'

We stared at him, slithered inside and slumped on the sofa, just in time for lunch and *World of Sport* with Dickie Davies.

2.2 RESTRICTED PLAYGROUND ACCESS

The weather-beaten black and white notice that hung on the recreation ground wrought iron gate had been defaced. In all honesty, it was a shoddy attempt, with a thick black marker. Though the message read clear: 'No W~~D~~ogs Allowed'. The £10 fine remained in place. Thankfully, no increase in that, at least. Only on a handful of occasions did anyone reference the notice while I played on the ground.

The local recreation ground (the Rec) was our Lords and Wembley, our Wimbledon and Yankee Stadium (ok, we played rounders, not baseball). Second only to home, my siblings and I spent more time on the Rec than anywhere else, often from dawn to dusk in the holidays. Even on school days, a day wouldn't pass except we'd be tearing up and down the Rec, involved in some mischief or other, much to our parents' chagrin.

The Rec housed two sections, an open concrete expanse with a couple of rickety football nets, and a playground with swings, a roundabout, a rocking horse and two slides. In addition, two rides, the Pancake and the Umbrella, both of which certainly wouldn't pass Health and Safety standards today, sat in the middle. The Pancake would spin at terrific pace, and falling off invariably resulted in injury, often severe, as the unfortunate individual would land on hard, uneven tarmac littered with broken glass. The Umbrella had the additional exciting feature of movement in all three dimensions (think of an actual umbrella without the handle fixed to the ground with the ability to pivot freely from the top). The ride proved livelier for poor individuals thrown into the middle, with hard wooden seats striking from all directions. It became an effective gang punishment technique, witnessing many a bloody nose.

Towards the top end of the open expanse lay a rectangular grey brick building known as the 'Youthy' (the Youth Club), a rectangular prison-like structure with tiny windows protected with steel bars, hardly allowing any light to enter. The words NF Rules, Wogs Go Home, Blacks Out, along with a host of other obscenities and swastikas, plastered the outside. Inside, it wasn't any more homely. Under the flickering neon lighting, the placed reeked of smoke and alcohol. Most indoor amenities had long since been vandalised, with a table tennis and mini-football table the last games standing. The rest comprised just empty space, with a few chairs pilfered from the school canteen. The Youthy provided some respite from the often-inclement weather, if nothing else. I dared venture inside a few times, only to be chased out by some older boys shouting:

> 'We've got a friend who you've not got, Enoch,
> Enoch...
> We've got a friend who you've not got... Enoch
> Powell...
> When the lights go flashing, we'll go nigger
> bashing...

NF, NF, NF!'

Eh, what lights are they talking about? I always thought. It wasn't that catchy, either.

The Rec witnessed many fights during those years, with the open space providing an alluring if not unyielding backdrop. Fights ranged from one-on-one encounters of the 'Right, I'll meet you on the Rec after school' variety, to full scale inter-gang related brawls, though few involved Asian gangs due to relatively low numbers. They mostly comprised youths from different areas within Burnley, all vying for top spot. Some of the gang fights were surprisingly violent, involving all types of creative homemade weaponry. We stayed well clear.

In the summer holidays, the youth organisers arranged skipping games, rounders, football, and netball, with seemingly the entire local community involved, a startling contrast to most communities nowadays. Still a little young for football and netball, I regularly played rounders. My well-developed hand-to-eye coordination playing cricket helped me score many home runs, increasingly my popularity, albeit for brief pockets.

2.3 SNOWBALLS, STICKS AND STONES

Tasneem represented the archetypal class swot: skinny, bespectacled, straight As, front row seat in class, and fearless admonisher of smokers in the playground. She decided before her 10th birthday on a career in medicine and plotted her academic trajectory accordingly. *Adored* by her teachers, *loathed* in equal measure by the knuckleheads in her class. She was also one of the few Pakistani girls in the entire school of around 500. That striking combination made her conspicuous and the target of some quite horrific abuse.

On one wintry occasion, while walking home from school, a group of pupils were waiting for her outside the school gates. They took offence at her recent competition success. An ugly scene, straight from *The Lord of the Flies*, ensued. They pelted her repeatedly with snowballs while chanting, 'Specky four eyes Paki!' in chorus. Her school bag and pink NHS glasses fell to the ground as she flayed her arms in desperation. The assault continued for several minutes until the History teacher ran into the fray and dispersed the crowd. A slow, tearful, and painful walk home followed.

Alas, the snowball throwers were her own classmates. Enraged by the incident, my father visited the school the next day, and she transferred to another class the following week. That helped, but the event remained with her.

By contrast, Amjad wasn't one to patiently endure, and more than happy to entertain anyone hurling abuse. He didn't let his wiry physique deter him, either. He even took on Popeye, the fearsome '*cock o' town*' (Lancastrian: toughest kid in town). Often, some child would come tearing down the street to call Tasneem to one of Amjad's scuffles, though I'm not sure what she did when she got there. While playing football, one despicable boy decided to start throwing stones, while cursing and flinging racial abuse. Amjad flew at him, resulting in a side-line scuffle, landing blows while on top. The PE Teacher turned MMA referee eventually separated the two, though he let the fight continue longer than strictly necessary while the boy received the chastening blows. The football game continued shortly thereafter.

2.4 SHATTERED DREAMS

Tearing down the street on my way home from school, I could already taste the Penguin chocolate bar and steaming chai tea. Few delights topped sipping the tea whilst slouched in front of the TV watching the afternoon kids' programmes on the BBC, with *Bananaman* and *Super Ted* taking centre stage. I turned the corner at terrific pace only to unceremoniously collide with a group of local teenagers.

'Ey, yer little coon, watch where you goin'?'

I ignored them and darted towards the front door.

'Ali Baba, do you live 'ere?'

'Yeah, so what?' I snarled back, clenching my fists, poised with my jiujitsu moves.

'You need to move out Paki. If you don't, wi'll start puttin' these windows through,' one barked. He spat in my direction, but I deftly evaded the ball of phlegm. It was seldom just spittle.

'Or we'll burn down the Paki's house!' one added.

Our house at the time, our fourth in the Burnley Wood area, was an old Post Office with a huge front window. *There are quite a few windows to break,* I thought. Breathing heavily, I ran into the house and slammed the door shut. I paused momentarily to see if they were still there, my heart pounding. I could still hear their racist vitriol outside. Now they knew my face and where I lived. *Perhaps my response wasn't a good idea. Drat.*

'Smelly jigs... Shouldn't be in our country. Jus' wait until the NF get in, and we can kick 'em all out.'

'Haha, yeah!'

Later that evening, just before 21:00, I found myself snoozing on the sofa. My brothers and sister had already gone upstairs to sleep, leaving my father watching the news. Suddenly, the letterbox clanged, twice, thrice, then a fourth time. Highly unusual – we didn't have visitors so late. My father opened the front door. I heard a bottle smash, followed by, 'Dirty Pakis, get out of our country!' The culprits ran away, with my father giving chase. I sprinted towards the door, but couldn't see anything in the darkness. A few minutes later, my father returned, breathing heavily and perspiring. He quietly swept the broken glass and double-bolted the door. We didn't speak about what had happened or why.

The next day, keen to play Sherlock, I discovered the

vagabonds had tied a long piece of thread around the neck of a milk bottle and used it to move the letterbox. They had knocked from around the corner, allowing a swift getaway. Quite clever. Although I wasn't sure the gang were responsible. It seemed far too creative.

A few weeks passed, and I hoped the gang had become bored and moved on. Maybe they weren't going to smash our windows after all.

ON AN AUTUMNAL SUNDAY morning a few weeks later, I awoke to a kerfuffle and raised voices downstairs. I felt an uneasy, sickly feeling, and crept down past the open door. I could see two police officers and my father outside in stern conversation. In the living room, my brothers and mother sat with dejected faces, and Tasneem in tears.

'What's happened?' I asked.

'Someone's thrown a big rock through the large window,' replied Amjad.

I sat down on the sofa, in shock, numb, trying to process what was happening. The boys had been faithful to their word. My wishful thinking they'd be satisfied with the bottle. Attached to the rock was a piece of lined paper with a couple of shoddy swastikas drawn underneath. 'Pakis Out!' and 'NF' had also been scribbled in barely legible writing. Things had gotten serious. The police expertly deduced the rock originated from the nearby canal. However, that's where their deductive powers ended. They quashed any hopes of trying to identify the culprits. These attacks were common in Burnley, and racially aggravated cases seldom pursued for fear of reprisal attacks. We simply had to accept what had happened and move on, a bitter and difficult pill to swallow. Amjad wanted to catch the gang and give them a proper beating.

Nobody raised any objections, not even Tasneem. But, aside from suspicion, we had no proof or means of identifying the perpetrators.

My father never replaced the window glass. Instead, it remained boarded with a patchwork of wooden sheets and planks. As usual, we didn't speak about the attack, but we were all increasingly concerned about the situation. The services of Bananaman or Super Ted would have been useful at that time. Sitting on the sofa, shivering, with the autumnal wind blowing through the shattered window, represented one of the genuine low points during the early years.

Those youths had spoken of deportation again, the forever and present threat throughout our childhood. The dangling sword above our necks. The fear of the National Front and expulsion was quite real. We'd seen Idi Amin[1] deport Asians from Uganda a decade or so earlier. So, while logistically complex, we knew it could happen. Ironically, many of those expelled from Uganda resettled in the UK. A second deportation would have been really bad luck. Hardly a day would go by without someone mentioning the threat 'when they kick us out'. We genuinely thought we might all be going back to Pakistan – probably back to Village 247.

2.5 MINI EXODUS

After weeks of fiery debate following the attack, my mother finally convinced my father that we should move from the area. My father initially dismissed her grandiose plans. She argued the situation would only deteriorate. What would follow the broken window? Would they try and physically attack us? Would they try to burn down the house with us inside? What would happen to her children? Would they remain focussed or succumb to a wayward lifestyle amongst all the feral activity? My mother remained resolute; we *had* to move.

However, moving out of the area wasn't a fiscally trivial

matter, with cheap housing perhaps the only benefit of living in the locality. Our house cost little over £1000, the one before a mere £500. My father's labourer's wage didn't spread far, particularly with four growing kids to feed. He also sent money back to his parents in Pakistan, and what little remained set aside in a savings account.

My mother concluded there was no escape without an extra income, and decided to take matters into her own hands. My father wasn't overly keen on her leaving the house for work due to the increasingly hostile climate. In any case, my mother's presence at home was paramount for raising the children. By good fortune, she heard one of her friends had recently acquired a home sewing job, providing a handy second income. It seemed her prayers had been answered. After a few enquiries, my mother met Eileen, a spirited woman with fierce, bushy, white hair. She worked for a small sewing company making uniforms for dinner ladies, cleaners, and the like. Eileen arrived several times a week, lugging bags ready for sewing. The bags were heavy, yet she managed to swing them with remarkable gusto. Thursday became the regular payday in the form of a small, square, brown envelope crammed with notes and coins, a number '12' neatly written in the top corner. My mother would carefully remove a few pounds for necessities, and then bury the remainder at the bottom of a huge black and silver trunk. The trunk still exists today.

So, when my mother wasn't looking after the children, cooking, or cleaning, she'd be working under the dim light of the sewing machine. I'd often wake early in the morning to find her sewing, and, long after we'd all gone to sleep, she'd continue into the small hours. I took the opportunity of her time (and stationary position) learning what the mosque failed to teach me in five years. I started afresh with the Arabic alphabet, and, after a few weeks, became fluent reading the script, soon progressing onto reading the Qur'an. While listening to snippets of motherly wisdom, I managed to complete an entire reading within a few months – all without a bamboo stick in sight.

Several years passed, with my parents skimping and saving every spare halfpenny. Yet, despite this, they still managed to buy us a string of computers, bikes, and eventually a six-foot snooker table, which snuggled very nicely in the old post office room (though we had to graduate from playing with marbles for balls, wickets for cues and shoes for pockets). Through their will and determination, they managed to gather £8000, still short of the £10,000 we needed to buy the new house my mother happened to see while visiting friends across town. Enamoured with the prospect of a large house across from a park, her resolve only increased. After discussions with friends, they negotiated several loans on friendly terms. We finally had the £10,000, and secured the property. A momentous day.

In 1987, we packed our belongings and finally moved across town, away from the ruffians and troubles. Life in the new house proved a little more predictable, thankfully. We had a decent crop of neighbours, a huge park, and most importantly, fewer windows.

2.6 RELIGIOUS INSTRUCTION

As often the case with first-generation immigrants, there's a desire to 'fit in'. Life is tough enough in a foreign land with little or no language skills and support. The last thing needed is another luminous sign advertising difference. After a long shift at work, many first-generation immigrants would join their colleagues down the local pub and sup ale, or something a little stronger. They blamed the inclement weather and general hard work. Many women would wear English clothes, rather than their own traditional Asian dress, all in a desire to integrate. Amongst Muslim women, the hijab was almost non-existent, and the niqab would likely have resulted in public lynching or a call to SETI.

Aside from the enforced mosque visits, our upbringing wasn't religious. We were cultural Muslims. Knowledge was in short supply, mainly as immigrants had little or no education, religious or otherwise.

We knew about halal meat, which wasn't available at the local Sainsburys or Kwik Save. We knew pork was a no-no, but why would anyone want to eat a pig anyway? Alcohol was generally taboo, aside from the medicinal pub visits. We occasionally prayed on Fridays, and twice a year on Eid. Oh, and, unfortunately, we couldn't eat Gummy Bears because of something called gelatine (thankfully, there are halal versions now). That represented the total of our religious knowledge and practice.

My FIRST YEAR at secondary school in Religious Education class:

'So, Muslims, do not believe in the Christian concept of vicarious atonement, that Jesus died for our sins.' Our teacher, Mrs Rawlings, a pleasant lady with strikingly silver straight hair and a dodgy leg, scanned the room. 'Er, do we have any Muslims in the class? Any Muslims in the class...?' She turned towards me, before pausing and squinting her eyes. 'Asif, you. Aren't you a Muslim?'

'Er, yes,' I croaked.

'So, what does Islam say about this?'

'Sorry, say about what?'

'Jesus dying for the sins of humanity?'

'Er, er, I'm not sure, miss.' The class erupted. 'Jesus is a prophet in Islam, not God,' I whispered with embarrassment.

'Yes, but what about his crucifixion? What about atonement?'

Silence. 'I don't know, miss.'

Ashamed and red-faced, I recognised my ignorance, and not just about this seemingly strange concept. I knew little about my faith. That had to change. So, at the age of 11 years, my path to enlightenment began.

2.7 TROTTER'S HIGH SCHOOL

We had a solitary grammar school in Burnley. Anyone showing a modicum of intellectual spark or fizz was immediately despatched on the big red bus. In the mid-80s, the school converted to a regular comprehensive due to a lack of pupils passing the 11+ examination. We knew one chap sent to the grammar school after a single day at another comprehensive. According to Burnley legend, he later became a brain surgeon post-graduation from Oxford.

After leaving primary school, I suffered a brief stint at the converted school, but left after a year due to the excessive bus travel, which triggered regular, debilitating migraines. I transferred to the local comprehensive my elder siblings attended. My new secondary school ranked amongst the worst in East Lancashire, quite a feat given the stiff competition at the foot of the table.

Much like primary school, the secondary school building showed signs of decrepitude. With limited resources, the teachers (mostly) tried their best. I spent the next four years at the school, an entertaining experience overall. I enjoyed a good rapport with my teachers, and regularly featured in the school cricket team.

Some five years older, Amjad and Tasneem had it especially rough at the same school, snowballs and stones aside. They seemed to have a 'who's who' of undesirables, rogues, and vagabonds in their years. Even the teachers were terrified of some of these pupils, let alone the other kids, let alone the tiny huddle of Asian kids. Many of the vagrants spent months in young offenders' institutes, and Paki-bashing rounds were all too common. Thankfully, by the time I arrived, the nastier pupils had moved on, and even their younger siblings were more civil. As I progressed through the years, a greater awareness of cultural and religious diversity became apparent, though progress still excruciatingly slow.

~

Mr P, my moustachioed high-school maths teacher, would often stroll into our class and announce with glee, 'You lot know what you're doing, get your books out and get on with it! You don't need me to tell you that! You're all adults now! You'll be out in the big wide world in a few months!' He'd then lean back in his leather swivel chair and pluck the latest copy of *Angling Times* magazine from his leather briefcase. With feet comfortably raised, fresh coffee in hand, he'd spend the maths hour engrossed in some fantasy fishing adventure. On occasion, after a particularly productive weekend, he'd show photos of his latest catch, lovingly lingering on each juicy carp or trout. Yes, for Mr P, teaching maths was an inconvenient and bothersome endeavour.

That might sound less than ideal for a pupil with impending GCSE exams, but the situation wasn't entirely devoid of merit. First, I enjoyed maths and didn't need much instruction from Mr P. In fact, I preferred minimum contact with him for non-fishing reasons. Second, Mr P's preoccupation with *Angling Times* left me and a group of friends at the back of the classroom with sufficient air cover to discuss many non-maths related topics: politics, football, cricket, *The A-Team* and particularly religion. Several years after the embarrassing incident in the RE class, I was an aspiring student of comparative religion (mainly Judaism and Christianity) and would assume the role of chief polemicist within the group.

With delight, I'd research topics the day before and then mischievously throw them to the group for discussion. Papal infallibility, confession, eschatology and the Trinity were popular topics with Christian friends. Only competitive games of paper toss (much better than the app version) punctuated our debates. A wayward toss would result in a look of disapproval from Mr P, albeit a brief look. Those maths lessons cemented my interest in comparative religion. As a bonus, I managed an 'A' in my GCSE Maths, too. Alas, not all my friends performed so well. As for Mr P, like Miss Bigelow of *Charlie and the Chocolate Factory* fame, he came to a rather sticky end.

'OK, you lucky pupils, in our next topic, we will be covering the Theory of Evolution, specifically biological evolution, Darwinism,' my biology teacher's voice tapered as he turned and grimaced at me. 'And, what's more, I'm not having *any* debates with you, Mr Rana!' His long bony finger extended towards me.

Double Biology on a drizzly Monday morning – what a way to start the week. Though, after all these years, Mr Harrison had finally sparked my interest. Why hadn't he told me we'd be covering this earlier? Unusually, I listened to the lecture without interruption or question, much to his surprise. I hadn't given evolution much thought until that point; as a teenager, I had too many other issues going on.

When the lesson finished, I headed straight to the library and hoisted several *Britannica* volumes from the shelf. This seemed far more important than my other lessons that day. In the monkish silence, I spent the next three hours reading the tiny encyclopaedia print. Now I had a headache, but understood the problem. At least for adherents of Judaism, Christianity and Islam, Darwin's Theory of Evolution presents an interesting challenge. The story, specifically around the mechanics of Adam and Eve's creation, is described in both the Bible and Qur'an.

According to Genesis, God created Adam and Eve and then rested on Sunday. The Qu'ran gives a similar creational account[2], but without the nap. In both narratives, no evolutionary process, no adaptation, and no common ancestor are described. A direct creational event occurred; a human followed by another. So, how, if at all, are the two reconciled? That left me puzzled for a few years. And, of course, my biology teacher and I debated both the theology and mechanics for many hours.

As a schoolchild, though, the Big Bang had a greater bamboozling effect than Darwin could ever pen. But not due to any questions around the infinitesimal singularity. Or the mega inflation occurring in a trillionth of a trillionth of a second. Or the order from chaos. Or the absolute majesty of the Universe as a result. Or the appearance of life. No, none of that. When I asked my Physics teacher what came before and what caused the tumultuous bang, he replied, 'Nothing.' Somehow, we got something, quite a lot of something, as it turns out, from 'nothing'. Since, scientists have tried to explain nothing in a way that appears to be something[3]. In any case, it always seemed peculiar to me, even as a child, that if someone believed a cream cracker had spontaneously materialised from a tiny singularity, they'd immediately be despatched to the psychiatric ward. But the entire Universe? That's ok.

DURING MY FINAL year at secondary school, the Head Boy, Deputy, Senior and regular Prefects were selected. I consistently achieved high marks during my tenure and participated in school teams, so concluded my name was 'definitely in the conversation' to secure at least Senior Prefect or Deputy Head Boy. But I didn't know the headmaster well, certainly not like I'd known Mr Brennan.

The headmaster ran through the chosen list during school assembly, starting with the Head Boy and ending with the final Prefect, enumerating some 40 names. I waited and waited and waited. He didn't call my name. *Perhaps there's been some terrible mistake?* I thought. *Perhaps he doesn't have the latest dot-matrix printout?* After assembly, I raced towards my form tutor and questioned my omission from the list. He remarked, 'Well, you've never attended a single prize-giving ceremony in four years! You haven't made yourself very popular with the Headmaster or the Deputies. If you weren't bothered about those, you're probably not bothered about this – that's their view!'

Lord, give me strength; have they been keeping records all this time?! Are they holding that against me? What about my general track record at school?

I hadn't made enough effort schmoosing with the Head or his Deputies, a strategy that wouldn't serve me well in corporate life. My record of achievement wasn't enough. I listened in silence, though didn't have the will to argue with my teacher or the Deputies.

Later that year, after our exams, we received the invitation to the final prize-giving event, a chance to meet fellow pupils and teachers for the last time before moving on to college. I'd managed to win a few awards, though, adhering to my general policy, had no intention of attending. My mother, on the other hand, made it quite clear we would both attend. I reluctantly capitulated.

We waited an age for the Head and his Deputies to assemble on stage as we chatted amongst ourselves. Eventually, the Head raised his hands to silence the crowd and began with the words, 'Anyone can make a silk purse from a roll of silk, but can you make a silk purse from a sow's ear?'

Hang on, did he just refer to us as sows' ears? I really shouldn't have attended this one, either[4].

2.8 GREAT EXPECTATIONS

Not wishing to confirm any stereotypes prevalent within the white British psyche, but there always seemed to be an expectation from our parents we would all do well at school, go to college and then university, quite a bold expectation given academic prowess wasn't prevalent within our lineage (on either side). I blamed Tasneem, the class swot. She set a Mo Farah pace for her younger siblings. She'd often give us a leg up in her spare time, too. Not content with completing the Junior Readers Awards herself, comprising written reviews for Bronze (10 books), Silver (25 books), and Gold (50 books) Awards, she proceeded to 'help' Amjad with his books. This sudden spurt of enthusiasm and prolificacy left his teachers wholly baffled.

My parents didn't take a hands-on approach when it came to schoolwork. Aside from asking if we'd completed our homework and if we were going to secure an 'A' in any upcoming exam, there was no checking homework, no attending parents' evening, no extra tuition, and certainly no fretting over forthcoming exams. But we didn't mind this (obviously). We didn't realise an alternative approach existed. We even signed our own report cards with their full consent, though this didn't always go according to plan.

'Piranha?' queried the teacher. 'Piranha? Who is piranha?'

'Er, that's P. A. Rana, miss,' I replied, cursing my poor forgery skills.

Despite this relaxed posture, my parents had great expectations. Following a beatific vision, my mother believed her (then) five children would follow five different professions: Doctor, Lawyer, Barrister, Dentist and Ophthalmologist. I'm unsure if she was simply covering all bases while thinking of her dotage, or whether she'd secretly investigated salary potential. Whatever the motive, having the whole gamut of professions on tap seemed like a good strategy, particularly with legal representation at multiple levels. However, I wasn't overly pleased with my dentist allocation. 'I don't really want to spend the rest of my life looking into people's mouths,' I retorted. My mother scowled at me. It was a short conversation.

2.9 STICK TO ACADEMICS

One of the (many) benefits of living in terraced housing was the ready-made and accessible track to play cricket and other sports. When a trip to the Rec felt too arduous, or we wanted a quick game after dinner, our backstreet offered a ready alternative. Ok, the cobbled corridors were narrow, sometimes difficult to negotiate through dog ordure, and on a 20° incline, but they sufficed our needs. We were able to hone our batting and bowling talents within those concrete slivers. We had the track, a simple bat, tennis ball, and an old milk crate as wickets, and suddenly we were Viv Richards at the crease, or Malcolm Marshall with the ball. We lost many tennis balls in people's backyards during those years. Sometimes we'd scale the back gate to retrieve it, only to be chased away by the owners. Other times, a barking dog would dissuade any rescue attempt, a sure way to keep ethnics away.

Of all the different sports we played, cricket was my favourite, and I practised with alacrity. Sure, we played football, but we suffered from the self-fulfilling 'Pakistanis can't play football' syndrome. The general footballing environment wasn't conducive to our presence either. In the 80s, crowds were just becoming accustomed to black footballers, who suffered (and amazingly continue to suffer) appalling racial abuse. Asians playing professional football may have caused a complete terrace meltdown. Amjad tried to make a fist of it, though, travelling with the school in overseas tournaments. His teacher remarked he wasn't strong or large enough to progress much beyond the school team. A combination of cultural opprobrium and ludicrous notions around physical attributes permeated the football scene. Vestiges still exist today, despite the talents of a skinny small chap called Lionel Messi.

Progressing on the cricket field appeared less fraught with obstacles. The success of Indian and particularly Pakistani cricketers in the 80s and early 90s helped. 'Nobody wants to face a team of Imran Coon[5] Pakis!' as one of my PE teachers wisecracked while watching me bowl in the nets. The lads sniggered, 'Imran Coons!'

At the peak of my cricket career, I played in four teams: School, Town, Club (U13, U15), taking the most wickets in all teams. However, that year proved to be my final season as a cricketer. First, my parents realised I was playing cricket almost every day and not doing much else. Second, as I grew older, people took the game seriously, whereas I only wanted to play for fun. I had been bowling since a very young age, and regularly practised with my elder brothers. As I grew older, my speed increased, and I felt comfortable with my action. I wasn't prepared for the criticism I started to receive, despite my great bowling numbers.

'Put more back into it, son. More back!' cried one coach during an U15 match (I was only 13 at the time).

What's he talking about?! I'll give him more back.

'Stop bowling too short, lad. What the hell are you doing?!'

Oh, be quiet, man.

The after-match drink also became increasingly uncomfortable. For a long time, we'd settled for *cris' 'n' pop* (Lancastrian: crisps and a fizzy orange drink that strangely irritated the throat). As we grew older, some of the lads started experimenting with alcohol, an uncomfortable position for me. The drinking culture became more apparent during the year, and if you weren't in the clubhouse *'suppin' ale wi' lads'*, you were considered an outsider.

I slowly grew disillusioned with the game, and it reflected in my performances.

My sports teacher asked, 'Asif, you don't seem to be enjoying your cricket anymore?'

I explained the situation to him.

'Well, to be honest, you're better off sticking to academics, anyway,' he advised.

Sage advice. Life as a military medium county bowler would

have been a banal existence compared to the exciting world of computing.

The final straw came when the coach dropped me from the Town Team. In his defence, I committed the ultimate sporting felony with a 'no-show' in the previous game. In my defence, some Einstein scheduled two matches on consecutive days. I missed the second. Ok, that's a miserable defence. The team still managed to win. As my reward, I missed the opportunity to play in the final at Old Trafford.

Lesson learnt.

2.10 WINDS OF CHANGE

By the late 80s and early 90s, monumental changes were sweeping the globe. We had the fall of the Berlin Wall, followed by German reunification, the collapse of the USSR, with accompanying repurposed vocabulary (glasnost[6] and perestroika[7]), the popularisation of mobile phones, the invention of something called the World Wide Web, and the creation of the Premier League. It took years adjusting to the new German national football team name. We could handle the other changes.

Even our insular Burnley enclave couldn't resist the onslaught. The thugs around town were outgrowing their imbecilic ways, and many had moved away.

Football hooliganism was generally on the wane after the Heysel tragedy, with much greater police presence at matches, increased CCTV, and harsher sentences. Mandatory seating after Hillsborough also added to the general increase in civility at football matches. We were also getting older and physically larger, no longer such easy targets.

Growing up on the streets of Burnley during the 80s instilled extraordinarily valuable traits within us: durability, resilience, determination, toughness, and the ability to endure a public whipping. Traits that professionals spend thousands to acquire in the corporate world. Frankly, if we could survive and thrive in that environment, we could survive anywhere. Our Spartan training combined with our fair play, 'no nonsense', traditional values upbringing would remain with us throughout our lives.

The special attention we received in those early years was solely due to our identifiable unwashed, brown folk status – economic immigrants from a faraway land, leeches on limited housing, medical and employment resources.

But within a few years, that would spectacularly change.

3. A FEW ACADEMIC MATTERS

'Meet every person with graciousness.'

— ETHICS OF THE
FATHERS

Before university, I spent a couple of years studying A-Levels. Fortunately, the new house my mother chose was a textbook's throw away from the college. Even better, a sprawling park, complete with boating lake, occupied the space in between. I really had little excuse not to attend every lecture, with a sharp pencil and front-row seat. Those two years were a joy, particularly strolling back home after a late afternoon double chemistry lecture to watch the latest episode of *Star Trek: The Next Generation*, sitting next to the fire, with tea and Jammie Dodgers at hand.

Though, as I packed my college rucksack ready for the start of term in September 1991, we could still feel reverberations from the first Gulf War, which (officially) ended six months earlier. The fallout wasn't especially directed towards immigrants or Muslims living in the West. Sure, the odd person mistook us for Iraqis and blamed us for British soldier deaths, but the war was generally seen as an attack on an oppressive dictator who'd butchered thousands of his own people and then ventured into neighbouring Kuwait with eyes on the grand prize, Saudi Arabia (some shrewd commentators suggested oil lubricated the decision to intervene and send troops). We, too, debated the war during our A-Level classes, and the possible ramifications further down the line. However, no one predicted the Second Gulf War some ten years later.

In the following years, Muslims and Islam fully entered the mainstream UK psyche with the Bosnian War. The footage of 8000 emaciated Muslim men and boys gathered in Srebrenica (declared a UN 'safe haven') to be later butchered by Serb forces still represents one of the most harrowing scenes since World War II. The perceived lack of Western interest, despite the conflict occurring on European soil, as distinct from the rather decisive earlier Gulf War, led to accusations of double standards. Many British Muslims volunteered to fight with the Bosnians with the (initial) blessing and support of the UK Government. The Bosnian genocide was eventually halted in late 1995[1].

Meanwhile, in the UK, as I trekked through university in the mid to late 90s, I cannot recall any personally significant racist, anti-Muslim or unpleasant incidents (other than a few horrific Domain Theory exams), and certainly no physical altercations. Perhaps due to my larger physique, or increased facial hair, or my renewed interest in martial arts. Perhaps society was becoming more tolerant of different ethnicities. Whatever the reason, there seemed to be less abuse around. However, the programming of my youth and associated physiological responses remained deep. Every reading of Steinbeck's *Of Mice and Men*, replete with its colourful language, every mention of the Kuhn-Tucker (pronounced *coon*) condition in Maths & Statistics lectures, even mention of the Sambo Martial Arts club, would send frissons of evocative sparks through my being.

3.1 STRANGLED BY THE CAM

Between my two A-Level years, I was selected along with a group of six others to visit St John's College, Cambridge and Keble College, Oxford. That particular honour involved the not inconsiderable trek from Burnley to Cambridge and back again, followed by Burnley to Oxford (and back again), all in a barely roadworthy white minibus. My shortest path analysis suggested a more efficient route possible, but my teacher irritably dismissed. He recommended I focus on the required entry grades and leave the driving to him. The visits were part of an attempt to increase state-school pupil Oxbridge attendance. Our college in Burnley and a host of others (private and state) were selected for the visit.

My parents, normally ultra-cautious about allowing overnight stays outside the home, seemed intoxicated by the idea of their son attending one of the two pre-eminent educational establishments. They both gave their blessing without hesitation. So, I packed an overnight bag, along with a couple of cans of tuna (well, you never know), for the first journey. My standard wear during A-Levels included BSCO jeans, shirt, trainers, and a rather distinctive scarf. A scarf that many people noticed, but few ever commented on. The following day, we started at 06:00 for a 200-mile journey to Cambridge.

Fast forward five and a half miserable hours, and we arrived at St John's College, a breathtakingly idyllic college surrounded by fine architecture, including the famous Bridge of Sighs. The College had made considerable effort to welcome its potential students: several hours of taster sessions with notable professors, meals within the Harry Potter-like dining halls, opportunities to meet and greet other students, and even goody bags.

Given my maths/computer science interest, I attended the first session delivered by a well-known Scottish maths professor, in a lecture theatre brimming with a hundred other very clever and enthusiastic students. The Tripos Maths system at Cambridge seemed like hard work. Just an hour of explanation made me hungry. After a further 30-minute Q&A of youngsters desperate for some ardent glory, boasting about how many A-Levels they were studying (one guy felt we all needed to know his seven subjects), we had a short wait before dinner.

With a luscious summer breeze rustling through the trees and the sun setting in the distance, what better way to pass the time than gazing into the River Cam? Except gazing wasn't enough for one of our Burnley lads. No, Pete decided he needed more excitement. He took a handful of gravel and launched like Fatima Whitbread into the river below. The stones mesmerically splashed below. In silence, with military coordination, we all took a handful and followed, one by one. We laughed at the spectacle, feeling quite pleased with ourselves. A group of private school pupils looked on aghast.

'We're just studying the Doppler effect!' I shouted as they looked away, mumbling. 'Ok, that's enough fun. I'm famished, let's go and wait in the dinner queue before we're evicted and sent back to Burnley.'

Our group marched towards the entrance of the magnificent 16th-century dinner hall to meet with our teacher. The others strolled inside as I tarried near the door, appreciating the scenery, the history, the long list of famous alumni: Herschel; Wordsworth; Wilberforce... Mike Brearley. *Imagine, I could be studying here next year.* Lost in the surroundings, I closed my eyes and inhaled deeply, then exhaled, then inhaled. *Yes, this is perfect.*

While still in an almost hypnotic trance, I vaguely recognised the shape of a man walking directly towards me. He stopped abruptly in front of me and looked at my scarf, then up at my face, then back at the scarf. Taking each side, he wrapped it around my neck and pulled. Yes, this stranger was actually trying to strangle me. Jokingly, of course, but strangle, nonetheless. I suspect there weren't many assaults outside the Hall, St John's College, Cambridge. Even in jest, a highly unusual move, given the size differential.

The man recognised the flag on the scarf tassels – the Palestinian Flag. 'I'm just about to go in for dinner. Do you want to join me?' I asked.

'Sure, why not,' he replied.

Noam, a research doctoral student, and I discussed the history of Jerusalem from the time of David to the present day, an absorbing dialogue. Of course, we didn't agree on many issues, but we needed a solution to the ongoing problem. On that, we agreed.

'That's what I like about you, Noam, you can think through a problem and follow a rational argument.'

'Sure, thanks, that'll be the physics training.'

'My experiences aboard this ship have taught me that most problems have more than one solution[2].'

'I think I've seen that episode,' he chuckled.

The conversation outlasted the Oliver Twist pea soup, dumplings and dried herbs dinner. The two of us continued chatting after most had left the cavernous hall. Quite a picture, I'm sure. I retired back to my en-suite room after 23:00, feeling even hungrier than before dinner.

Right, where are those tuna cans?

Strangulation attempts aside, I found visits to both universities slightly uncomfortable. I hardly spotted a brown face throughout. Though perhaps more importantly, what about food? Burnley to Cambridge/Oxford wasn't exactly a short distance. Manchester seemed a better option for undergraduate studies.

3.2 MISTAKEN IDENTITY

'You see, the problem with you Pakis is that you all look the same! I can't tell you apart!' quipped one of my school chums.

It's a comment etched into my earliest memory banks. Aside from the occasional aberration, Tom was a good lad and meant well. Ironically, many years later, I realised this 'other-race effect[3]' represented an interesting, if not controversial, area in neuroscience (it works with other species, too).

During my college years, while walking back from town, happily minding my own business, a strapping ginger police officer, probably topping sixteen stones, stopped me and asked in a broad Lancastrian accent, 'Are you willin' to take part in a police line-up, lad? There's been an incident, and we're tryin' to get volunteers for the parade.'

Amazingly, I hadn't been stopped or questioned by the police before. My only interaction had been during school visits with the Alsatian dogs. That didn't help the relationship.

'Er, what does that entail, exactly?' I asked.

'Well, you'll get £5 for a start. You stand in line for a few minutes, and you'll be on your way.'

The £5 caught my attention. 'Right... Where do I go?'

'Come to Burnley Police Station at 17:00 today.'

Hmmm. That crisp £5 note would feel good in my pocket. 'But hang on... What if I'm picked from the line-up?'

He shook his head. 'Don't worry. You won't be,' he replied confidently.

Later that day, I returned to town and the local police station, an impressive sandstone building. As I lined up with the band of potential Asian rogues, staring into the one-way glass ahead, my old chum's comment came flooding back.

'All you Pakis look the same...'

Hmmm. Maybe this wasn't worth the £5 after all. Lord, I hope the victim is Asian, too... I thought, unknowingly pre-empting the other-race effect science.

First facing forward, then the side pose, then back again. It was a swift process, over within a few minutes. Back at the front desk,

'So, who did the victim pick?' I asked the Sergeant. 'Number 5 looked really dodgy to me.'

'Here's your £5 son. On your way now.'

I trousered the note and sped home.

SEVERAL YEARS LATER, while studying at university, the communal house phone rang late one Saturday evening. We didn't receive many calls, and my general aversion to answering the phone continued well into my late teens. I tentatively answered, expecting interrogation from my parents. It was Zak, an old school friend, who also studied in Manchester, though at a different university.

'Asif! How are you!? Long time! Hey, why don't you come over and have dinner tomorrow night?'

'Zak, how are you? Good to hear from you after all this time! Forgive me, but, what do you want?!'

'Why would I want anything? Can't two old friends just meet and reminisce over past times, past struggles?'

Zak, my buddy, had a habit of calling me when mired in trouble, typically when the quicksand tickled his ear lobes. I remember him ringing me a few days before his final year A-Level project deadline. I didn't sleep much that week.

'Hmmm... Ok, I'll come over around 7 pm,' I replied.

'Great, see you...' Zak was never one to spend more than 10p on a phone call.

The next day, I arrived at his dilapidated student residence halls clutching the smallest box of *Quality Street* sold in the local minimarket. He lived on the outskirts of Manchester in a rough area.

'*Assalaamu alaikum* (Arabic: Peace be with you – a customary Muslim greeting), Asif. Great to see you. Please, please come in.' I followed him into his tiny, spartan room, a prison-style bed, a wardrobe, and a desk with a white wooden chair about the only contents.

'This is great timing. I recently went home and have chapatis and chicken.' It wasn't long before we were munching spicy curry, merrily eating and chatting about old times in the communal kitchen, a welcome treat from my regular frozen meal schedule. Food often did the trick with hungry students, a strategy I'd seen before – three chapatis later, I felt suitably softened and indebted for whatever lay ahead.

'Let's have tea and biscuits back in my room. It's more comfortable in there.'

'Sure, why not.'

Now, not many impoverished university students would conjure a silver teapot and tray at this point. But Zak, despite his modest means, liked to do things properly. We continued chinwagging as the tea brewed, sitting on the threadbare, industrial brown carpet. He began to pour steaming tea from the long silver spout. 'So, Asif, I'm glad you came. Actually, I'm in a spot of bother.'

I grinned and shook my head. 'Yes, I gathered something was wrong.'

'You see, and, here's the short version. I have a maths exam coming up, and if I don't pass, I'll be kicked out of university.'

'Eh?! How have you got yourself into that position?!' I cried, mouth crammed with a custard cream. 'You need to do some serious revision!'

'Well, as you know, I've never been good at maths.'

'I know... So how exactly do I help you? You need tuition?'

'Er, not exactly. No, no, it's all a little late for that.'

'I'm getting a feeling of déjà vu, Zak.' I sipped my tea before dunking another custard cream. 'Then what do you need from me?'

'Well, you need to take the exam!'

'Eh!?' I spluttered, choking on the tea. 'That's crazy. How can I do that? I can't just waltz into your university and take an exam for

you! There are rules and regulations! There are security proce-
dures! Protocols to follow!'

He grinned at me and poured more tea into my cup.

'For a start, I look nothing like you! I have a beard, and you're
bald!' I pointed to the copious locks of hair on my head and then to
the glistening baldness of his dome. 'You wear glasses, and I don't!
Our skin complexion is completely different! Our noses are
different shapes! They will know I'm not you. Look at your
University ID and look at me! Stevie Wonder would know the
difference!'

'Asif, Asif, come on... All Pakistanis look the same! You know
that!'

Zak began roaring with laughter. I paused before laughing
uncontrollably, too, nearly spewing tea across his brown carpet.

'Are you sure they will kick you out if you don't pass?'

'Yes, they've told me.'

'And when is the exam?'

'Tomorrow morning, 09:00.'

'Tomorrow?! For goodness' sake, this gets better and better.' I
shook my head, took a sip of tea, and sat back leaning on the
prison bed.

That night, I tossed and turned. Of course, I didn't want Zak
thrown out of university. But on the other hand, if they caught us,
we'd both be ejected. *Is it worth the risk? Not sure, but it's quite
exciting.*

I woke early and sat in the kitchen with images of some great
heist whirring through my mind. I grabbed the Weetabix packet
and managed to tear the white wrapper, making a mess on the
table.

My housemates were getting ready for university. 'Are you
coming with us?' one asked.

'Er, not today, I've got a few things to do. You guys go ahead.' I
took a large spoonful of soggy cereal and watched them disappear,

leaving me in solitude. *I can't possibly go ahead with this. It's too risky. Let him fail, that will teach him a lesson!*

An hour later, I saw Zak waiting outside the maths building. I shook my head again in disbelief. 'I cannot believe I'm going along with this!'

'Look, don't make so much noise, you're attracting attention!'

'I swear, I'm going to swing for you, Zak! Don't tell me I'm attracting attention!'

'Shhhh, just put these on...' He offered his cap and green scarf.

'I'm not wearing those! That's ridiculous. The scarf won't even cover my beard.'

He thrust them towards me.

In a scene cut straight from *Four Lions*, I looked like a guilty man in ludicrous disguise. 'This won't even get me into the building! I should take this scarf and strangle you myself!'

This maths undercover subterfuge worked my heart harder than any HIIT session. I joined the other students outside the exam room, keeping my head down, trying to avoid everyone's gaze. It's a good job Zak didn't have many buddies. One by one, each student showed their ID to the invigilator before entering and taking their designated seat.

Lord, I'm done for here, I thought. *I can escape. Run. Quickly back out. It's not too late. Oh yes, it is.* Like a man condemned to the noose, I edged towards the invigilator with my heart now thumping beyond operational thresholds, my leaden feet barely moving across the polished floor. This was a one-way mission. I showed the invigilator Zak's ID and smiled. 'Hello...' I squeaked.

The invigilator screwed his eyes before yanking the ID closer and then looking up towards me, then back at the ID. I continued smiling. He nodded. 'Right, please take your seat, Zak.'

Goodness' sake, open your eyes, man. That's not me! What on earth is wrong with you?! Stop me now!

I slowly turned away. Once inside, I carefully reviewed the

exam rubric. The most difficult part of the exam was remembering not to write my own name. After an hour or so, I'd polished off all the questions, and I slowly raised my head to survey the room. Most of the students were still beavering away, heads down. I didn't want to raise any suspicion, so remained in my seat for another 30 minutes before the others started to disperse.

With my jugular venous pressure still at dangerous levels, I walked out of the room, down through the maze of corridors and out into the brilliant sunshine. Zak greeted me with a beaming smile. I hurled the scarf and cap on the ground and walked away. 'Never again!' I shouted.

Zak performed very well in his exam and managed to complete the year and overall degree.

Crikey, we really do all look the same.

3.3 WATERFALL SUPPORT

Doc Cooper, my eccentric chemistry teacher, was quite a character: erudite, loquacious, affable, and an enviable trendsetter in his brown leather sandals and knitted short-sleeved sweater. Darn good teacher, too. I thoroughly enjoyed two years studying with him.

'What I like about your lot is that you look after one another. Parents, kids, brothers, sisters. We've lost that in our culture. As soon as our kids reach 18, we kick them out. They return the favour and put us into old folks' homes years later.'

I laughed. 'Yes, our lot! Though we're slowly catching up on both fronts. Give it a few more years, and we'll be doing the same thing.'

In the late 80s, when Amjad and Tasneem packed their suitcases and headed to Sheffield University, the very thought of paying any tuition fees felt taboo, if not offensive. On the contrary, each term they were handed a healthy stipend to pay for accommodation, books, food and the like. The generous allowance allowed

Amjad to buy a tidy sum of Manchester United shares with the money left over (quite profitable in the 90s).

Once they'd graduated, I packed my bags for university. Thankfully I didn't pay any tuition fees either, though grants had remained static for some years, so didn't stretch quite so far. Amjad, who now worked, helped finance me through university (Tasneem was still negotiating her way through medical school).

By the time my younger brother and sister left for university, the Government had withdrawn almost all support. Stipends no longer existed, and exorbitant university fees introduced. Fortunately, we were collectively able to support our younger siblings. Rather than a quick conversation a few nights before departure, we now had emails and Excel tables detailing the percentage contribution. We were happy to help, and all managed to graduate from university without taking student loans.

My final week at Manchester university, and after weeks of walking instead of taking the bus, dining on the ultra-value range at Lidl, I had the paltry sum of £2.75 to my name. Thinking of ways to raise some quick cash, I marched to the university bookstore, hoping my once expensive textbooks would still be worth a few quid. Alas, no. What a silly idea. After bartering for 30 minutes, I slammed the books on the counter while scowling at the store assistant. I pocketed the £10 and left in a huff.

Fasting the remainder of the week could see me through, but not an easy option in June. By Wednesday, I had eaten the last tin of beans and the final slices of mouldy Lidl bread, while strange cultures sprouted in the remaining half-pint of milk in the fridge. I needed a good night's sleep to chew over the problem. *Everything will be clearer in the morning, I'm sure. I hope.*

The following morning, I awoke to a strange tingling sensation on my head. Jumping out of bed and flailing my hands like a man on fire, a couple of cockroaches dropped to the floor and scurried away. Well, at least they seemed content. So too were the mice patrolling my room looking for any morsels to nibble.

My dire predicament left me with only one option: Amjad. I traipsed to the nearest phone box with two 10p coins in hand. Without the assistance of any roaches, I awoke the next day and checked the mail. Amongst the usual junk, I found a brown manilla envelope with a handwritten address. I ripped it open to find a single, crisp, £50 note. It looked wonderfully pristine. Yes, suddenly I finally understood Charlie's euphoria finding that last Golden Ticket. The £50 secured my food, water and final bills for the rest of the week, allowing safe passage back to my parent's house.

Doc Cooper was right. The waterfall support method worked well for our lot.

3.4 UNEXPECTED ORTHODOXY

Running late for my train. *Drat, I'm not going to get a seat again.* I darted through the Euston doors with my heavy rucksack, only to be greeted by what looked like a scene from the 'Feeding the Multitude' (Matthew's version). I looked at the great mass of travellers on the concourse with eyes fixed on the departure board as though waiting for revelation. *Bank holiday weekend and this train will be absolutely heaving.* I didn't fancy standing for the journey. I'd already tried that once. For some reason, I thought the fare would be halved or something. The ticket inspector quickly set me straight.

Yet another trip between Euston and Manchester while studying in London. I'd managed to clock a fair number of miles on that length of steel carbon, and learnt a few tricks how to pre-empt the concourse announcement along the way. *Right... occupied plat-*

forms... trains arriving... trains departing... that little x-factor... probability... and... put the lot on... Red 13. Grabbing a latte on the way, I barged my way through the crowd and waited by the platform screen ahead of the barrier, head down, collar up. *If I've miscalculated this, I'm standing all the way. Come on, come on...* A few minutes later... bingo. 'Ladies and Gentlemen, the next train to depart from Platform 13 will be the 12:30 Virgin Train Service to Manchester Piccadilly.' I glanced back at the hungry crowd racing towards me as though I was still clutching the loaves and fishes.

Good job I wore my new trainers: down the incline, through the barriers, quick flash of my ticket and onto the train. Phew. I wandered the length of the train and found a table seat unoccupied close to the door. Perfect. I settled into the window seat, clutching a latte and grabbed my Domain Theory textbook. *Three hours of interrupted study,* I thought, stretching my legs. Just the right preparation for my exam next week. *Now, where's my notebook?*

'Excuse me, is anyone sitting here,' an unusual accent whispered from above.

Two men sporting tremendous beards and distinctive hats peered over me. *Well, these guys are certainly outdoing me on the follicle activity front,* I thought. Two children, maybe seven or eight years old, accompanied the men.

'Er, no, looks like they are free,' I replied, offering the seats as though mine to give away.

The elder of the two men and the children sat down without removing their gaze from my good person. The younger man stood awkwardly leaning on the headrest of the seat in the middle of the aisle. I looked across to the adjacent table with a free seat and then to the standing man, then back again to the free seat. *Surely, you're not going to stand for the next three hours. Just sit down over there, mate. Perhaps he hasn't seen it? Perhaps he thinks he'll get a discount if he stands? Well, I can assure him he won't.*

Anyway, important revision awaited me. I opened my book and

began reading. Five minutes later. *What possible benefit or application would this have? Why am I even studying this, for goodness' sake?* With their wide, glistening eyes, the children opposite, intrigued by their new travelling companion, continued to stare without any awkwardness, as children do. I continued reading the book, trying to ignore them, and started making notes with my black Bic biro. My eyes twitched every so often, eager to see how my four travelling companions would spend the next three hours. The kids seemed content with my theatre, while the older man read what appeared to be a prayer book.

Providence had engineered an opportunity simply too good to miss. Surely, I couldn't squander the next three hours on Domain Theory? *I'd better make the first move.* 'So, do you live in Manchester?' I asked the older man sitting to my left.

The children's mouths dropped in cartoon style as I finally pierced the silence.

'Er, no, we're just travelling to Prestwich. We live in Stamford Hill.'

'Aha, I used to live in Manchester until I moved to university in London.'

'Ah, very good,' he replied.

'I know Prestwich well. I used to travel through often on way to my parent's home. Quite a large Jewish population in parts?'

'Yes, that's right...'

'My name is Asif, by the way.'

'Aha, I'm Joseph, this is David, Daniel, and Jonathan standing.'

I glanced again at Jonathan. I felt uncomfortable watching him continuously twitch, changing positions as though in some SAS stress endurance test. 'Why doesn't your friend sit down? There's a free seat just there, look.' I finally blurted.

'Well, actually, he's too shy to sit next to the lady. We try to avoid any contact with non-related women.'

I looked across again. I'd only focussed on the free seat and the incredulity of a 3-hour standing journey. 'Ah, I see. That's interesting.' I turned to Jonathan. 'You can sit here if you want. I'll find another seat.'

'Oh, that's very kind, I'll be ok. I'm used to standing. It happens quite a lot on public transport.'

The first 15-20 minutes resembled the early rounds of a cagey boxing match, with the boys providing a captivated audience. We trod carefully, getting our range, being extra polite and careful not to say anything that may offend.

Ten minutes later, everyone felt more relaxed, and the conversation started to flow freely. Given the similarities between Judaism and Islam, we weren't short of topics either. Our gathering generated considerable attention from fellow passengers wandering up and down the train, and those sat nearby, an unusual sight to see an Orthodox Jew and Muslim deep in conversation. A couple, a few seats away, munched on popcorn while listening to the discussion. The snack may have been mere coincidence.

We spent the next two hours discussing points of commonality and difference between the two religions: the nature of G-d[4], credal belief, sources of law, prophethood, rituals, written vs oral law, religious signs and symbols. It was a spirited discussion, with both men and the children now fully participating. However, we hadn't touched the thornier issues yet. I took a sip of coffee and cracked open some shortbread biscuits before offering them to the children.

I'd spent a little time learning Hebrew, given its similarity to Arabic, and I'd also dabbled in Aramaic at university. They belong to the Semitic group of languages, spoken by Semites[5], no less.

'So, I presume you all speak fluent Hebrew?' I asked, turning to Daniel while mentally prepping a list of Hebrew verbs ready to conjugate.

'Yes, Yiddish and Hebrew.'

'I see. I don't know any Yiddish, I'm afraid. I know a little Hebrew, though.'

'That's impressive! Do you speak Arabic, too?' asked Joseph.

'I'm learning. The two languages will come in handy when I eventually visit the Holy Land. I think they're the two official languages of the country?'

'Yes, something like that.' Joseph's expression changed as he glanced at Jonathan.

'I presume you visit Israel often?'

The group remained silent.

'No, no, quite the opposite. The last time, I was three years old,' Jonathan finally replied.

'That's odd?'

'Not really. Many Orthodox Jews don't support Israel or its policies and practices. Look, Asif, we are a people in exile. The Torah forbids we should have our own state until the Messiah comes.'

The Messiah again. 'Fascinating. You're waiting for the Messiah. Everyone is waiting for him, in one guise or another. Let's hope he doesn't disappoint when he arrives.'

'Actually, we lived well in many Islamic lands for centuries, better than most European countries. It's mostly in the last 60 years the relationship between Muslims and Jews has deteriorated.'

'Yes. I'd love to visit Jerusalem and the historical sites. That appears tricky at the moment.'

'Yes, agreed.'

I glanced at my watch, we had 10 minutes before arrival into Manchester Piccadilly, and only a couple of minor topics remained.

'So... Jesus. We Muslims believe he was a great prophet of God, a position between the Christians on one side – who deify him – and Jews on the other, who reject him. Do you agree with that? What is your orthodox position?' I asked. 'If he wasn't the Messiah, who was he?'

'Well, our definitions of the Messiah are probably different. We certainly differ with the Christians.' Joseph took another full bite of sandwich. 'He was a Jewish teacher, but not the promised Messiah. Others may describe him less favourably. I wouldn't use such language.'

'What about Muhammad[6] (ﷺ)?'

'He's not mentioned often in our books, Though I believe he was a prophet sent to spread monotheism amongst the Gentiles. And, importantly, Muslims uphold the Noahide Laws. Anyone doing so will have a place in the world to come. As the Rambam...'

'Ah, The Ramban,[7] I said. 'we need to discuss the Ramban...'

'Ladies and gentlemen, we will be shortly arriving into Manchester Piccadilly...' interrupted the train announcer.

'We believe God sent Muhammad to Jew and Gentile,' I quickly added. 'Well, I'm afraid we're out of track. We'll have to continue next time...'

'Or we could go back to London and continue the conversation,' Jonathan quipped. 'I can sit down for the journey, as well!'

'I don't think my mother would approve; she's made roast chicken ready for my return.'

The group roared.

'Does she make chicken soup[8]?'

'For sure. My mother makes a cracking bowl of chicken *yakhni*!' (Urdu: broth).

3.5 SNOOKERED BEHIND THE MALODOROUS BROWN

As a Postgraduate student at Imperial College, I suffered from a few undesirable habits. One of the least desirable involved missing my entire morning lectures and tutorials without any good reason. The practice appeared to be a hangover from my A-Level days, where I adopted a similar strategy, much to the irritation of my maths lecturer (she'd almost swing for me in the afternoon lectures). Not content with simply missing the lectures, I'd then saunter into university just before lunch and head towards the cafeteria, picking out a fresh tuna baguette with sparkling mineral water. With catch in hand, I'd dive into the Muslim prayer room for the next hour. There, students from dozens of countries would gather, compare woes, copy notes and chat before afternoon prayers.

On one occasion, while engrossed in my sandwich looking over the morning notes I'd managed to acquire, a first-year student came and sat close. I hadn't seen or spoken with him much in the first few weeks.

'So, what are you studying?' I asked, chewing on my baguette.

'Trying to study Chemical Engineering,' he replied, weary and downbeat.

'Ah, that's good. Do you like it here?'

'Yes, though it's hard work. They push you very hard. I wasn't expecting it to be this difficult. I hope I'm still here next year.' The emotion and worry apparent on his face.

'Yes, high standards here. Don't worry, you'll get the hang of it. The first year is tough, with the adjustments, though I do recommend you attend all your lectures and take copious notes. The course is more difficult if you don't.'

Confused, he replied, 'Well, of course. I go to all my lectures and take notes. Sometimes I'm even on the front row, not that it helps much.'

'Do you have one of those fat pencil cases?'

'Of course! These questions are strange!'

'Er, never mind. So, where are you from?' I asked, quickly moving on.

'I'm from South London.'

'Ah, yes, I should have guessed with that accent. It's quite distinctive. Actually, there are a few famous snooker players from that area.'

'Er, yes, I went to school with a famous snooker player,' he replied.

I lowered my sandwich onto the napkin below. 'Really? Who?!'

I edged forward in delight. 'We've been watching snooker since the early 80s. We played for hours and hours as kids. My younger brother was really quite good, knocking in breaks of 80 at the age of 7, you know. You can tell me, I'm suitably qualified.'

Diplomacy (and the possible threat of legal action) prevents me from revealing his name, so let's call him 'Johnny Davis' for now.

'He was a complete bully! He terrorised us! Paki-bashing, he called it. Him and his mates used to scour the playground for us at lunchtime. Said we smelt bad. 'Smelly Pakis!' he used to shout. He was a big lad, even at 16.'

Poor chap, I could see the trauma surface, but too late now. I roared with laughter, causing a couple of tuna flakes to traverse the wrong pipe. I took a gulp of water to regain composure. 'Yes, I've heard the term once or twice. The classic, Pakis smell bad, eh?'

'Why are you laughing?!'

'Sorry, that's really funny, though I can imagine it wasn't funny for you at the time. It's quite a good claim to fame. Don't worry, he's a reformed character now. I think. I hope.'

Never mind his claim to fame. I've used it myself a few times myself. 'I went to university with a chap who took a right mauling at the hands of Johnny Davis.'

3.6 IMPERIAL RESISTANCE

3rd floor, Computer Science Building, Imperial College, London. *Why don't they just knock down this place and rebuild?* I wondered, scaling the depressingly bland stairs. I arrived at my tutor's room, knocked on the door and then slowly turned the handle. It needed a dash of WD40, as did the professor.

'Aha, hello, professor...'

A musty, stale aroma of old books and body odour slapped me in the face. *For goodness' sake, open a window, man.* He didn't get out much, the professor.

'Aha, Azeef, come in, sit down.'

I did as instructed.

'One moment...' He continued reading from a thick wad of papers squinting his eyes. The professor wore a tired chocolate half-sleeved sweater with matching tan shirt sporting a sizeable collar – a look straight from the Open University. A sheen of perspiration covered his bald head, with a few wispy white strands desperately clinging on. A shaggy grey beard completed the look. He sat behind a dusty desk, the rickety chair no more salubrious. Piles of stacked theoretical computing books sprouted from the floor like stalagmites, making it difficult to navigate within the space, and three large blackboards covered the wall space. I'm surprised shrubbery hadn't sprung around him.

'Right, I wanted to go through some comments on your thesis. Now, where did I put them...' He placed his hands on his head, revealing large sweat patches under his arms. I tried to avert my gaze. He continued rummaging into the swamp of papers on his desk. 'Ah yes, here we are. Right, we've had the moderator response back. The summary is that you've done well with this research, though the moderator has made a few observations that you ought to address.' He handed me a dot-matrix print of the commentary.

I scanned the sheet. 'Hmmm. Ok, yes, right. Well, the comments seem reasonable.'

'Yes, I thought so. I don't think they will take long for you to address.' He paused again. 'So, what are your plans once you finish here?' he asked.

'Not sure, maybe continue in research. I think that's my preference. Though I've been offered some positions in industry.'

The professor looked at me earnestly as he stroked his wispy white hair. He took off his spectacles and placed them on the table. 'Well, you could continue here, you know. I have some open doctoral research positions. Some areas that I think may interest you.'

Somehow, the thought of spending the best years of my life in a similar office didn't appeal. 'Well, I appreciate that, thank you.'

'Look, Azeef, let me give you some advice. Between you and me, if you want a career as an academic, a serious academic...'

I edged forward in my seat. What pearls were about to flow from the professor? He did have 40 years' experience under his mortarboard. 'Oh, yes?' My eyes widened, nodding my head in anticipation.

'You *really* need to focus on your research.'

'Ok... Well, I like to think I'm reasonably well focussed...'

'I mean completely focus; this religious stuff seems to occupy quite a lot of your time.'

Religious stuff?! That's what I liked about the professor; he didn't mince his words. 'Well, it's not a wacky hobby I indulge on the side. The world over, are there are not many successful academics who are Muslims, or generally people who follow some faith or another? And, for about 400^9 years, Islamic civilisations made extraordinary contributions to science and technology. Didn't seem to do them any harm?'

'Well, that's all well and good, but I need someone who is *extremely* focussed. It's just some advice for you. Take it or leave it.'

I'd received a few unexpected comments over the years, but this topped the lot.

'Right anyway... are you happy to address those moderator points?' He lowered his gaze again.

I continued staring at him. 'Yes, I'll do so this week.'

'Right, excellent, I'll see you next week. Please leave the door ajar on the way out, it's rather stuffy in here.'

I grabbed the sheet and left the room. Well, at least he helped make up my mind. *Maybe I'll send him a Brut set as a parting gift.*

3.7 WITNESS PROTECTION

There was a time when a pair of polite, usually Caucasian, well-heeled Jehovah's Witnesses would visit each year, sometimes twice, without fail. I enjoyed the visits, and not just for polemics, either. I'm not sure what happened, but they don't knock anymore. These days, I see their active outreach work centred around the busy commuter train and underground stations. On my morning walk to the station, I'll see the familiar literature neatly laid out with two people happily engaged in conversation. 'Don't mind us, we're just happy people having a chat,' they say without moving their lips. 'It doesn't matter if you take a booklet or not. Impressively, a different couple attends each day, no matter how inclement the weather. Perhaps some sophisticated algorithm in the cloud selects locations and pairs.

The change in general strategy seemed sensible. After all, most people don't appreciate interruptions at home, let alone interruptions with discussions about God. Though I'm not convinced targeting the commuter population is an effective alternative. Happy for the statistics to prove me wrong.

My first encounter occurred towards the end of my university tenure.

The intercom buzzer rang.

Drat... I wasn't expecting anyone, and knee-deep in a swamp of computer code that refused to yield. Deep in the matrix, I chose to ignore. A few minutes later, it rang again, this time longer and louder. *Oh, go away, I'm busy. How about if I try this...hmmm or this... Nope.* The third ring blasted louder than my smoke alarm. *Right, this better be important.*

I snatched the intercom phone. 'HELLO?!' It sounded harsher than intended.

'Oh, hello, my name is John. Sorry to disturb you, but we'd like to talk to you about God.' He spoke with a clear but rather bland tone.

God?! At 09:00 on a Saturday morning? This was dedication. A tough choice, glancing between my computer screen and intercom. It seemed rude to turn them away after all that buzzing. Perhaps I would be their only client for the day. *Let me help them reach their targets.*

'Err, ok. In that case, you'd better come straight in. Up the stairs, flat seven, on your left. I'd avoid using the lift.' I clicked the security latch button. A few minutes later, the pair stood outside my front door as I eyed them through the spyhole: the risk assessment. *They look genuine.*

'Aha, hello, please come in. My name is Asif. Let me take your coats? Would you like some tea or coffee? A Penguin or biscuit?'

John turned to the woman for approval. 'Sure, and yes, please, tea is fine. This is Anna.'

Once all settled and relaxed, I began. 'So, tell me about Jehovah's Witness theology. How does it differ from mainstream Christianity? What are you witnessing exactly?'

'Well, we are Christians, for a start! Our name comes from Yahweh or Jehovah. We don't believe Jesus is God or co-existent with God, and we reject the Trinity.'

'Oh, that's a good start, so we agree on that!' I poured the tea. 'Would you like sugar?'

'No, none for us, thanks.'

'We're doing well here. I don't take any sugar either, there's enough in the biscuits.'

We chuckled in unison. Right on cue, John opened his black case and removed a pristine Bible. 'Here's one of our Bibles.'

'Ah, I haven't seen this translation before. I do like the King James version, if only on literary merit.' I flicked through the Bible, landing on the opening chapter John 1:1. The Bible effused a distinctive new-book smell. 'Don't you think it's a little odd that you have your own specific Bible translation, though? Why don't you use one of the others? There's a huge selection. Look, I've got a few here.' I pointed to the array of Bibles on my bookshelf.

'Well, we think those have been inaccurately translated in some places,' Anna interjected. 'Hmmm. Ok. Perhaps those don't serve your specific theology?'

'No, no, ours is accurate, from the original,' she replied.

'Which original? Which language was it translated from?'

They stared at me blankly. Ignoring the silence, I began to read... 'In the beginning was the Word, and the Word was with God, and the Word was a god.' Odd. That does sound a little different to the standard translation. Not that we would agree with the mainstream Christian position anyway! I suppose that's one of the benefits of Biblical scripture, there's quite a lot of latitude – which manuscripts to select and reject, how to translate different words from translations of Hebrew, Greek and Aramaic.'

Anna shiftily glanced at John. Both remained silent.

'Thanks for the Bible, though, I'll add to my collection.' I placed it on the table. 'Anyway, I do remember reading about the exact number of people who will eventually be saved, according to your theology. Now, what was the number? Something like 150,000?'

'It's 144,000, actually, from AD 33 to the present day.'

'That's quite a specific, tiny number, considering the number of Christians over the years. I mean, that's probably only a small percentage of Jehovah's Witnesses in the world today?! That's not a great ad for the group!'

'Well, I'm not sure we're supposed to take the number literally.'

'No. I wouldn't if I were you.'

We continued chatting about points of difference and similarity, with me doing most of the talking. 'So, I remember watching a movie once about a family of Jehovah's Witnesses and the father wouldn't accept a blood transfusion for his daughter? Is that correct? Even in a matter of life and death, you wouldn't take a blood transfusion?'

'No. The Bible forbids taking blood to sustain the body.'

'Really? Where?'

'Many places, Genesis, Leviticus: "If any man of the house of Israel or any foreigner who is residing in your midst eats any sort of blood, I will certainly set my face against the one who is eating the blood, and I will cut him off from among his people."'

'Well, that's eating blood! We'd agree on that point. It sounds a tad extreme. You would rather your son or daughter died?! What about the preservation of life?'

As they mulled over the question, I opened the shortbread biscuits and fanned them neatly on the plate. I reached behind the sofa, took my own black case, and placed it on the table. Removing some literature, I handed to John. The two watched in horror at the role reversal.

'Actually, do you know anything about computer coding? Perhaps you can help me?'

'I'm afraid not,' blurted Anna. She sprung to her feet with impressive agility. 'Right, I'm sorry, we need to go now.'

'What, already? We're just starting!'

'We have other appointments, I'm afraid. If you can get our coats, please.'

Anna grabbed my pristine Bible, and without even handing me a *Watch Tower* magazine, the two hurriedly left the flat. Quite rude. I wanted that Bible, too.

Right then, back to this code.

4. ROAD TO EXIT

*'Accept whatever comes to you woven in the pattern
of your destiny, for what could more aptly fit
your needs?'*

— MARCUS AURELIUS

Throughout college and university, my career aspirations wavered year to year: English, Engineering, Actuarial Science (yes), IT. I enjoyed studying languages, and excelled at the Analytical Sciences and Maths. Towards the end of the academic stretch, I also developed a renewed fitness interest. Where might these skills prove useful? What about my Arabic, Urdu and Punjabi and, er, subterfuge skills? My university lecturer didn't tap me on the shoulder or slip me a blue envelope after a Computational Complexity lecture. Just as well, that probably wouldn't have worked out.

Finding the right industry proved a little tricky (we're a fussy bunch), and the acclimatisation period took a tad longer than I expected. It's not easy deprogramming bad college and university habits.

Once I started work, I realised the traditional career and workplace cloth cut an uncomfortable fit. The ordinarily greasy corporate pole seemed too slippery for a regular agitator, non-conformist type. But, as an enthusiastic graduate, I tried my British best. However, no matter how much I struggled, I couldn't force myself to play the bizarre and exhausting game of schmoosing, appearing in the right places, connecting with the right people, thinking how every utterance might affect my career. Making the right managerial propitiations seemed far too much effort and an irresponsible use of cerebral capacity. I enjoyed the impartial 'let's follow the evidence, wherever it takes us' approach, rather than constantly toeing the party line.

Moreover, what was the point of all that effort if I could be jettisoned at the whim of someone higher up the food chain?

4.1 THE LOOK

Now before we go much further, I need to explain an important concept that I'd initially sensed growing up but didn't pay much attention to, as it played second fiddle to verbal and physical abuse. It became more apparent as I grew older: 'The Look'. This will no doubt be familiar to anyone housing a helix of non-Caucasian DNA. Familiar, certainly, to those who'd fail Adolf's Aryan Race Test. I suspect the lower the score, the greater the familiarity. Allow me to clarify with an example:

One stormy autumnal morning, I arise to find my wooden front gate violently flapping in the wind. Not bothering to change, I lace my trainers and bolt to the back shed in the pouring rain. Fiddling with the lock, I open the door and scour the array of paint pots, tools, toys and junk. *Goodness' sake, this shed needs a good clean. Come on, come on... Aha, there! A piece of sturdy green rope.* I sprint to the front of the house. It now feels as though I'm in the middle of some thunderous sea storm, standing on the deck of the Ontario. As

I try to remember my nautical knots, the rain continues to lash down, and I'm entirely drenched. *Right, over, under, through, pull tight... Hmmm. This isn't working. Lord.*

I momentarily glance away, and my eye catches the gaze of a seemingly pleasant, elderly chap, soldiering past, not overly concerned with the stormy weather. *He's seen it all. He's not bothered by any of this! Different generation. Not like this current one!* I smile at him and nod my head. It was a smile and nod of, *'Look at how preposterous this is! Yes, I'm getting soaked! Isn't this all quite amusing? Haha!'* That kind of well-intentioned smile and nod. The dear old chap turns to me with a look of utter, utter revulsion. Think Greta Thunberg glaring at Donald Trump. He screws his eyes, looks directly at me. *'Don't smile at me!'* his rotten scowl wordlessly says. *'What are you doing in my country anyway, you dammed Paki?!'*

How was I so sure? Well, my radar is finely tuned after all these years. I smile, nod my head, and continue grappling with the knot.

4.2 UNCOMFORTABLE OCCUPATIONS

As with most students, I ran the excruciating job application gauntlet: job fairs, tome-like application forms, psychometric tests, day-long assessment centres (sometimes longer), and, of course, the desperately agonising group exercises. All that pomp and ceremony to secure a graduate job in some administrative function that likely wouldn't exert a schoolchild.

I tried to avoid most of the larger, popular organisations for that reason. Instead, I focussed on the obscure and niche. After a handful of interviews, I secured a role working for a software house in Camberley developing neural network simulations. All fancy, *Star Trek* technology. However, these weren't any whimsical simulations. No, these modelled war field scenarios used by militaries across the world. The neural network part fascinated me; precisely what I wanted, following my university degree. However, the war field content presented a moral issue. I didn't want to spend the best years of my life developing software for military purposes. Alas, an intriguing opportunity, but I politely declined.

'IF HE DOESN'T WANT to drink our wine, then let him drink our water,' quipped one of my early employers, while scowling, as though he'd just seen Beelzebub. He happened to be a famous millionaire Dragon-type character. I didn't appreciate the comment in front of the whole development team. His fire breathing may have impressed or intimidated others, but it wasn't working with me. I joined the company as a software developer, and didn't realise the umbrella organisation also owned a company that sold a range of costly wines (though I'm no expert in this area). Yep, my first project involved developing an elaborate new wine shopping experience.

I felt uncomfortable. My Parisian manager wasn't the most sympathetic, with his investigative line of questioning. 'But what iz za problem Azeef? We are not asking you to drink za wine, ha?! Just write Java code and drink water!' The words tumbled from his mouth while his face reddened like a plump tomato. Between the two positions, the millionaire and Inspector Clouseau, I'd decided I'd had enough by the end of the week.

Il n'y a pas plus sourd que celui qui ne veut pas entendre.

'ASIF, I've got a great role for you!' The agent sounded even more ebullient than usual.

'Aha, what is it?'

'Well, it's in the gaming industry. I think you're ideal.' I could sense he was punching commission percentages into his large desk calculator.

'That's great, I've worked on a few computer games in the past. I interviewed with Mirage Software shortly after university. They developed *Rise of the Robots*, great game.'

'Er, that's good, but gaming as in betting, gambling. It's a great role; can I send your CV over to them today?' he continued.

'Eh, betting? Oh, I don't work in the gambling industry.'

'Why on earth not?!'

'Sorry, it's a problem from a religious and moral...'

'It pays very well,' he interrupted, 'you can practically set your own salary. And there's a 50% bonus on top of the salary! Are you sure? I can probably get you an interview this week!'

That seemed like an awful lot of money for a graduate. I paused, momentarily considering his Faustian bargain.

The Islamic position on wine[1] (generally intoxicants) and gambling is the same. Some benefit may exist from partaking, perhaps temporary delight in the case of wine, or winning a tenner on the 2:50 at Haydock with gambling. But overall, the harm outweighs the benefit[2]. Consequently, both are proscribed. The prohibition includes every link within the chain: collecting the grapes, pressing, bottling, transporting, and selling, with or without the computer code.

'Er, sorry, mate. Though do let me know if you've got anything in the computer gaming industry.'

4.3 PILGRIM'S RETURN

In the late 1990s, after a couple of working years, I managed to save enough money for the *Hajj* (Arabic: Pilgrimage). Like most people, I was wholly ill-prepared for it. Sure, I'd heard trench tales from friends and relatives, but, frankly, how difficult could it be? The hubris of youth. I left my house in two pieces of white cloth resembling two large bath towels held together with only a handful of strategically positioned safety pins, an unnerving experience for someone who prefers to layer on clothing. There were around 25 others on the same £1000 'no-frills' package on the flight to Jeddah. More luxurious packages were available, but for several times that amount.

Hajj is the fifth pillar of Islam, after the testimony of faith, prayer, almsgiving and fasting. It's the pilgrimage to the ancient city of Makkah (Mecca) in the heart of that impenetrable golden Arabian desert, a journey wearied by sandals and drenched with tears for millennia to the sacred house of God. According to Muslim tradition, rituals of the Hajj date back several thousand years to the time of Abraham and his (second) wife Hagar, who had settled in the Makkah valley with their son Ishmael. The Ka'ba, the cubic building now adorned by black velvet cloth, lies in the centre of the city. Muslims believe Adam[3] built the structure as the first place of worship on Earth, but it was destroyed and washed away along with the impious in the great flood of Noah. However, the foundations remained, and the structure was rebuilt by Abraham and his elder son, Ishmael.

Each year millions of Muslims from every city, every town, and every deep ravine on Earth gather on the plains of Makkah. In scenes reminiscent of some ancient biblical event, pilgrims gather, dusty, dishevelled, heads uncovered, wrapped in two sheets of white cloth, under the blistering Arabian sun. Spiritual significance aside, the vast numbers involved, air and land transportation, water, food, accommodation, sanitation and encompassing infrastructure represent some of the most logistically challenging for any single event on Earth.

The actual Hajj event comprises a set of rituals spread over six days across different sites within the precincts of Makkah. Circumambulating the Ka'ba, trekking back and forth to (symbolically) stone the devil, wandering around the plains of Arafat, not to mention the mundane activities of sourcing food and queuing for the bathroom, all require considerable patience, discipline and physical stamina to complete. Anything to reduce loo visits is generally a good strategy. The experience can also be quite costly, particularly in current times. Consequently, only the financially and physically able are obliged to perform the pilgrimage. Alas, none of my grandparents from Pakistan ever managed to make the journey.

Once out of the airport, around 12 hours after landing, we arrived at the hotel in Makkah before the start of the event. I realised how few frills were on offer. Off the bat, I found myself in a large room with the 25 others and possibly half that number of mattresses arranged in rows, with insufficient space for a rodent (or cockroach) to navigate. *Ok, not too bad,* I thought. *This is a pilgrimage, after all.* Then I discovered the single bathroom we'd all have to share. *Ok, this may be a little tricky.*

Trekking around the different Hajj sites during those days, I clocked more than 100 miles, all in my brown leather sandals and two garments (which weren't so white towards the end). I reckon sourcing food contributed a good number of those miles. Despite this, the Hajj is perhaps more mentally and emotionally challenging than physical. Never did I believe such masses of humanity could gather in such confined places. In an email to work colleagues after, I likened the feel to a capacity Wembley crowd, only a factor of ten greater. Trying to keep calm and spiritually focussed with such gargantuan groups arguing, pushing and jostling for the best position requires a supreme effort. My placid demeanour only wavered a handful of times, and only under extreme provocation.

A few particularly memorable moments from the trip included: arriving in a baggage holding area that was the equivalent of a Google Data Centre; witnessing hundreds of thousands of pilgrims gathered on Mount Arafat, creating a bizarre snow-like effect in the middle of the desert; and an over-enthusiastic chap throwing his slipper at the largest stone pillar (representing the Devil), instead of the customary small pebbles. But the most memorable moment involved climbing to the top floor within the mosque and gazing at the mass around the Ka'ba below, like a single amorphous body, swirling around and around, a sight that never wearied the eyes. Gathered on those great tracts of earth with several million others, all dressed in the simplest garb, all calling to God, was a uniquely humbling, emotional, and spiritual event.

Two WEEKS ON, with blistered feet and red chafed thighs, and weighing a good 5kg lighter, I hobbled back onto a government airport coach with my suitcase and two sports bags. The dark brown décor and thick dusty curtains reminded me of school coaches back in the early 80s. My throat felt laced with stinging nettles, having succumbed to the temptation of drinking ice water in the desert tents (despite many 'don't feed the Gremlins' type warnings). And, to top it all, I'd been struck down with a spiky new influenza strain.

A bumpy, stuffy two hours later, we arrived at Jeddah airport. *Nearly there, very nearly there.* Amidst the maelstrom and jostling bodies, I could see the glorious prize ahead: our Boeing 777. But I had to negotiate a few more obstacles first. Present in body, absent in mind, I waited amongst several hundred others huddled near the large glass doors, all hoping to be called through to passport control.

Some daring pilgrims tried to squeeze past the airport guards; all were ignominiously sent back to the group, often quite forcefully. I decided to wait, lost in my own foggy cocoon, drunk with emotional and physical fatigue. To the right, some last-minute fisticuffs had broken out between two groups, both vying for early entrance to the departure area. They'd already forgotten what they (should have) learnt over the previous two weeks: patience, humility, and discipline. To the left, another group decided to start banging on the glass barrier, hoping to gain the attention of the Saudi airport officials. *They certainly achieved that*, I thought, as they were dragged away.

Half an hour later, my moment came. The guard motioned me to move, and with the renewed vigour of a marathon runner on the final stadium lap, I hurried through the departure check-in area. After a cursory passport check (even the officials simply wanted to herd people onto flights), I stepped onto the BA plane and collapsed into my seat with a mixture of euphoria and exhaustion. I stretched back, as much as one is able in an Economy Class seat, and placed my head on the rest. It didn't matter I couldn't recline beyond 80°. It felt like the most sumptuous, comfortable seat, I'd ever experienced. The aeroplane lights remained dimmed as the remaining passengers silently boarded, all in similar states of haziness.

At 03:00, in the dark cabin, the only noise came from the whirring murmur of the air vents above. I ripped a blanket from its plastic packaging and wrapped it around myself like a baby in swaddling clothes. Yes, it was good to be going home, back to Blighty.

4.4 SUITCASE LADEN WITH SUSPICIONS ITEMS

If my father ever penned a money-saving 'How-to Guide', I'm convinced it'd sell millions. Over the years, I've marvelled at his frugality, ability to spot a bargain, and creative approach to solving the banalest problems. I was a little bemused when he offered to *acquire* the plane tickets for Amjad's wedding in 1999. Working for an airline, I'd made my own arrangements.

'I'll take care of your tickets to Pakistan. You two don't worry about a thing.'

Amjad and Tasneem glanced at each other. I chuckled. *This will be interesting.*

'Don't worry, we can book the tickets,' Tasneem interjected. 'There are direct flights from Manchester to Lahore. I'm in surgery the following week, so I don't need any delays.'

'No, no,' my father insisted, 'I'll get a better deal than you.'

A week later, in a scene reminiscent of *Rocky IV*, the pair sat on a hard, wooden bench surrounded by a throng of other passengers, all desperately trying to keep warm. The outside thermometer had frozen at -10 °C. Overhead, a flimsy plastic covering flapped in the wind, and snow beat down incessantly, smiting their faces. Teeth clattering, they stared ahead at the Russian aircraft in silence, vowing to make their own travel arrangements in future.

Ingenious. I didn't even know a route via Uzbekistan existed. You can take the man from Village 247, but not Village 247 from the man.

IRRITATED, hot and bothered. That's how I felt touching down in Islamabad. They assigned me possibly the worst seat on the plane, just ahead of the WCs, with my knees touching the plane wall ahead. Thankfully my travelling companion didn't mind me turning my legs 30° towards him. My stomach churned with hunger to the point of nausea due to my strategic refusal of food, thereby limiting trips to the aforementioned WCs.

I'd just arrived from Heathrow for Amjad's wedding, the final family participant to land. I negotiated my way to the baggage collection area, a dimly lit, drab hangar setup with a thick soupy stench of sweat and heat. The carousel had seen better days, perhaps it was still pedal-powered by someone behind the brick wall. On this day, though, it had decided to stop carouselling, which meant two poor airport workers had the unenviable job of manually shifting each piece of luggage. I felt exhausted and a little guilty watching the pair graft. My fellow passengers appeared less sympathetic. Half an hour later, I spotted my new Samsonite hard-shell case and raced towards it, handing each worker a crisp 100 rupee note, which they accepted with alacrity.

Right, next job, an internal flight to Lahore. I edged towards the ticket sales booth through the multitudes and noise. A stern-looking woman sat behind the counter. 'Acha... iq ticket... chayda,' I began. Alas, my local language skills hadn't improved much since the last trip. She understood the message. 'We only have business class tickets on this flight, or you can wait another three hours for the next flight.' I took a few deep breaths and grudgingly swiped my card.

Under the searing Islamabad sun, I glared at the odd-looking contraption slouched on the tarmac. It looked familiar. *Where have I seen it before...? Hmmm. Yes, that's it, Indiana Jones, 15 years earlier. Not sure which one.* I didn't realise anyone still flew these things, let alone for commercial use. The aircraft was, in fact, a turboprop Fokker F27. Fortunately for me, I hadn't studied the Fokker 'Notable Accidents & Incidents' list beforehand. I later did check, and it boasted quite a few entries.

Lord, I'm not getting on that plane! Unfortunately for me, I didn't have another method of getting to Lahore to meet the rest of my family. Travelling in Pakistan with a giant neon sign declaring 'GULLIBLE WESTERN TRAVELLER' hovering above my head, I didn't fancy taking my chances via another route. I had little choice, except risk life and limb and squeeze on the tiny Fokker plane. Perhaps I could convince myself I was Indy. I should have packed my brown Fedora hat and whip.

I crawled up the tight staircase and navigated to my 'business class' window seat. A good move. Even this seat barely accommodated my frame. No sooner had I settled than a stewardess appeared and offered a hot lemon-scented towel. Given the circumstances, I didn't feel that would help much. I accepted the gift nonetheless, and dabbed my brow with a citrus cloth for the first time in my life.

'Ladies and gentlemen, we have a technical problem. Take-off will be delayed by a few minutes,' announced the pilot in a thick Pakistani accent. *Oh great...*

I peered forward and caught the pilot springing from his seat. He jostled towards the exit to join a throng of airport officials, all attempting to close the aeroplane door. *This is a little unusual. A new entry into my bizarre incidents log.* Unfortunately, despite balancing on his toes, the pilot couldn't reach the top of the door. The stewardesses gathered to watch the show from inside the plane, and volunteered the tallest to join the effort. This meaty woman of equally impressive height reluctantly edged outside and grasped the top before firmly dragging the door down. She'd have made a decent wrestler. The door slammed shut with a thud. *Crikey, I hope it hasn't been damaged and opens on the other side.* I looked around the cabin. Nobody else seemed the slightest bit worried.

When I'm on a plane, I generally try to convince myself there isn't really 40,000 feet of clear blue sky between my good person and the hard ground. That's not so easy in a Fokker flying at such low altitude where every minute landscape detail is visible below. A turbulent and hair-raising 40 minutes later, I arrived at Lahore Airport to find a mob of enthusiastic relatives waiting outside.

Amjad's wedding was an eye-opening, culturally insightful though hectic affair, an elaborate event spanning a week across Islamabad, Lahore and Faisalabad and a host of smaller towns and villages whose names I've forgotten. Much had changed since our trip back in 1981. I enjoyed the sounds, the hustle and bustle, the multitude of cuisines, but not so much the driving. No, the driving felt like the *Crazy Cars* computer game, the short-cut between Lahore and Faisalabad proving particularly perilous.

Given the pound's strength against the Pakistani rupee, we could dine out most nights. And we dined well. I was often volunteered by relatives to foot the bill. I met hundreds of people, all somehow related to me. They tried to explain how, but my eyes glazed after a few minutes of explanation[4].

I marvelled at the vestiges of British colonial past dotted around the country. Railway stations, churches, schools and colleges all exuded a very familiar architectural feel. Arriving at Lahore Railway Station felt like arriving at Marylebone for my morning commute (yes, people mostly complain about the trains in Lahore, too).

We may have been the same hue, spoke the same language (ish) and enjoyed the same food as the locals, but my siblings and I were clearly foreigners. And the locals delighted highlighting our foreignness at every opportunity. We walked differently, dressed differently (even wearing the same clothes), spoke differently and thought differently.

'We should visit the book market today,' Tasneem announced, the day before my departure. *What a great opportunity to find some bargain, perhaps even antique books,* I thought. With no dissenting voices, after a full breakfast, comprising parotta, yoghurt and chickpeas, we jumped into the mini-jeep and headed towards the market in downtown Lahore. We arrived early to avoid the midday heat and crowds to find a multitude already browsing. But what a sight! A bibliophile's wonderland: rows upon rows of tables laden with books on every conceivable subject. A dusty, little grimy Waterstones in the open air, popular with locals and tourists.

My eyes widened as I scanned the technology books: Java, C++, UNIX, Visual Basic (yes), all at a fraction of their regular price back in Blighty. Most of the books were special 'Indian Edition' sold in the Indian Subcontinent – crude copies, poor print, and paper that would barely pass latrine quality standards in the West. However, the content appeared identical to the originals.

And, frankly, at 5% RRP, I could strain my eyes a little to read the print. I also grabbed a stack of Arabic books, given my recent interest in learning the language, piled them into whatever plastic bags I could find, and heaved them back to the mini jeep.

That night, I had the tortuous task of packing my suitcases, about half a dozen quarts into a single pint pot. With enough encouragement, and after exhausting every possible packing permutation, I zipped the two cases. *Goodness' sake, I just need to move them now.* They were rather dense. I could imagine the conversation with Customs back home: 'Are you packing dark matter in these? You do know that's an illegal substance to traffic?' Escaping from Pakistan wasn't difficult, once I'd paid the 3-fold baggage fees plus 'a little extra' (albeit grudgingly).

Around 18 hours later, I arrived bleary-eyed at Manchester Airport. An airport official greeted me with the familiar, 'Excuse me, sir, do you mind opening your suitcase?' I wasn't surprised. I flicked open the clasps, and the top sprung open like a jack in a box, a few books vaulting onto the floor. The official inspected them before handing them back to me.

'Right, please come with us, sir.' Two officials led me into a tiny room with a square black table and three uncomfortable IKEA chairs. A dark window adorned one side of the wall. The burly guard hoisted my suitcase on the table – an impressive feat.

'Right, what were you doing in Pakistan?' No pleasantries to get us started. No offer of tea or refreshments. The elder of the two men wore a nasty expression from the moment he laid his accusative eyes on me. The younger seemed more amiable. Perhaps they were trying the good cop/bad cop routine.

Still a little foggy from the long flight, I replied, 'Er, I was at my brother's wedding.'

'And did you travel anywhere else while you were there?' the younger man asked.

'Quite a few places around Lahore and Faisalabad, all part of the wedding event. Look, I'm just glad to be back on terra firma, to be honest. Why are you asking me all these questions? I'm shattered and would like to go home.'

'Terror, what?!'

'Er, ground, just back on the ground. We experienced a lot of turbulence flying here, and the airline assigned me another awkward seat.'

'Did you go anywhere in the north? Any training camps...?'

Aha, now we're getting somewhere. He referred to military camps used to train Muslim fighters before being dispatched to different theatres of war. Attitudes towards the camps had shifted a full 180° in the space of two decades. In the 80s, they enjoyed full Western support during the Soviet Afghanistan invasion. By the 90s, they were considered a little irksome, but were mostly tolerated, particularly during the Bosnian conflict. However, by the early 2000s, post 9/11, most had been forcibly closed or bombed, and some operated underground.

'No, no training of any kind. I did consider some IT training, though. Time didn't permit, I'm afraid.'

The two paused, pondering over the next line of questioning. 'And why do you have all these books?'

'Well, I work in IT and...'

The younger man interjected, 'But you also have Arabic books.'

'Are the two mutually exclusive?' I snapped. 'I am learning Arabic.'

The two dumbfounded automatons floundered, failing to remember the next section of the script. *Lord, I need to get out of this room.* I was beginning to feel the walls contract around me.

'Look, I work in IT. Actually, I'm a bit of a geek, and I program a lot, C/C++, Java. You see, all these books were incredibly cheap. I work for *this* airline,' pointing to my badge. I paused for breath. 'I'm also a keen language student. There's really no sinister pathology here. Everyone can move on.'

They turned their attention to my British Airways badge. Suddenly the mood flipped. We'd shifted from a deep Siberian freeze to a fresh spring meadow in a few seconds. The two eyed my passport again, then badge, and finally at each other.

'Ok, we're sorry to have inconvenienced you today, Mr Rana. You're free to leave.'

I shook my head, squashed the books back inside my suitcase, slammed it shut, and hurriedly left the room.

4.5 ARABIC LESSONS IN NEW YORK

I've only been to America once, thankfully pre 9/11, but despite that, the reception was frosty, and that's being quite charitable; sufficiently frosty to dissuade a return visit. But the whole experience could have been much worse, I suppose. In a parallel universe, I could have been accused of being an undercover Al-Qaidah operative on a clandestine mission, for example – by my wife, post 9/11, at JFK airport... Oh, wait, that *did* happen to a friend of mine. Now, before you jump on the blower to MI5, his wife was suffering from severe psychiatric issues at the time. From all the nightmare airport scenarios Muslim males can face in our time, that's probably topping the table. Poor chap. The US authorities interrogated him for 10 hours, before eventually releasing him late in the night. To make matters worse, they only gave him one cup of water, a soggy biscuit, and a single napkin. They didn't use the water or napkin for anything else, mind. Thankfully for him, his suitcases contained ample psychiatric medicinal evidence to substantiate his wife's behaviour. His impeccable history helped, too. Incidentally, he's still happily married.

As FOR MY own visit to America, I had an unusual mission, and not one that I particularly wanted to endure (more on that later). The mission, as described on the card before it self-destructed, *seemed* reasonably straightforward: fly from Heathrow to New York, hop over to New Jersey, have lunch with the professor at the Marriott, hop back to New York, and return to London just in time for work on Monday morning, 09:00 sharp — all in around 48 hours. Unfortunately, I couldn't swing an extra day off work due to an important (boring) meeting Monday morning. I bought a company 'standby ticket' to further complicate matters, which meant I wasn't guaranteed a seat on either leg. It also meant the considerable ignominy of prowling around the check-in area like a cat burglar, hoping one of my would-be passengers had broken down on the M25 or forgotten a passport. Failing to secure a seat on the London flight would have been embarrassing but sufferable. However, the prospect of being stranded on the return leg didn't bear contemplating. Plus, 'IT Consultant Marooned in New York' would have made an excruciatingly banal movie plot, and I didn't want to play the lead role.

I arrived at Heathrow with my laptop bag and luggage case and headed straight for the check-in area, ensuring my BA airline pass was on full, resplendent display. The attendant looked at my passport and then ticket. 'Ah, you're on a standby ticket – one moment.'

'Yes,' I said, tapping my badge. 'Airline staff.'

She punched a few keys on her terminal. 'Yes, don't worry, there are quite a few free spaces on this flight. You'll get on.'

I smiled. Of course, I'd already taken a sneaky peak at the numbers the day before, one of the benefits of working for an airline company. But the prospect of a last-minute booking surge always loomed.

'Any chance of an upgrade to business class?' I asked, nudging my badge again. The attendant glanced at the badge and then down at the terminal again.

'Er, yes, there are lots of free seats.'

'Aha, marvellous!' I exclaimed.

I took my documents and headed towards baggage control, before walking straight through, feeling rather pleased with myself. Airport security barely noticed me waltzing through. My first trip to America and the Big Apple, and I was looking forward to the journey. As part of my pre-flight routine, I'd checked the aircraft model, a Boeing 747-400, a fine plane with a good safety record. Things were going well.

Once onboard, I grabbed my book, notepad, and pen, then placed my bag in the locker above. I sat back in my roomy business class seat. *Oh yes, this is very comfortable.* The flight passed uneventfully, with the serenity only punctuated by the occasional pocket of Atlantic turbulence, thankfully nothing too bone-shaking. The *Summa Theologica* kept me entertained through most of the flight. As the wide blue expanse below grew ever narrower, I started chatting with a Finnish lady, a lecturer in linguistics at the University of Helsinki, travelling with her children. Another language aficionado, what good fortune. The opportunity to discuss language agglutination and verb conjugations between Finnish and Arabic was too good to miss. I had learnt a little Finnish while writing my thesis at university.

'You see, both languages are quite similar in that regard...' I started, before being interrupted from behind.

'Excuse me, sir, you need to complete this landing card.' I turned around to see an airline stewardess thrusting a batch of cards in my direction.

'Sure.' I took one and handed the remainder to my Finnish companions.

I scanned the card and the questions, using my customary exam technique; just to assess the lay of the land. *I'll come back to any difficult questions,* I thought. *Ok, name, address, passport number. No fruit and veg, no grain. No lumps of cash in my bag. I haven't touched any livestock. No terrorist affiliations... obviously. Haha, I* thought, *these questions are easy!*

A few minutes later, I polished off the remaining checkboxes, and turned back to the Finns.

'But can you beat this: ها - ون – كتب – ي – س – ف three prefixes and two suffixes on the root.' I wrote carefully in disjointed Arabic to emphasise the point. There was no way she was going to trump that one. I sat back, satisfied.

'That's impressive but look at this...' she responded.

'Ladies and gentlemen, we will soon be arriving at JFK Airport. Please return to your seats and fasten your belts.'

I smiled. 'We'll have to continue this another time – perhaps on the journey back to London.' I placed the landing card and pen back in my top pocket and sat back.

Twenty minutes later, we landed at JFK airport. I bade farewell to the Finns, as I struggled off the plane and down through the jet bridge, then through a series of narrow corridors. The décor appeared depressingly grey and dull. A stuffy aroma filtered through the passages. *Is this the famous JFK airport, in one of the most famous cities in the world?* I felt I'd been transported back in time to circa 1965. Heathrow seemed modern and vibrant by comparison, even my favourite Terminal 3.

By the time I'd reached passport control, I felt flustered, and was perspiring heavily due to the humidity and long trek. The queue rapidly dissolved ahead of me, and suddenly the immigration officer nodded at me. I blearily handed my passport and landing card to him. The man wore a short, greying moustache and an unyielding, matter-of-fact expression, clearly a powerful man in that three-foot-square cubicle. *Oh great, just what I need, a hot and bothered Mr Mackay type.* He opened the passport, looked at my photo, and then at me. 'And, what is the purpose of your visit?' he demanded, as a deep furrow spread across his brow, his face still stern and unflinching.

Resisting all my creative and voluble instincts, 'Er, just meeting a prospective relative,' I uttered meekly.

'Eh? Prospective? What does that mean? Where do they live?'

'Er, Paterson, New Jersey.'

'How long are you staying?' His tone wasn't becoming any more cheery.

'Just a few days.'

'That's a very short visit.'

'Yes, I have to return to work on Monday morning.'

He paused. My terse approach seemed to be working.

He squinted and focussed on my passport once more, before moving onto my landing card. As he flipped it over, his face froze. 'What is this on the back of the card?'

Eh, what's he talking about?!

'Excuse me?'

'These scribbles on the back of the card? What are they?'

Oh wait... Lord, that's my Arabic lesson with the Finnish lady. I must have written on there by mistake.

I paused for a few seconds.

'Er, er... That's just an example of Arabic verb conjugation with...'

'What?! What are you talking about?' he interrupted, his voice becoming increasingly irritated.

'Look, it was a mistake. I mistakenly wrote on the card.' I spoke in a slow, deliberate tone.

He focussed hard at the card again, the focus of a man grappling with the mysteries of dark matter or quantum physics. I could see the cogs and wheels whirring in his head. *What are these squiggles? Is this some encoded message for terrorist operatives in NYC? What is he planning?*

'Look, it just says "So they will soon write it" in Arabic.'

'They will soon write what? Who are they, and what will they write?' he demanded.

'It's just an example, it means nothing. I wrote it by mistake on the card. I thought I was writing in my pad.'

He shook his head and picked up the desk phone. 'Can you come down here? Something to check.'

A few moments later, his colleague appeared. Mackay handed the card to him, before whispering a few unintelligible words.

'Sir, stand to one side until we get this checked.'

Oh, for goodness' sake! I've got people pouring over my verb conjugations! How ridiculous. Now I had the embarrassment of other passengers walking past, nosily rubbernecking. *There's nothing to see here, people. Move on.*

An excruciating ten minutes later, the man appeared again with my card.

Mackay beckoned me forward. 'Right, you shouldn't be writing on the landing card – it's a very important document.'

'Yes, agreed. I'll be sure to avoid that in future.'

'Yes, do that. You could easily land in trouble here, and you don't want that, do you?'

'No, no, we wouldn't want that.'

'Right. Just make sure you leave on time.' He stamped my passport and handed it back.

Eh? Leave on time? Did he really think I wanted to stay there for a moment longer than necessary?!

I managed to meet with the professor at the hotel as planned. The meeting didn't go well. Around 36 hours later, I travelled back from Newark airport. Thankfully, leaving the country proved much easier than entering. As we touched down in Heathrow, I breathed a huge sigh of relief. *Glad that's over. Don't want to go back there in a hurry.*

I looked at my watch. It read 06:30, Monday, 11th September 2000.

4.6 EGYPT: LAND OF PHARAOHS AND CAMELS

'Asif, I just came back from Egypt, but had a rather bizarre experience. Can you shed some light on it?' a colleague asked over lunch.

'Sure, I'll give it my British best. What happened?'

'Well, while snorkelling in Sharm El-Sheikh, one of the tour guides offered me 100 camels in exchange for my wife. A straight swap on the spot. He was willing to deliver the camels to any destination.'

I paused. 'Hmmm. Quite a wealthy tour guide. Perhaps he was offering on behalf of some rich Sheikh. Did he mention what colour of camel?'

'Eh?! What does that matter?!'

~

OUR WORK PIPELINE in early 2001 resembled Old Mother Hubbard's cupboard – bone dry. I needed a distraction, rather than working on mundane client proposals and generally trying to look busy in the office. Something a little more intellectually stimulating... *Right, let's go and see Peter O.*

After an hour's worth of lively debate with my manager (door closed), I'd managed to swing a full 30 days off work, citing 'pursuit of outside academic interests'. He eyed me dubiously, possibly enviously, as I described a potential opportunity in the Land of the Pharaohs. He finally agreed, albeit reluctantly, though probably so I'd stop talking and leave his office so he could continue with his day.

Aside from anything else, I needed a break from the banality of staring at my 22" monitor each day. My attempts to learn Arabic over the previous few years were not yielding enough. I needed a more intensive, more immersive, and more interactive experience. What better way than combining a 'holiday' with a rigorous Arabic course in the heart of Egypt? So, after a brief survey of options, I found an ideal course: 8 hours 1-1 tuition each day followed by another 6 hours homework at night, for 30 days. That sounded immersive enough to me. Cairo had the added benefit of a short 5-hour plane journey, plus a comparatively low cost of living.

I dialled the Internet using my 56kb/s modem and ordered a large canister of mosquito repellent and sun cream in preparation for the adventure. I didn't need much else, other than a few clothes and books. Shortly before departure, I called the Arabic Institute to ensure someone would collect me from the airport. Trying to negotiate my way to the accommodation in downtown Cairo seemed a little too daring for my liking, particularly on my first trip.

After assuring me he would personally be at the airport, the manager whispered, 'Whatever you do, don't wear a *thawb* (Arabic: traditional dress) or speak any Arabic when you get to the airport.'

I thought about telling him it didn't matter how quietly he spoke; mobile phones had ears and long memories. *What on earth is he talking about? I'm arriving in an Arab land. Why wouldn't I wear local dress and flex my linguistic muscles a little?* 'Er, ok, if that's what you advise,' I replied. 'You don't want them to get the wrong idea. I'll explain when you get here,' he added.

He sounded serious, so I asked no further questions.

I landed at Cairo Airport a few days later, dressed in my tracksuit bottoms and sports top. I looked like a genuine tourist and could easily have been on my way to Sharm El-Sheikh for two weeks snorkelling in the Red Sea. Perhaps that's what he was implying. Coasting through customs along with the other holidaymakers, I spotted him on my way out. He had my name neatly printed on a white piece of cardboard.

'Assalaamu alaikum...' I greeted him with a huge smile.

'Walaikum salaam...' he answered

'It's good to be here,' I beamed.

'Yes, yes, my car is just outside. Please come, come.'

As we stepped outside the gloomy airport into the searing light, a hot gust of wind blew in our direction. It felt like opening the oven door after a 15-minute 200°C preheat.

'Quite warm at the moment, I see.'

He laughed. 'Yes, it will get hotter this month.'

I placed my luggage in the boot and got into his car. After a few more pleasantries, I asked why he'd instructed me not to speak Arabic or wear local dress.

'Well, we had a few brothers from the UK who made that mistake. Their dress and trying to speak Arabic meant hours of questioning at the airport. You see, they were mistaken for militants trying to cause trouble in the country. You don't want to end up in an Egyptian jail. Trust me, brother. They aren't like your jails in England.' He spoke remarkably proficient English. He was right, though. Egyptian jails were known for their brutal conditions and once inside, many people effortlessly disappeared.

'We've had a lot of bombings and attacks in the country recently, lots of attacks on Westerners, tourist places. The government is worried people from outside are involved, providing support.'

'*Allahu Must'aan* (Arabic: May God help us!), I only want to learn Arabic!'

'Yes, it's too sad. Too sad. So, better avoid any potential problems while you're at the airport. Don't worry, you're ok once inside. Mostly.'

'Mostly?'

'Well, people are routinely monitored.'

Great...

Around an hour later, we pulled up outside the three-bedroom villa. However, this villa didn't have a lavish pool and surrounding thick foliage. It wasn't overlooking the Nile, either. No, this villa resembled student accommodation back in Blighty – lots of grey concrete, spartan décor with few amenities. Zero distractions, too, which wasn't necessarily a bad thing. Inside I met my fellow house-mates, three other students of Indian/Pakistani extraction, two from America and one from Canada. All had landed in the past few days; we'd all chosen the same Arabic course. We swapped stories about entering the country and the general immigrant Muslim experience in the US and Canada, remarkably similar stories. Our discussions continued throughout the night, only halted by the morning call to prayer.

My state penitentiary-like room appeared carefully crafted for a serious student: concrete floor, no Internet, no TV, a mini desk with interrogator's chair, and a single bed with a mattress that made the floor seem comfy. A solitary window allowed a handful of rays. During the night, mosquitoes butchered my legs and feet, despite copious applications of repellent. I decided to purchase a high-powered fan that I positioned to blow across my body. While the mosquitoes busied themselves at night, during the day, armies of ants crawled around the kitchen, accompanied with armour-plated cockroaches. It took several hard slipper wallops before these critters finally perished. It appeared the Egyptian 'roaches had taken a different evolutionary path to their more benign British cousins.

The Arabic tuition continued for the entire month, with only a couple of days holiday. My language skills flourished, though I still struggled with Cairo taxi drivers, who spoke the colloquial dialect rather than classical Arabic (think Shakespeare landing in the middle of Newcastle city centre). On two days off, we visited the Central Cairo Museum and the Pyramids of Giza. Aside from the frustration of many taxi drivers all vying for our attention, the Museum was a fascinating place. As expected, there were lots of relics from Ancient Egypt, but the real jewel lay inside the specially cooled mummy room. Entrance was allowed only after parting with a further 100 Egyptian Pounds. In the centre of the room lay the astonishingly well-preserved body of an Egyptian

Pharaoh, possibly Ramses II[5] – the Pharoah of Moses. He looked like a mean hombre, even after 4000 years.

The more perilous experience occurred visiting the Pyramids on camelback. First, I had no appreciation of camel mass, or how swiftly they could run. I also repeatedly told our guide I'd never patted a camel, let alone ridden one. He assured us we'd be safe, though that didn't prevent him from instructing the camels to gallop across the desert, in a scene direct from *Lawrence of Arabia*, the great pyramids in the background. I nearly lost life and limb that day. Though, perhaps most disappointingly, the camel wasn't an expensive red either.

4.7 WHITE VESTS

A glorious summer's day in the middle of the school holidays. Aside from the England vs West Indies Test Matches (which looked like a foregone conclusion), what better way to enjoy it than frolicking in the countryside nearby? After breakfast, Sajad and I decided to ride our new bikes and explore the area. He'd recently pestered my parents to buy him a new drop handle, while I managed to acquire a hand-me-down BMX from a neighbour, so we had two superb engineering specimens.

Five minutes into the ride, we joined a busy main road. Sajad, keen to test his new bike, put his foot down and sped off. I didn't like riding on busy roads, so continued close to the curb at a steady pace. Out of nowhere, a small blue car appeared from behind. I could sense it getting closer and closer, until it clattered into my back wheel. The jolt knocked me clean off like a springboard diver. I flew headfirst through the air onto the hard pavement, while my bike continued screeching down the middle of the road. Meanwhile, the driver parked in a nearby spot and walked towards me.

I writhed in agony, my trousers torn, face bruised, and burn marks covered my arms. As though in a hazy dream, the driver, a silver-haired lady, peered over me, shook her head in headmistress disapproval, and then proceeded towards the church opposite.

Long before the days of mobile phones, 'no win no fee' and 'where's there's blame, there's a claim', and from a combination of shock and inexperience (what do I do here?), I remained silent and motionless. *Come on, lady, do something. I'm in pain here. At least help me before you go and pray? What happened to the Good Samaritan?* Nope, nothing. Not a jot. She disappeared inside.

Aside from dissuading me from road riding for many years, the incident focussed my attention on the church opposite and its distinctive signage. I had walked past the building on countless occasions, and vaguely recognised it as some type of modern church. However, on that sunny June day, sitting upright on the pavement with my mangled bike heaped in the middle of the road, my senses sharpened. Now, with remarkable clarity and presence of mind, I stared at the sign: The Church of Jesus Christ of Latter-day Saints. *What denomination of Christianity is this? One too many 'of's in the title,* I thought. *Who on earth are these latter-day saints, anyway?*

'It's QUITE warm to be wearing that thick vest, isn't it? Particularly after a game of football. You're making me uncomfortable just looking at you,' I quipped, while grinning at my work colleague Dave

'Well, these are special vests.'

'What, some designer vests? I quite like the *Peter Storm* variety.'

'No, these are special vests from the church. We wear them all the time.'

'Eh? Why would the church care what vests you wear?' I asked.

'Well, they're called Temple Garments. They remind us of our commitment to God. There's an element of modesty, too, and protection from evil.'

'Ok... I see why you don't mention them amongst the footie lads. I suspect they wouldn't understand the nomenclature, either. Well, at least you get free underclothes. That saves a neat little sum each year.'

'Er, not quite. We still have to buy them.'

'Oh... Well, at least they look comfortable.'

'Hmmm. Not that comfortable, they're ok.'

'You're not selling this particularly well.'

I enjoyed chatting with Dave. We'd spend hours discussing religion and philosophy, though mostly when we should have been developing computer software, despite repeated warnings from the gaffer.

Our conversations in the middle of the office sparked amusement and delight. Everyone knew Dave as a devout Mormon and me as a Muslim. There appeared a genuine appreciation that we could discuss our faiths without getting emotional and upset with our often radically differing beliefs.

I valued having Dave on the team. He provided a refreshing air cover. When I mentioned I wouldn't be attending the Christmas party one year as 'I didn't believe the Christmas story or that Jesus was born on the 25th of December', my manager retorted, 'Asif, don't worry about it. No one actually believes in the Christmas story except Dave.'

Amusingly, Dave spent the best part of two years trying to convert me to Mormonism. I appreciated his effort. He even offered me some quality white vests and said he'd 'put in a good word' at the Church. In return, I invited Dave to a local mosque and fed him spicy chicken biryani while we discussed theology.

He prepared me well. Years later, I'd shock many (invariably) young, well-dressed name-tagged men with my knowledge of Mormonism. They'd quickly move on.

4.8 ON GEESE AND PROFESSORS

Quite early, my parents made it clear we would all be going 'back home' to get married, so we shouldn't get any smart ideas. Aside from the aforesaid vocational vision, my mother dreamt about a batch of daughters-in-law, all busy under the same roof, ready at her beck and call, a little like the musical *Seven Brides for Seven Brothers*, minus a few brothers. The marriage threats created more amusement than anything else. We incessantly teased each other, particularly poor Tasneem. I'm unsure if the 'Declaration Form' even existed, but the mere mention sent shivers of terror through her bony being. Legend has it, she'd have to sign the form to allow any potential husband into the country. She vowed never to pick up a ballpoint. My father had selected someone from Village 247 as a match for her. A strange combo on paper. His incarceration a few years later put a spanner in the works.

On one occasion, I recall my father arriving home and congratulating my seven-year-old younger brother. It wasn't immediately apparent what he'd done to deserve the plaudits, but it later emerged that one of my aunts had just given birth to a daughter, and a potential match had been made. Consanguine marriages were the norm (and still occur). In our case, at least, these marriages were more 'recommended' rather than 'forced', though we heard many tales of unsuspecting boys and girls on family visits to Pakistan returning a few months later with a related (or unrelated) spouse. Thankfully, the forced, abduction type is becoming less common, due to increased education and better vigilance from UK authorities. In addition, as youngsters began delving into religious knowledge, they realised forced marriages were expressly prohibited. Kids quoting scripture left many parents quite shocked.

'COME, LET'S HAVE A CHAT.' My Uncle's raised brow suggested trouble. A few weeks earlier, Tasneem and I had arrived in Pakistan for a couple of weeks holiday. As soon as the suitcases slammed on the dusty hard floor, my aunt cried, 'Look, here are your wedding clothes all prepared for you!'

'Oh, I didn't realise I was getting married! No one told me about the plan!' Tasneem quipped.

My Uncle guided me down a steep set of dark stairs into his musty basement office, a room with a single flickering, flimsy incandescent light dangling from the ceiling. A small wooden table sat towards one end, flanked by two white plastic chairs. His office looked more like an Egyptian interrogation cell. Perhaps he would strap me down and pull out a range of sharp, metal objects, or a jug of water and cloth.

'Sit down...' He flipped open his Marlborough packet and swiftly lit a cigarette, before taking a deep puff. 'So, what do you think of Tasneem marrying my son?' He spoke in English to ensure no misunderstanding.

'Well, there's only one problem with that. She's not interes...'

'My son is interested. He'd like to move to England,' he interrupted.

'Right, but *she's* not interested, and nobody can force her.' I surprised myself with the forthright tone. Perhaps emboldened by the support I'd managed to secure from my influential Aunt Shameem, a few days earlier.

He paused as a wry smile spread across his face. It looked like a scene from a budget Bollywood film. 'Your sister lays a golden egg,' he continued, referring to her medical occupation. My uncle always had an eye on the financial vista.

'That may be true, but she doesn't want to marry your son.'

He took another deep puff, then another before spluttering and coughing in my direction, his disappointment etched on his face.

'I really think we should move on,' I said.

'If you're very sure there's nothing that can be done?'

'Yes, very sure.'

'Ok, ok. Jameel will be disappointed.' He sighed. 'Let's go and get fried fish on Allamah Iqbal Road.'

'Good idea, fried fish, yes. That'll cheer everyone up.'

'Yes, you can treat the whole family. And guests from Faisalabad. And guests from Karachi.'

It's NOT uncommon to see a list of requirements from potential parents-in-law: cash in the bank, salary, housing, cars, and so forth. Sometimes the specification can be very precise, as with the professor in New York.

He eyed me dubiously through his circular, black-rimmed spectacles. He clearly didn't want to be sitting in the Marriot hotel foyer talking to a prospective son-in-law. With his rotund physique, waistcoat and bow tie, he reminded me of Penfold, Danger Mouse's trusty sidekick. A little cleverer, mind. 'So, where do you work?' he finally asked.

'For an airline company.'

'Haha, an airline company? Doing what!?' He smirked, speaking with a native Indian twang.

'IT, computers, mainly programming.'

'Oh, I see. I thought you were serving people in the sky,' he chuckled.

'You mean cabin crew? No, I'm mostly on the ground.'

'Your job probably doesn't pay much?'

'Well, it's quite good for a graduate job, £25K a year, about $40K.'

The professor shook his head while stuffing a scone into his mouth. 'Is that all!? How can you support my daughter with that?!

No, no, you need to earn at *least* £50,000 before we'd even consider a marriage proposal.'

'Eh? Fifty thousand pounds?!'

'Yes, at least that.'

I pushed back in the easy leather chair and took a sip of mint tea. I later found out the professor, a high-flying surgeon in New York, raked in more than $250K each year, excluding private consultancy.

'Yes, £50K,' he repeated, 'AFTER tax.'

I violently coughed. To add insult to injury, it took several minutes to work out the gross UK salary required for £50K net. The meeting didn't last much longer after that, and no spectacular wedding in New York City followed.

4.9 A DIFFICULT DAY

On a characteristically banal Tuesday morning. I woke at the usual time and prepared my two semi-boiled eggs, lightly buttered wholemeal toast and 100ml of orange juice. As I munched through the toast, my mood suddenly brightened. No long commute today, and no client site, thankfully. Just a leisurely drive to my local office a few miles away. The office, nestled amongst thick green foliage and with gushing water in earshot, more resembled an opulent country hotel than an office.

I took my time, that day. With laptop bag in hand, I sauntered into the main building just after 11:00, placed it on one of the window hot desks and headed straight to the canteen, my usual habit. No problems are solved without my latte. *Now, what's on offer today? Might as well check the lunch menu while I'm here.* I grabbed the coffee, an apple and a banana. *Sure, let me take an orange, too. Crikey, I need a bag for all this.* I prized this office more than any other. The distance, ambience, and comfort all delighted.

But most of all, refreshments were all free. Hitting my 5-a-day targets here was a cinch.

Back upstairs, I eased back into my mesh seat after tweaking the seat levers, and started my laptop. *Great,* I thought, as I leaned back, casting my eye over the green expanse outside. *This is precisely what I need. Quiet time in the office. No meetings. No enraged client demanding the impossible. No tomfoolery. Time to plan. Catch-up on emails. Time to think, without any distractions.*

I took a sip of coffee. *Ouch, too hot.* It tasted different. New coffee beans, perhaps. I didn't care for the taste. *Oh great...* I scanned my inbox for any messages from my manager. Over the last few months, our relationship had become increasingly frosty, and I sensed a major disagreement brewing. Paul annoyed me, frankly.

Engrossed in my inbox, responding to emails, and flicking between the sports pages, I lost complete track of time. Whispers of excitement from behind briefly caught my attention. I ignored them. *Aha, here's another message from Paul, the clown. What's he moaning about now?* 'Have you seen what's happened in New York?' The voices continued behind me. *What are they mumbling about? Can't they mumble quietly?* The mumblings continued, louder and louder. I turned around and saw a crowd huddled around one computer. *Please be quiet. I have important work here.* I continued scrolling through the long list of unread emails. A few moments later, the group had swollen, along with the noise level. I grudgingly rose from my seat and walked towards the group. 'What's happened?' I asked.

'There's been an attack on the World Trade Centre in New York.'

I stared at the grainy video footage on the BBC website. It resembled a computer game. *Surely someone hasn't flown a plane into the building.* My earlier annoyance rapidly morphed to shock as I stood glued with the rest of the group.

The video, now on loop, showed one plane hit the first building, followed by the second, with the subsequent house-of-cards collapse, amidst hundreds of people screaming and rushing from the scene in terror, enveloped in dust. I had an awful feeling about this. Quietly, I extracted myself from the group, grabbed my coffee and stuffed the laptop and fruit into my bag, before heading straight home.

Along with most of the population, I watched the continuous news footage that day without leaving the flat, except for evening prayer at the mosque. This attack felt different, more significant, compared to previous attacks in the West, at least. And it wasn't long before the American finger pointed towards the 'Mozlems'. Yes, 'the Mozlems did it'. Down at the mosque, we weren't convinced (it took a while for Al-Qaidah to claim responsibility). Outside, we mulled over the events in hushed tones. Aside from the unequivocal illegality of such an attack in Islamic Law, the operation required meticulous planning and logistics – not our strong suit. Islamic scholars from every land condemned the attack, including the Grand *Mufti* (Arabic: cleric) of Saudi Arabia. Meanwhile, George Bush promised swift and severe retribution in the new world order of 'good vs evil' and 'with us or against us'. A few days later, he declared the 'War on Terror'.

As Tony flew to stand side by side with George, I didn't leave my flat much, and continued to work from home and the local office. Coincidentally, I worked in the Travel & Transport division for the consultancy, and all projects were immediately halted. Paul scheduled our monthly meeting for the same week. Travelling to the office in remote Surrey always felt like a faff. But given the events of the previous week and the collapse of just about every project, I thought I'd make an effort. I sensed it wasn't going to be the usual somnolent meeting.

'Azeef, don't worry,' he looked me directly in the eye with a sympathetic face. 'If there are any signs of, er, *prejudice*, or anything of that sort, I want you to report back immediately. The words crawled from his mouth with the enthusiasm of an obdurate toddler before school. I wasn't sure what he was going to do, exactly, but I appreciated the sentiment. 'We won't tolerate any of that behaviour here. But the Travel & Transport industry will struggle for a while. We need to broaden your work base.' *Well, that sounds surprisingly reasonable. Perhaps I had misjudged him all this time.*

'We'll find you another project, don't you worry.'

I left the meeting feeling surprisingly buoyant and upbeat, the most optimistic since around 14:00 on the 11th of September. I was quite impressed with him for the first time. At least he was trying to understand and help. I bounced into my car and headed home. This good news deserved luncheon.

Seven days later, Paul called me back to the office: same chair, same positions. Paul's demeanour was more earnest this time. 'Look, Azeef, things are tough for everyone at the moment. The company isn't doing well...'

'Er, yes, I know,' I replied.

'I'm afraid we need to make some changes.'

To paraphrase Hirohito, 'It appeared the situation had developed, and not necessarily to my advantage.'

'Right... But only last week, you said...' spluttering the final words.

'Look, I'm not prepared to rehash old conversations,' he replied firmly with accompanying unnecessarily animated gesticulations.

'I'm not sure I understand. Are you telling me to look for a new job?'

'Azeef, you can interpret my words in any way you wish.' There followed an elongated pause, as we stared at each other like prize-fighters before a big fight.

'Are you having this discussion with all my peer group?' I finally continued.

No response. *Rehash old conversations?! What on earth is he talking about.* It'd only been a week. What had happened? As angry as I felt, my endorphins levels had plummeted. I refused to continue the conversation with him. I left without asking further questions. Thoroughly annoyed, I crawled into my car and headed home. As a relatively junior person in the corporate world, I wasn't sure how to react. *Can he threaten me like this? Should I go to HR? What would they do anyway? They'd probably side with him.* I dialled a few colleagues and asked if they'd also been summoned to HQ. None had.

A light rain fell from the drab sky as I stepped outside my apartment that day. I needed a Nando's. *That spicy peri-peri chicken pitta will soon revitalise spirits, if anything can.*

'Usama, Usama! Usama, Usama!' I turned my head and saw a group of youths gesticulating with their fists. *Aha, perhaps these lads are jesting with their friend, Usama, whom I can't see?* I scanned the area. Nope. It's me. *There are some similarities, I suppose.* 'Terrorist, terrorist!' they screamed. Raising my coat collar, I reciprocated with a wave and walked on into Nando's.

Predictably, the grisly end arrived soon after the meeting with Paul. I probably need to track him down on LinkedIn and send him a (free) copy of this book.

5 . EASTWARD MIGRATION

'Who lives sees, but who travels sees more.'

— IBN BATTUTA

You know that feeling when you don't quite fit? Perhaps it's the name, or the face, or the affiliation? You don't belong, and people around are not shy to highlight the fact. A little like a Manchester United fan hazily wandering into the Kop at Liverpool. Or perhaps a burqa-clad woman arriving at Charles De Gaulle Airport with a halal meat sandwich, asking for asylum. You just know something isn't quite right.

Post 9/11, the mood had changed beyond anything we'd previously experienced. Our culture and colour now played second fiddle for the first time. There was a new game in town, and the Muslim face wasn't fitting. Life for the average Muslim in the West suddenly became incredibly uncomfortable and constrained. Physical attacks on Muslims and those who generally looked a bit foreign soared. Mosques were targeted and firebombed. I recall a group of youngsters staying in a local mosque overnight to confront an angry mob wielding batons and broken glass bottles. Schoolkids were beaten up in the playground amidst raucous chants of 'Bin Laden! Bin Laden!' Muslim women, who represented obvious, soft targets, often felt the violent fury of opportunists seeking an outlet. Tensions reached boiling point within the community, with Muslims constantly fearful of reprisal attacks, in addition to the general anxiety about the possibility of another major terrorist attack occurring, perhaps on UK soil.

Against this backdrop, and my unfortunate end with Paul, late 2001 seemed like an ideal time for a break, a change of scenery. To somewhere warm and sunny, maybe with a bit of sand. So, after scouring the international IT market, I found a perfect role within a few weeks. And, remarkably, after a short telephone interview, I was offered the job within a couple of days. I stuffed my suitcase and two sports bags and headed to Riyadh, Saudi Arabia, though, I forgot to pack sun cream.

During my sojourn in Riyadh, I worked in the (well air-conditioned) Head Office for Al-Rajhi Bank, the largest retail bank in the country. At the peak of a Riyadh summer, the roadside digital thermometers often displayed an eye/armpit-watering 49°C. Rumour had it, at that point, a little hack kicked in to prevent the device ever displaying 50°C. Officially, at that temperature, all workers had to be sent home. I secretly hoped that included office workers, in addition to the poor guys labouring in the sweltering heat (obviously). Even when I landed, October temperatures rose to 38 °C.

But at least I was away from the heat in Blighty. Surely life in Saudi would be a doddle for a card-carrying Muslim.

5.1 WAR ON TERRIBLE ETIQUETTE

'I don't know. I don't care. It's not my problem.' I peered through the door to see a distraught Filipino chap in his early 20s, almost in tears. The HR manager looked busy, annoyed, and important.

'But, sir, my family.'

'I cannot help you,' came the response, with scathing contempt. 'Now you leave!' He pointed towards the door. I continued staring at the HR Manager. Hang on one minute. I recognised *the look*. Except this was the Saudi version. The young man ambled to his feet, shuffled his papers from the table, and left the room, lowering his head as he walked past.

Right, my turn. I knocked on the door and popped my head around.

'Assalaamu alaikum...' I started.

'Yes, what do you want?' *Barrel of laughs, this chap.*

'It's my first day here, Mr Saleh told me to bring my passport.'

'*Min Bakistan?*' (Arabic: From Pakistan?) He spoke with the familiar Arabian twang, replacing Ps with Bs.

I walked into his office and grudgingly placed the passport on the table. Close to my side. It felt like detaching a limb. Maybe that would have been easier.

He gawped at the book with eyes widening, before a broad smile replaced his stern brow. 'Ah... Bri-teeesh...'

'Yes, Bri-teeeessh,' I scowled.

'Ahmad, Ahmad, Bring tea, *yalla yalla* (Arabic: get a move on). Blease, Blease, Mr Asif, sit down, *habeebi*' (Arabic: my beloved- a common term of endearment, less profound than it sounds).

I grimaced. 'Habeebi, have you read the chapter on good manners and character[1]? You may need a quick review.'

WE BRITS ARE CHAMPION QUEUERS. Champions at redrawing maps and carving territory that's not ours to carve, too. We're the Michael Phelps, the Carl Lewis, of queuers. Rain, hail, or shine, we'll queue with remarkable humility and fortitude. Not only that, but we're slow to challenge non-conformists openly, often preferring to raise eyebrows, puff cheeks, and seek similar disapproval from fellow queuers.

But this stoicism isn't displayed with equal vigour outside these green isles. No, in some places, the queue operates in reverse ('Last In, First Out' rather than 'First In, First Out').

Opening a bank account (and many other mundane activities) isn't a straightforward endeavour in the Middle East. Most frustrating and amusing is perhaps the driving license experience, which involves collecting a plethora of rubber stamps from different departments, but precious little driving. You'll also often hear the words '*bukrah, bukrah*' (Arabic: literally tomorrow, tomorrow—though usually meaning at some unknown point in the future), when the office admin can't be bothered to deal with you at that particular moment, which can be a tad frustrating after waiting for a couple of hours.

Even while working for a bank, opening an account wasn't a trivial affair. In classic style, I had to travel to a specific branch on the outskirts of the city, as only that specific branch could open my account. Bemused, I hopped in a taxi and travelled to the city edge, clutching a bunch of forms, IDs, passport photos, and medical reports I'd collected from Harley Street, London. After prayer at the local mosque, I hurried through the crowds to the bank. Much to my delight, I arrived first, and stood close to the bank counter, waiting for the clerk to raise the curtain.

A large LED screen displayed the bank was now open and ready for business. What better way to spend the next few moments than trying to best my *Snake* high score on my trusted Nokia 6210? Engrossed in the game, I didn't notice someone creep up behind. 'Excuse me, sir, do you know what time the clerk will be here? I'm in a rush.'

'Oh, sorry, I just arrived myself. I'm hoping he'll be here soon. Don't worry. My turn won't take long.' He stood around 5' 5", a diminutive chap with a squeaky voice. 'So... where are you from?'

'Ah, I'm from Manila, sir. I've only been here a few months. I need to send money to my family back home.'

'Aha, I see...'

Many of these guys were young and imported into the Middle East to work as labourers, house help, office boys and the like. As we continued chatting, a Saudi man with a thick moustache and black briefcase brushed past the queue rope and bollard, walked in front of the Filipino, and stood directly ahead of me, as nonchalantly as you like. He didn't even turn to look at us.

Eh? What just happened here? I glanced at the Filipino, who was now avoiding eye contact, staring at the ground with a *'sorry, I don't want any trouble, guv'* look.

Have I just missed something here? There's a queue. Perhaps he didn't see it? I tapped him on the shoulder, and, in the clearest monotone, schoolteacher English, said, 'Excuse me, the queue starts here. You need to go to the back of the queue.' I pointed just to ensure there was no misunderstanding.

He gawped back at me in shock. *Why is this Bakistani guy telling me to queue?* Unsure whether to move, he continued to hold ground. My gaze, firm with indignation, morphed to disappointment, the look of disappointment you might give a naughty schoolchild. Reluctantly, he grabbed his black briefcase and moved behind, jostling the young Filipino back a few paces.

I looked back again. *Oh, come on, say something!* I urged, with my telepathic powers. *Say something, man!* His eyes seemingly held down with lead weights. Nope, he wasn't budging. I turned back around, shaking my head and sighing.

But at least now there seemed to be some movement behind the desk. The clerk raised his curtain, and I bolted forward like Carl off the blocks.

'Assalaamu alaikum – I need to open an account,' I gushed.

'Ok, show me papers...'

He scanned them and paused before shaking his head. 'Bukrah, bukrah, habeebi!'

5.2 A FISTFUL OF (TAX-FREE) DOLLARS

'If you continue...' I'd switched to my measured monotone again, 'We'll take this outside and settle it the old-fashioned way, like men.' *Eh? What on earth was I saying?!* I don't think I'd ever used that phrase before, let alone at work. It left Mr Hamidi dumbfounded. I don't think there's a precise Arabic equivalent, but my enraged face gave him a clue towards its meaning.

A few days earlier, I had sent a list of issues with the impending 'Go-Live' of the new Internet Banking system, a first within the Kingdom. Rather than a discreet note to the manager, I'd (innocently) sent the list to the entire team, including the senior managers. Mr Hamidi hadn't taken it well, and proceeded to blame me for all the problems. Ashamedly, Mr Hamidi's behaviour had pushed me over the edge.

'Right, I'm going to report you to HR. I will not tolerate this behaviour. They will deal with you,' he screamed.

'Yes, why don't you do that!' I snarled, continuing to stare at him.

I stormed out of his office, slamming the door behind me. *I've had enough. I'm off. Back to Blighty.* Ten minutes later, my line manager had pacified me and explained if I wanted to stay in Saudi, I'd have to fine-tune my approach. Otherwise, my Bri-teeesh character would land me in serious bother, and I *really* didn't want to sample time in a Saudi jail.

EVERY MEETING at work in Riyadh seemed like a gathering of the United Nations General Assembly. We had Americans, Malays,

South Africans (black and white), Spaniards, Canadians, Italians and Indians, to name a few. I reckon 50 nationalities occupied that office alone. Something lured all these people to Saudi, and it wasn't the Pied Piper of Riyadh.

Sure, some liked the climate, some the relative safety (except for brief risky pockets), and some the general mystique of Arabian lands. However, the attraction for most was quite obvious: the tax-free dollar. Yep, we paid no tax of any discernible kind: no income tax, no council tax, no car tax, no TV tax, nothing. This was mostly thanks to the generous government and price of crude oil. When I spoke about taxation to the locals, they looked at me aghast, almost ready to draw swords. I chuckled each time I frequented the petrol station, parting with the equivalent of £5 to fill my car. Yes, if you wanted to save camel loads of money, Saudi was the place to be.

Now, I'm no fool. I, too, trousered the tax-free dollars. But for me, the cultural and religious experience also played an important role in my presence. Saudi, home to the two most sacred sites in Islam, *Makkah* and *Madinah*, provided a radical change of location from my first 27 years or so. I fully immersed myself in the local culture. I lived amongst the general populace, rather than in the opulent compounds, and made many local friends. I studied Arabic at King Saudi University in Riyadh. I also enjoyed the local cuisine and adventures (night-time trips to the desert were fun). In addition, I got to know people within the enormous ex-pat community. I'd often visit their villas in the fortified compounds. Some of these compounds were so large they housed half a dozen open pools, gymnasiums, supermarkets and 18-hole golf courses. Yes, a comfortable existence.

One day, after returning from visiting a friend, and feeling in a philosophical mood, I decided my fellow countrymen were squandering a great opportunity while remaining in their lavish cocoons. I didn't blame them. It was all relatively easy to slip into a routine and stay isolated: early start, early finish, back to the compound, maybe a quick swim, dinner, and then lounging with friends, especially with copious amounts of disposable wealth to spend at the many shopping malls.

So, I took it upon myself to pen a few words to the ex-pat employees of the bank in an email entitled: 'More than a Fistful of (Tax-Free) Dollars.' I explained the opportunity to discover the local culture, people, language, and history. I picked around 100 English sounding names from the email address book and, *ping*, sent the email. Easy. By the following morning, I'd received half a dozen emails thanking me for the note.

'Great note, thanks, Asif,' one read.

'Interesting. It's quite easy to live in a bubble here,' read another.

'Fistful of dollars!' chuckled one more.

Feeling quite good about myself, I took a break, and wandered downstairs for a latte. Ten minutes later, back at my desk, the desk phone rang. 'Hello, is that Mr Asif...'

'Er, yes, speaking.'

'This is Sameer. Mr Hudaif wants to see you in his office.' Mr Hudaif was the head of HR at the bank, a no-nonsense character, mostly feared and loathed. I hadn't previously met him.

'Er, ok. Now?'

'Yes, now. He's waiting for you.' Sameer, his dutiful secretary, sounded serious. *Why on earth would he want to see me anyway? Lord, it's probably about my 'let's go outside' comment with Mr Hamidi,* I thought. I was hoping everyone had forgotten about that little incident.

I took the lift to the 10th floor. Only the bigwigs from the bank enjoyed offices up here – just a row of senior bods and their secretaries. Yes, everyone needed a secretary.

'Any ideas what this is about?' I asked, walking past Sameer.

'No, but he is angry about something.'

Lord, so much for my keeping a low profile. I knocked on the door and crept inside. His corner office occupied more square footage than my apartment. By contrast, our unruly technical team camped in a grotty space half the size. Mr Hudaif wore metal-rimmed glasses and the familiar red headdress. He sat behind a heavy mahogany desk stretching across the room.

'Assalaam alaikum, you've got a great view from up here,' I remarked, avoiding his gaze while surveying the Riyadh expanse below. I may have been pushing my luck again.

'Walaikum salaam, Asif... Blease sit down. I am very busy. Blease.'

I tentatively took a seat.

'Now, you sent an email yesterday?' I thought for a moment. *Email, email, I send lots of emails... What's he talking about?*

'We had some complaints about it...' he continued.

Email... Aha! The dirham finally dropped. *That* email. My 'dollars' email.

'Ah, yes. I'm surprised anyone complained. It was quite bolite, and I received emails thanking me.'

'Well, some others didn't abbreciate it. Some senior managers. You're a technical specialist, right?'

'Yes, I work in the IT department.'

'It's better you stick to the technical issues and leave the advice, barticularly on group emails.'

Eh? 'Ok... Yes, it would appear so. Thanks for the advice. Was there anything else?' I asked.

'No, that's all.'

Phew! At least he didn't know about my other little run-in. I stood up and walked towards the door. *Well, that wasn't so bad,* I chuckled.

'Oh, Asif...' came the voice, 'Mr Hamidi mentioned the other incident, too. That's two strikes. Blease close the door on your way out.'

5.3 PISTOLS AT DAWN

The year 2003; an *annus challengus*, if ever there was one. A couple of years after 9/11, while Afghan war embers were still smouldering, Tony and George decided a single war in the region wasn't quite enough. The world needed another major conflagration point, another radicalisation honeypot. So, on the back of a dodgy dossier and a collation of the unwilling, a second war in Iraq to remove Saddam Hussein began, some ten years after the previous unsuccessful attempt by George's father, George. Amidst these major trouble spots, sporadic attacks across the globe were happening with painful regularity. It appeared the entire world was ablaze, and those pesky Muslims were seemingly at the heart of it all.

Meanwhile, less than 1000 kilometres south of the Iraq border in Riyadh, we, too, felt the effects. In the space of a few months, militants had attacked multiple Government and Western targets. I'd experienced a near escape myself, walking close to the Interior Ministry, an unusual, spaceship-type building in the middle of Riyadh, on my way to the local restaurant. An almighty clap suddenly jolted me from thoughts of my tandoori chicken and biryani dinner. The noise reverberated around the densely populated buildings nearby. As though flimsy trees in a storm, they shook violently, requiring some deft footwork to avoid falling debris. Extremists within Saudi Arabia were stepping up their game. So much for my 'life will be dandy in Saudi' forecast.

The Government swiftly deployed protective measures across the country, including gargantuan white concrete barricades around official buildings and Western compounds to stop would-be suicide attackers. Army personnel, trying to look mean and surrounded by sandbags, guarded the entrances with heavy-duty artillery, ready to mow down anyone who looked remotely suspicious. For that period, it felt we were also living in the middle of a war zone. Suddenly, meeting friends inside the compounds became a hazardous activity. With my long flowing *thawb* (Arabic: traditional dress) and beard, I could feel the crosshairs marking my torso each time I visited.

Another nasty phenomenon emerged during this period: early morning targeted shootings, something hitherto never seen in Riyadh or the broader Kingdom. Compared to major cities in the West, Riyadh resembled Teletubbies-land, an atmosphere appreciated by many ex-pats. The first shooting appeared an isolated incident, but another followed a few days later, then several more. Fatalities resulted. The targeted shootings sent shockwaves around the Western ex-pat community, particularly the Americans.

The morning after the second shooting, a melee greeted me as I entered the office. A crowd had gathered around an empty desk, anxiously murmuring amongst themselves.

'Where's Jim?' I asked, sensing something terrible had happened.

'He left the country last night,' a South African colleague responded.

'Eh? I just spoke with him yesterday. He seemed, ok?'

'Half a dozen Americans and Canadians left last night. A group of Brits are also planning to leave today.'

I'd worked closely with Jim for a while, a brilliant guy, well mannered, a genuinely amiable chap. He must have felt his Canadian roots were a little too easily mistaken. Ironically, Jim was also a Muslim convert. Yes, the atrocities don't discriminate.

5.4 NEAR MISSES

'Ladies and gentlemen, welcome to this Saudi Airlines flight to London Heathrow.'

I settled into my seat and gazed at the dazzling display panel: 5000, 5500, 6000, 6500 feet. I always feel nervous taking off. It seems the riskiest operation, blasting away into the skies. If the plane explodes into a thousand pieces, surely it will occur on take-off. Thankfully, it seldom happens.

'Please keep your seat belts fastened until we have reached our cruising altitude,' the voice continued. The rough English translation never quite matches the poetic Arabic, though admittedly, 'Our noble travellers, for your delight and comfort...' may have raised the odd eyebrow.

The ascent progressed well... 7000, 8000, 9000 feet. *Phew, over the worst.* I relaxed my hand from gripping the side rest, almost leaving a handprint. *Now, where's my book.*

As I reached down, a flash of light suddenly engulfed the cabin, followed by a jolt and then a thunderous crack, all in quick succession. *What on earth was that?!* My pulse, already teetering on Heart Rate Zone 5, hit a vertical climb.

A scene copied and pasted directly from an aeroplane disaster movie ensued, as hysteria swept the passengers. Even the cabin crew forgot the emergency rules playbook and joined the frenzied tomfoolery. I surmised the left engine had exploded, and we were now 10,000 feet above Riyadh with a single engine, though the plane continued its ascent, thanks to the wonders of modern aero engineering. Not a single 'what have you done?!' stare, either — one small benefit of travelling Saudi Airlines rather than British Airways. There were far too many suspects on the plane.

The gasps and shrieks continued as we circled above Riyadh, though not a peep from the captain yet. We continued circling for 15 minutes, jettisoning fuel to reduce weight, before the plane could land. Impressively, only at that point did the captain announce our return to Riyadh in a measured and reassuring voice. The cabin crew ordered everyone into the emergency position by howling up and down the aisles. Ten minutes later, we had returned to the Riyadh tarmac, as euphoria replaced pandemonium. After my first and only ride on an inflatable chute, I couldn't help take a few snaps of the frazzled Rolls Royce engine, an impressive though chilling sight.

I'd never travelled on Saudi Airlines except between London, Riyadh, and Jeddah, and aside from the odd exploding engine, I couldn't fault the service: efficient, clean, and teetotal, to boot. I wrongly assumed services to other locations enjoyed similarly high standards.

A FEW MONTHS LATER, my mother had arrived in Lahore and 'requested' I join her. She reckoned she'd found me the perfect wife: religiously committed, respectable family, and a medical professional, no less. My mother was in no mood for a debate, either. The flight between Riyadh and Lahore measured a tolerable 1500 nautical miles, less than four hours by air, and I hadn't been to Pakistan for a few years. I reasoned a week's stay couldn't do any harm, even with the interview. A week would provide enough time to meet my mother and relatives, see a few sights, and hopefully exit without getting a runny tummy.

I returned to Riyadh airport and breezed through check-in and baggage control with a personal best time, before arriving at the gate. I noticed all the passengers were Pakistani males, dressed in shabby, traditional attire. *Aha, of course, this plane stops at Peshawar in the north of Pakistan before flying to Lahore. All these people must be taxi drivers.* I'd gotten to know quite a few drivers in Riyadh, with my two daily taxi journeys – they came from Peshawar, and all dressed in traditional fashion.

I scrutinised the plane from the viewing area, like Attenborough discovering a new species of ape. *What on earth is this monstrous machine?* Not a Boeing or Airbus, or anything else I recognised. Perhaps Eastern European. Saudi Airlines clearly reserved their best planes for more high-profile Western routes. I settled into my seat, along with 200 other passengers, including 195 taxi drivers from Peshawar. The aircraft looked even more bizarre from the inside, with the seating layout triggering a level of disorientation. The rugged, all-male cabin crew were handpicked for the trip. Curiouser and curiouser. From my seat, I could see a grey, tatty and sagging curtain that barely stretched across the cockpit area: no bulletproof door, no locking mechanism, no intruder prevention wizardry of any description. In fact, I could see the balding head of the pilot and the wiry neck of his accomplice. *Lord, anyone could make a beeline for the pilot and hijack this plane. Though perhaps they know, no one will.*

No spicy pretzels, tiny cans of coke, juices, or Perrier mineral water were offered, either. But at least the biryani tasted like biryani, novel for aeroplane food. A few hours later, the plane landed at Peshawar, and the taxi drivers exited. That left me and a handful of others on the plane, now a little like a private jet rinsed of every luxurious feature. Next stop, Lahore.

The meeting with the prospective wife and family predictably lasted no longer than 30 minutes, much to my mother's mortification. The girl's aunt took centre stage, asking a range of awkward questions. As the meeting progressed, I batted with increasingly terse and hostile responses. You know things aren't going well when guests request only water and not a grain more. The final straw came when I suggested speaking directly with the girl, who wasn't actually present in the room. That caused some offence, and they scurried from the house, leaving my mother and me sipping tea in silence. After a few minutes, I turned to my mother, 'Well, how do you think that went?'

She glared at me. 'You do know the girl is a doctor?'

'That's great for her, but we're not compatible. Besides, can you imagine the aunt visiting every year?!'

～

AFTER THAT NEAR-MISS, a few days later, I climbed back on the plane of unknown origin to Riyadh. At Peshawar, a middle-aged chap with a salt and pepper beard wearing traditional northern Pakistani dress sat next to me. He smiled at me nervously, fidgeting with the booklets in the seat pocket. It appeared he'd arrived directly from tilling the land, given the sweat gathered on his forehead and the overpowering body odour.

'Are you ok?' I asked, in my broken Urdu. 'You seem nervous.'

'Yes. This is my first time on a plane. It's my first time away from Peshawar. I'm going to Saudi to work as a taxi driver. I'm quite scared.'

'Look, don't worry, I'm a seasoned traveller. I'll ensure you arrive safely.' At least, I think I said that.

'OK, thank you. Just one question: how do I get a cup of water here?'

I chuckled the chuckle of a kingpin sitting on his throne. 'That's no problem on an aeroplane! Just ask one of the cabin crew. Look, this guy here. Are you sure you just want water? Everything is free, don't worry! You've already paid for the ticket!'

My travelling companion raised his hand, as though a first-year student at school, and mustered, 'Excuse me, please can I have a cup of water? Thank you.'

The steward looked at the man with a bewildered expression, nodded his head, and walked away. I smiled at my companion. 'Don't worry, he'll bring it now. He's just gone to get you a nice cup of cold water, which you'll soon be enjoying. The biryani on this flight is really good (thumbs up). Better than any other plane.'

'This is very good! So, tell me, brother, how does this plane take off and stay in the sky without falling down?' he continued in Urdu.

I sat thinking how to translate Bernoulli's theorem and Newton's Third Law into Urdu... 'Acha...' I began, clearing my throat. 'Right... you see...you know...well...' I looked around the seats. 'Pass me that piece of paper...' It was a flimsy piece, just right. 'What will happen if I blow over the top of this paper, like this...?'

He looked puzzled. 'Bhai saab (Urdu: dear brother), I'm just a simple farmer. I don't know. I think it will just fall to the ground?'

I chuckled again. 'Watch...' I blew hard across the top of the paper, and it curled upwards.

Shocked, 'Bhai, Is this some kind of *jadoo* (Punjabi: black magic)?'

'No magic, just some simple physics...'

He wiped the sweat from his forehead. 'Bhai, where is my water?'

'Er, I'm not sure. It's ok, lots of people ask for drinks. He's probably forgotten. Just ask again. There he is, look.'

We replayed the event, and again, five minutes later, no water. *Why is this cabin chap intent on embarrassing me in front of my new travelling companion?*

'Right, enough. I'll speak with him.' I called the same steward, and, in my monotone voice, 'He's now asked for a cup of water twice. I don't know what the problem is, but please bring for him! We don't want to ask again!'

Aghast, the steward's eyes bulged. 'Yes, sure, sir, I'll bring immediately, right away.'

Within thirty seconds, my companion was sipping cool water from a white plastic cup.

On my return to Riyadh, I sent a lengthy email to Saudi Airlines about the shocking service onboard the Lahore flight in general, and specifically the steward's miserable performance.

Several weeks passed, and not a single drop of water.

5.5 PARANORMAL ACTIVITY @HEATHROW TERMINAL 3

From 2002 to 2005, Heathrow Airport became my second home. I flew more than twenty times between London and Riyadh, always, regrettably, from Terminal 3 (before the revamp). Despite its dilapidated state, it felt like my patch, my turf. I knew it well, every corner, every cranny.

My first few flights were uneventful. I would dutifully obey the airport rigmarole, following the rubric to the letter. In the early days, post 9/11 and the 'Shoe Bomber' debacle, the measures introduced were tortuous. As I evidently ticked a good number of the 'this guy's shoes are probably laden with Semtex' boxes' criteria, I didn't want to glance or even breathe in any way that could possibly be misconstrued. Moreover, given the frequency of my flights, I didn't want any unnecessary time spent with a bright light shining in my face, reclined at an 80° angle.

On the third or fourth occasion travelling outbound from Heathrow, I collected my wallet and paraphernalia from the grey tray and took my trainers before lacing. I'd deliberately avoided wearing boots with a thicker heel. No sooner had I completed the final knot, I heard a matter-of-fact voice: 'Excuse me, sir, please can you come this way.'

I looked up and saw a short, muscular black man in a crisp, well-ironed, white, half-sleeved shirt peering over me. I rose to my feet. He looked even shorter from up here. I rolled my eyes in disappointment. 'Sure....' I replied, before following him into a dull room with a couple of green plastic chairs and a small table. *Hang on, this all looks quite familiar.* At that point, I realised the purpose of the large glass display sandwiched between the baggage check and the duty-free outlets: one-way glass.

My endorphin count languished below 10%, and I was keen to exit the room to buy a few bits at Dixons Duty-Free before boarding the flight. *Ok, think Geoff Boycott... Straight bat, straight bat...* I thought.

Q: Can I see your passport?

A: Sure, here you go.

Q: Where are you going?

A: Saudi Arabia.

Q: Where in Saudi Arabia?

A: Riyadh.

Q: Why are you going there?

A: I work there.

Q: What do you do?

A: I work in IT.

Q: How long have you been there?

A: About six months.

I smiled, batting all the questions straight back without any hesitation, like a *Mastermind* professional, with my gaze firmly fixed on Magnus.

'Ok, that sounds reasonable,' he nodded.

'I'm pleased you agree.' I just couldn't resist a little wisecrack. 'Any more questions?'

'No, no, you can go.'

'Ah, thank you.' I took my bag and passport and left, smiling as I walked past the window. I was soon browsing new laptops at Dixons, and boarded the flight without any further incident.

A few months later, I experienced an almost identical sequence of events: same inquisitor, same location, same questions, same answers. I recognised him from the previous encounter, but thought it better not to comment. My answers were a little sharper, my tone a little more irritated, my glare a little fiercer. However, the outcome was the same.

Roll on another few months, and... Surely not again! *This guy can't possibly stop me again!* Did he suffer from amnesia? We stood in almost identical positions. Even my characteristically placid demeanour started to waver. Time for a bit of swagger. No more Geoff Boycott; enter Viv Richards.

I looked him in the eye. He knew me, and I knew him. We both silently acknowledged our previous meetings without saying a word.

'Can I see your passport, sir?' A miserably sheepish, limp request.

'Look, to save us both some time, let me answer your questions. Saudi Arabia, the same as last time you asked, and the time before that. Unfortunately, I'm going back to work, although, frankly, I'd rather just stay at home. I work in IT. It's quite banal, but pays well. There's also the lure of the tax-free dollar in Saudi Arabia. No, I don't have any terrorist affiliations or sympathies. No, I don't think *Al-Qaidah* are great guys. No, I don't think carpet-bombing entire countries is a good strategy to spread democracy. No, randomly killing individuals on the street and taking children hostage in a school isn't sanctioned by Islamic Law.' I paused for breath and looked at his startled face. 'You seem to be the only one who works here,' I continued. 'Why don't they ask someone else to play Magnus Magnusson? It would liven up the experience. Lord knows, the experience needs livening.' I paused again. The monologue was cathartic, potentially hazardous, but cathartic.

The man continued to stare, dumbfounded.

'How are Sandra and the kids?' I asked.

'Eh? Who's Sandra?'

'Why do you keep stopping me and asking the same questions?'

'I'm sorry, sir, we're just doing our job. Trying to keep our country safe. We just pick people at random, sir – there's *no profiling*' (Translated: you look decidedly dodgy, mate).

'Random?!' I exclaimed. 'Why don't you just update the Mischling Test and be done with it? I've studied probability theory quite a bit. I'm not that lucky. Why keep up with this pretence? Do you have any more questions? Do you?!'

He'd lost the will at this point, or sensed a right hook coming. 'No, sir, none.'

'Then I suggest you crack on and find those people who want to do us both harm. You're not an automaton. You're better than that.' I'd moved the boundary far, perilously far. One phone call and he could ruin my day, my week. Though it'd probably be more exciting than my week back at work.

'Ok, sir, you're free to leave. Thank you for your time again.'

A few minutes later, I was browsing books in the duty-free area. That random selection algorithm never did pick my number again at Heathrow Terminal 3.

5.6 ROCKY RAGHEAD

I'd never heard the term 'raghead' until Prince Harry popularised a few years ago when he referred to a camouflaged comrade in Afghanistan: 'It's Dan the Man...you look like a raghead.' Odd, considering my lexical strength in this area. Though it does appear more popular in the US. The term refers to the turban or head covering used by Muslims (mostly Arabs) and Sikhs. Aside from any other consideration, the turban cloth and head coverings can be very expensive, hardly rags.

While in Saudi, I dressed in the traditional long garment, much to the bemusement of my fellow Westerners. I'd also wear the head covering occasionally, though I never tried the *eqaal* (Arabic: the black wrapping cord). It's generally a good idea to keep your head covered and wear loose clothes in a sweltering, dusty environment. In summer, I'd find myself profusely sweating simply from the short walk between my apartment and the taxi (at 07:30).

However, there is one notable downside to wearing the long flowing garb (the Pakistani traditional dress *shalwar* and *kameez* suffer the same problem).

After spending more than two years abroad, I had to return to the UK for technical IT training, so I thought I'd make a little effort to look smart on the course, and buy some new trousers. I'd try and look the part, at least.

Now, there's no shortage of expensive stores in central Riyadh – Louis Vuitton, Hugo Boss, Gucci, all housed in the most sumptuous, glistening shopping malls and towers. Ignoring all those stores, I headed towards the backend of the building, straight into Debenhams (ok, it was surprisingly upmarket in Riyadh). Once inside, I bought a pair of trousers, eventually deciding on waist size 36", rather than my usual 34". When shopping, I'm constantly solving the shortest path problem in my head. How can I purchase what's needed and leave as quickly as possible? Consequently, I never try on anything in the store (there's also the discomfort of changing within the 2ft square cubicle). Surely size 36" would fit. I'd even have a couple of inches spare for the belt.

A few days later, as the departure date drew closer, I remembered my baggy trousers. *Let me just slip these on and tick the box,* I thought. I removed them from the expensive Debenhams packaging, and pulled them on. *Eh?* I could barely close the clasp. *Aha, they've mistakenly given me 32".* Scrambling from the trousers, I checked the size tag. *Lord.* Somehow, I'd ballooned from a slim, trim 34" to a 38", after a couple of years of good living, eating out and zero exercise in Riyadh. My loose *thawb* had successfully hidden the creeping waistline. Hardly surprising, given my daily regime, comprising a steak and egg breakfast at Kudu (a bit like McDonald's), followed by a chicken sandwich and chips for lunch, with a full evening meal at a local restaurant.

Crikey, how much do I weigh now!? I barely topped 80kg back in Blighty. Hurling the trousers across the room, I rushed from my apartment and hailed a taxi. 'Bhai saab, Ollaya javaoh, tee korah nah bachavoh.' (Urdu-ish: Brother, go towards the shopping mall, and don't spare the horses).

He shook his head in terror. 'Where? Where? Horses?!'

'Go to the shopping mall! The mall!'

I needed a set of industrial-strength scales. As I tentatively lifted one foot, then the other, I stiffened myself for the result. The dial violently swung to the right, oscillating between 95kg and 90kg, eventually settling on 92kg. I needed a few moments, and slumped on a nearby chair, watching the passers-by. Suddenly I could only see waddlers, with long flowing garbs and bulging bellies.

Right, no time to wallow in self-pity. Something had to be done, PDQ. I jumped to my feet, cleared my diary for that afternoon, and trawled the sports shops of Riyadh for the largest, grandest elliptical cycle available. I had it delivered on the same day, too. It took four men to carry the cycle into my apartment on the first floor, where it sprawled the entire width of my bedroom like some alien reptile.

Queue *Rocky IV* training regime.

5.7 7TH JULY 2005

I arrived at my desk with my now customary healthy meal: grilled chicken sandwich, salad, and mineral water. *Right, let me tuck into this little lot.* I took a large bite and opened my email. *Drat, the share trading website is down again. What is it now?! Lord, my phone is about to start ringing anytime, and I can already see Mr. Saleh stomping this way.* I took another bite and bolted towards my colleague.

'Neil, have you checked the site? It's down! I'm already getting emails!'

'Asif, is your family ok in the UK?'

'Eh? Er, yes... Have you checked the share trade website? It's down. The customers will be complaining soon!'

'ASIF, HAVE YOU SEEN THE NEWS?'

I shook my head. 'No, what news?' I looked over Neil's shoulder to see the headline on the BBC website: '*Suicide bombers attack London*'. My face froze in horror as I continued to stare at the screen.

Without saying a word, I walked back to my desk and began clicking through the morning's events. It appeared the bombers had followed a similar strategy to the 9/11 attacks. The horrific pictures showed the chaos, mangled buses, bloodied casualties being carried from the scene, and the unforgettable image of the man in the white mask. The scenes of carnage looked all too familiar, yet no less difficult to watch. But this wasn't an unfamiliar location in some remote area. This was London. I'd frequented two of the locations, Edgware Road and Aldgate, on many occasions.

The 7/7 attacks were the first suicide bombings on UK soil. Tragically, four young men, aged 18, 19, 22 and 30 respectively, believed the slaughter of 57 innocent people, along with their own deaths, would achieve some noble objective – an idea bewildering to the most pious Muslim and irreligious non-Muslim alike. Moreover, the quartet somehow believed their action was sanctioned in Islam. Three of the bombers were British-born sons of Pakistani immigrants, the fourth a convert. In a pre-recorded video, the bombers justified their actions by citing the recent wars led by the UK, and injustices against Muslims around the world.

I spoke with family and friends on many occasions in the immediate aftermath. The incident set the Muslim community back again, after a relatively quiet period. I felt an uneasy guilt watching the maelstrom from afar, knowing the ferocity of the impending backlash.

A University of Leicester study noted faith-hate crimes against Muslims rose 600% after 7/7, compared to 2004. Crimes ranged from stabbings, physical assault, verbal abuse, harassment, and mosque vandalism.

Though worse still, our faith had been violated. Again.

5.8 SCIENCE AND PSYCHOLOGY

I managed an early escape to the restaurant below our office a smidgeon before noon. I'd realised 11:56 was the sweet spot: early enough to beat the crowd, and late enough to avoid refusal from staff to serve luncheon. A welcome break away from the nonsense, tomfoolery and irascible Saudi managers. *Great, spicy chicken biryani on the menu.* That's precisely what I needed. A little quiet time away from the team and project. Grabbing my tray, I headed towards a corner near the window, for a 30-minute retreat into the recesses of my mind before the next batch of afternoon meetings.

I'd ingested no more than a few morsels of biryani when I heard a familiar voice, 'So, as someone reasonably devout, you must believe the Earth is 6000 years old?' Greg, one of the British ex-pats and a colleague at the bank, stood behind me. He enjoyed throwing difficult questions my way.

'Do you mind if I sit down?'

'Well, actually, I just wanted a few minutes.' He placed his tray on my table and grabbed a seat from a nearby table.

'So, what do you think?'

'Of the 6000 years, you mean?'

'Yes, isn't that what most creationists think?'

I paused and took another slug of biryani. 'I'm not sure? What's a creationist?'

'Someone who believes God, or some other higher power, created the world and Universe?'

'Aha, well, I believe some of that, but probably not in the way you think. I reckon that the 6000 number is on the low side. Shakespeare's foot slipped when he wrote, 'The poor world is almost 6000 years old[2]'. Do you know how the 6000 number is calculated?'

'Erm, no, actually,' he replied.

'Well, it's based on a combination of historical accounts in the Bible and the genealogy of Jesus back to Adam. Luke and Matthew's disagreement is trivial in the grand scheme. Though, we do have quite a lot of evidence suggesting the Earth is much, much older – around 4.5 billion years, according to fossil records, bits of rock and such.'

'Er... Ok, so you're not denying the scientific evidence?'

I chuckled. 'That's amusing. You've been reading too much, Dawkins. I've been studying science and religion for most of my life. Why do people see religion and science as two great combatants? Why must we follow one path or the other? There's a disturbing growing radical atheism movement that's as dangerous as its counterpart on the religious side.'

'Do we need a creator to explain anything? It seems science can do the lot. What is the strongest argument for the existence of God?'

'Strongest for who?' I quipped. Rob chortled. 'For me,' I continued, 'there is no other workable explanation, probably due to my analytical background. Consider the extraordinary, precise physical constants underpinning the universe: if any were even slightly untuned, there would be no atoms, stars, or galaxies. The unimaginable complexity of life. The digital nature of DNA code. There's an astronomically long list of near individually improbable events multiplied. All these are all prints, signs and wonders, the providence of a Creator, and not the result of a collection of unguided, random processes. These parameters and variables have been specified, leading to our existence here on Earth. We just do our best to screw it up.'

'Agreed with that.'

'You see, when I walk into the cafeteria at King Saud University and see a complete mess on the floor, *I know* the students created it, despite their protestations describing a set of random, unguided processes. So, how about the entire Universe in all its magisterial splendour? And I don't accept this something from nothing baloney, when scientists describe nothing as actually something. Wouldn't it be so desperately depressing if we ate, drank, slept, looked at our phones, died, and simply returned to dust, with no answers to the questions? No, this is what it's all about.'

'No justice,' interjected Greg.

'Indeed, no justice. We also have this concept of the *fitrah* in Islam.'

'Fit what?'

'There's no terse translation of the word. It's a natural inclination for a person to know God, to know his existence, without complex theological explanation. No need for the Quinque Viæ[3]. The *fitra* is present in all peoples in all cultures the world over. This is why, in almost every culture, in almost every part of the world, in every deepest ravine, in every elevated plain, some form of higher power or deity is known and worshipped[4]' I stood up and grabbed my tray, 'Right, on that breezy note, I do need to get back to the office. Important meet in 5 minutes.'

'Second question,' Greg continued. 'What exactly makes someone wake up early in the morning and say to himself, "Today, I'm going to strap Semtex to my body, calmly walk into a crowded area, and blow myself up, along with everyone else around me?"'

I sat back down. 'Another good question. There isn't a simple answer to this one, I'm afraid. But what's the difference between that person and the one who picks up a gun in the morning and goes on a shooting spree at a school, knowing he will be shot dead at some point by the police? Or the one who leaps in front of a high-speeding train?'

'Hmmm. But in the case of these Muslims, is it their religious conviction or what?'

'That's not the pattern we see from these people, certainly not in the West. If you go through the list, you'll see most of them are hardly religious. Look at the 9/11 guys. Many seemed to be looking for a way out. Perhaps if I'm having suicidal thoughts or major personal issues[5], I might as well hang my hat on the religious peg.'

'But they think they'll be martyrs in heaven, having a great time.'

'Killing innocent people, generally causing mayhem and chaos, doesn't get you a direct pass into heaven. Anyone with a tincture of

Islamic learning would know that. But if you take a particularly vulnerable person, someone with little understanding, add some imagery of atrocities perpetrated against Muslims around the world, throw in some out of context Qur'anic verses...'

'Yes, I can see why it might be appealing. A little like "I want to become rich, so I'm going to rob a bank,"' replied Greg.

'Er, yes, nice analogy. Though don't try robbing this one. Not in Saudi.'

5.9 RAINY EXIT

'Quick, quick, it's raining!' Shmaila, my wife[6] screamed.

I sprung to my feet, almost somersaulting in the air, and raced towards the window with the exuberance of a child.

'Yes, you're right! That's amazing! *Alhamdulillah!*' (Arabic: Praise be to God)

Rain in Riyadh was a rare delicacy, usually only happening twice or thrice a year. But when the rains came, they came with Biblical vigour, often causing spectacular flooding, even in modern downtown Riyadh. While the municipality had spent billions of riyals on modern infrastructure and skyscrapers, they didn't feel a drainage system necessary. Not that we cared.

We both raced outside, as though riyals were falling from the heavens, savouring as many drops as possible and strolled around, at the bemusement of everyone else who dived for cover (we stopped short of jumping into puddles). No quantity of riyals could ever match the feeling of that wondrous rain. How lucky we were in Britain to have such an abundance on tap.

I TARRIED around four years in Riyadh. Remarkable when I consider the shaky start. When I tell people the duration, they look at me as though I'm insane, or a man sleeping on sacks of money (neither are true). Sure, it may not be everyone's cup of *qahwah*[7] (Arabic: coffee). Sure, a fair amount of acclimatisation is required, mainly if you're coming from the West. Sure, the bread and milk don't *quite* taste the same. But the experience quashed my idealistic thinking and broadened my outlook on many issues. While not reaching Bajan levels, the relaxed lifestyle also had its benefits (except when trying to open a bank account or get a driving licence). 'Embrace the difference' has always been my motto.

However, in Saudi Arabia, there are some unusual rules and regulations, and I'm not referring to the goings-on down at the 'Square of Justice' after Friday prayers. For one, changing jobs isn't a trivial matter, as the employer controls residence within the country. It's also one of the few countries in the world requiring a VISA to *exit*. Yes, you can arrive at the airport wearing loose, comfortable trousers, fully hydrated and moisturised, and with half a dozen suitcases, but without the shiny employer exit stamp, the skinny airport officials will refuse entry. In any case, after four years, I fancied a change, and my employer wasn't playing ball.

5.10 ESCAPE FROM DUBAI

In August 2005, rather than return to Blighty, I decided to stay in the region and perhaps return to Saudi on a 'clean passport' a year later, a common trick. I'd been offered a role at a well-known organisation based in Dubai, quite a senior position, with a chubby ex-pat package, a tricky proposition to reject. I packed my belongings (elliptical cycle included) in large white containers and despatched them to the UK, while I hopped on the short flight to Dubai. A trial period in a new country without cubic yardage of additional baggage seemed a wise move.

In a new role, a few weeks is a reasonable yardstick for me to gauge compatibility. Unfortunately, after only a few days, I was already having second thoughts. Sure, Dubai housed more malls, attractions, and futuristic buildings than you could shake a stick at. The (all you can eat) buffet dinners at the furnished apartment hit the mark, too. I wasn't complaining about more tax-free dollars either. But I found the humidity unbearable, and the traffic, crowds, and superficial façade all disagreeable. It all felt too artificial. Fine for a week's holiday, but not the place I wanted to live.

My boss, James, had great expectations. He'd already chauffeured me to different sites around the Emirates, and shown me blueprints of the new Head Office building – a stunning structure in the heart of Dubai. He also introduced me to the CEO of the organisation, a Billy Bunter's father type character. James wanted me to transform the ragtag, fugitive group of 30 individual IT cogs into a lubricated Bugatti W16 engine, something he'd miserably failed to manage in several years. To further complicate matters, he was planning time away and wanted me to run the department in his absence. How could I possibly escape, morally and logistically? I felt like Frank Morris staring at his Alcatraz ceiling. The following day, I bought a nail file and started chipping at that plaster wall.

I realised the coming month-end was the perfect opportunity for my escape. By that time, the company would owe me a couple of weeks salary, enough to justify my existence in Dubai. The money would slam into my account on Thursday, along with reimbursement of expenses I'd incurred since entering the country (someone had to cover all the costs). That gave me Friday to collect and prepare my belongings. I'd come into work Saturday morning (another thing I didn't appreciate), and leave the same evening on a BA flight back to Heathrow. Sounded like a decent plan.

Later that week, after Friday prayers, I grabbed my brown leather swag bag and tiptoed towards a cashpoint with the newly minted card I'd received that very morning. I emptied my account of every last dirham, and then headed towards a nearby money exchange booth. I handed over the notes, and the Indian cashier returned the equivalent pounds sterling in wodges of sparklingly new £50 notes. Quite a lot of £50 notes, no questions asked. It felt like the diamond smuggling *Only Fools and Horses* episode. I stuffed the wads into my bag and bolted back to my hotel room to gather the rest of my belongings and patiently wait for the morrow.

The following day, I nervously sipped coffee while sitting in my office. Crikey, this absconding was genuinely stressful.

James popped his head around the door. 'Any exciting plans for the weekend?'

'Oh, just one or two things, nothing extraordinary,' I replied.

'Well, I'm preparing for my holiday. By the way, we need to discuss the new office first thing on Monday. Got some exciting news.'

I nodded my head awkwardly. He was a decent chap. Only a fool or a man bereft would walk away from this opportunity. *Hmmm, perhaps I should stay after all. Do I really want to return to a post 7/7 Blighty? The abuse, the difficulties, the harassment. I could just stay here in Dubai and enjoy the sun, the villa with swimming pool, the tax-free dollars, and an army of people at my beck and call. Yes, I should stay, and call Shmaila over as planned.* But an hour of debate later... *Surely it can't be that bad in Blighty? It'll be boring in Dubai, anyway.*

That evening, I was sitting on the BA plane with my bag safely in the storage unit above. Along with the cold, bland chicken and white rice, the return flight served the most horrendous turbulence I'd ever experienced. I'm sure a ride inside my Zanussi washing machine would have been smoother. Amongst the jolts, dips and climbs, I had a little time to think about what lay ahead at Heathrow, particularly with my track record of facing difficult questions. I didn't look dodgy in any way, returning after 7/7, bag brimming with wads of crisp £50 notes. Drug's cartel money, terrorist funding, money laundering? Take your pick. *Lord, just help me through this one.* Plus, the guilt about my hasty exit still weighed heavily.

Back at Heathrow... 'Ah, sir....'

My face dropped. *Drat, here we go...* I had no story prepped. Or if I had, the turbulence had knocked it clear from my mind.

'Well, that all seems to be in order. Have a wonderful day, sir,' the airport official smiled, handing back my passport. *Alhamdulillah.*

I had a frosty call with James once back home. He eventually understood my reasons. I think.

6. BACK TO BLIGHTY

'The strongest of all warriors are these two – time and patience.'

— TOLSTOY, WAR AND PEACE

I felt a queasy trepidation touching down on the Heathrow tarmac. Four years away seemed like an eternity, despite my regular, short visits. Now I had to negotiate this new post-7/7 Britain. I needed a job, a car, and somewhere to live. Plus, 'reintegration' back into work life. How difficult could that be?

One thing was for sure, I didn't want to return to permanent employment in the UK, not after my previous experiences. The freelance gown seemed a better fit. It would give me the autonomy, flexibility, confidence, and level of control that I wouldn't have achieved working as a regular employee, but also allow me to build project teams. Freelancing sheared away the blubbery, fatty layers wrapped around corporate life. Now, specific talent and proficiency (mostly) outweighed all other considerations. No schmoosing or political manoeuvrings required. Freelancing also provided opportunities across many different organisations and industries, broadening my exposure and adventures.

One of my first outings back in Blighty was to a large car supermarket in West London. The £50 notes were burning a hole in my brown leather bag. I visited the market one Saturday morning. While browsing the Volvo vehicle range, I noticed groups of men and women huddled around Skoda cars, speaking in hushed tones. It felt a little unusual, out of place, but I couldn't quite explain why. They appeared different. Sure, they were all white, dressed in usual weekend attire. Yet their behaviour resembled something 'we' would typically do – we Pakistanis. When we want to buy a new car or house, drop-off or collect someone from the airport, or go to the hospital, we don't go in ones or twos – nay, we often go en-masse: brothers, sisters, parents, uncles, aunties and friends.

Overcome with curiosity, I wandered over, buzzing around, miserably failing to remain inconspicuous. As I eavesdropped on their conversation, I realised these white folks weren't from these Isles at all. They were actually all Eastern Europeans, Poles, in this case. Over the last four years or so, while I'd been abroad, large numbers of immigrants had arrived on these shores, numbers far eclipsing anything in the 60s and 70s.

And so, on that day, for possibly the first time, I felt a feeling of Britishness, a Britishness amongst a group of Caucasian immigrants, a truly bizarre experience.

Hang on... Perhaps this post-7/7 Britain is going to be easier than I thought?

6.1 INTERVIEW TECHNIQUES

Ah, the famous Threadneedle Street, home to the Old Lady herself. I always enjoy walking around that area of London: so much history, so much tradition. You can picture Holmes and

Watson racing through the narrow, dimly lit streets on their way to solve another crime.

Alas, no deerstalker, pipe or dastardly crime to solve for me. A sweltering afternoon in August, under a fair amount of duress, I approached the 100-year-old financial institution, pushed open the wooden door, and stepped inside the grandiose foyer. It looked like they'd kept a fair amount of original décor. With F22 Raptor-like tracking, the receptionist immediately locked onto my position and followed my every movement. As I approached, she gave me the usual 'Why are you here? Are you lost?' version of *the look*.

'Can I help you?' she asked, in her best headmistress voice.

'Hello, yes, I have an interview with Percival.'

She scanned me up and down, and hesitated before asking, 'Right, if you're sure – what's the name?'

'My name is AH-SIF RA-NA,' I replied, with my simplest phonetic pronunciation.

'Ok, let me call him.'

'That'd be marvellous.' Suppressing my garrulous instincts, I smiled, nodded my head, and leaned forward to take what appeared to be a *Werther's Original* sweet from the ceramic ornamental bowl on the counter. Well, why not? I didn't have a great feeling about this. Might as well make the most of the opportunity.

'Hello, Percival, there's a, a...' she looked up. 'What's the name, again?'

'AH-SIF,' I repeated.

'Yes, Mr AZEEZ here for you... He says it's an interview. Is that right? Ok, right, yes... Yes, ok.' She turned to me. 'Ok, you can take a seat, he'll be with you shortly. Here's a visitor pass.'

Did Miss Trunchbull really think I'd made up the tale? 'Sure, thanks.' I stepped back and sat down on one of the lazy leather seats. *Phew, it's hot in here, even hotter than outside.* I looked around and couldn't see any air vents. They hadn't managed to install any air-conditioning yet. The usual array of magazines and newspapers covered the wooden, lacquered desk. Most of the papers carried the same story: '*43 Civilians Dead in Latest Iraq Attack*'.

Lord... I picked up one of the papers and started reading. Five minutes later, a stout, balding chap with round wireframe glasses entered. I glanced up and smiled.

'Azeeq...?'

I stood, towering over him. 'Yes... Percival?'

He offered a limp handshake with his fleshy, soft hands, and then glanced at the paper I inopportunely still held. His gaze shifted between the paper and my beard like a game of pong. 'Right, er... This way, please.' I followed him through a cavernous and stuffy set of tight corridors to a small open-plan office. No pleasantries. No chit-chat. No, 'Did it take you long to get here?' Not even awkward pockets of silence – just one long stretch. Around thirty employees sat working behind large monitors. We walked through to a meeting room clearly designed for Lilliputians.

'Right, sit down, please.'

Between the two of us, the tiny round table and the chairs, space and oxygen were in desperately short supply.

'Right, what do you know about the problems we've been experiencing?'

Aren't you going to offer me a cup of water, at least? Come on, man, its sweltering in here. 'Well, er, not a great deal, the agent didn't reveal much.' I loosened my tie a little. 'Sorry, I just need to take my jacket off. It's hot outside, and inside.'

He stared at me without saying a word, as I slipped my jacket behind the chair. 'Right. So you weren't briefed about the problem?'

'Not specifically. Can we go through it now?'

Percy paused. He shook his head. 'I don't think you can help us here.' His skin became a slightly darker shade of red.

'Oh, really? And, why do you say that?' My sarcasm restraints were about to shatter.

'Well, we, er... We have a *very* high-performing team here, and we work on complex problems.' He pointed a chubby finger towards the team behind the door.

'Percy, have you actually read my CV? That's what I do!'

'Er, no... I haven't.'

'Didn't you receive a copy? Not to worry, I have one here.' I handed him the neatly stapled sheets.

Without bothering to look, he placed them on the table. His finger twitched, poised, as though waiting for the 'Skip Ad' button to appear on a YouTube advert.

'Are you sure you don't want to walk through the problems while I'm here?' I asked. I didn't need to be Nostradamus to see how this was going to end. And I didn't have the will to debate with Percy, or even engage in cerebral banter. *Why on earth would I want to use my talents and expertise here, anyway?!* Now, I'm not a violent person in any way. Never have been, except under extreme provocation. But Percy needed a solid right, and, frankly, *nothing* would have delighted me more at that moment. Bruce Lee would surely have forgiven me. But it wasn't an option.

'Ok, Percy, I understand. Perhaps this isn't going to work out.' I stood, and reached for my jacket.

'Ok, let me see you out.' He sprang to his feet, probably faster than he'd moved in quite a while.

I followed him out to the main foyer. No further words, no handshake, no eye contact, no 'all the best, I hope you get another role'. I walked towards the receptionist again, handed over the badge, and smiled. 'These aren't *Werther's Originals*, but I'll take another couple.'

Exiting the suffocating old building on that sunny day was like rising for air after being strangled underwater for 10 minutes by a malevolent cartoon villain. The temperature had dropped a few degrees, as a fresh breeze swirled outside – a befitting tonic.

Home, James, and don't spare the horses.

THOUGH, I often find that interviews can be quite entertaining. When sufficiently motivated, I try to inject some life into them, whether I'm the interviewer or interviewee.

A few years later, at the end of one interview, I discovered my interviewee was a devout Catholic. We proceeded to plot the historical timeline of Adam to the present day, highlighting the differences between Islamic and Christian beliefs along the way. He seemed to enjoy that much more than the interview. I would have hired him too, but he was an awful programmer.

'Asif, can we continue the discussion over coffee?'

'I'm afraid not. I do need to get back upstairs, back to work, I'm afraid.'

In another interview, my interviewer asked, 'I see you worked in Saudi Arabia?'

'Yes, for around four years.'

'What were you doing there?'

'Well, I gained valuable experience at the Bin Laden Corporation.'

There was a short silence, followed by cacophonous laughter, as the interviewer thumped the table in utter delight.

It wasn't *that* funny. But I landed the job a short while after.

'YOU KNOW, I was never going to hire you,' one of my managers announced over dinner. We'd spent two years working on an IT Programme. The longest two years of my life, frankly.

I raised my eyebrow. 'Why on earth not?'

'Well, I needed the right person to deliver this project. I wasn't expecting someone fresh from the Caves of Tora Bora.'

I laughed. 'Well, those caves are really tough. If you can deliver in that mountainous terrain, you can deliver anywhere.'

He roared. 'Yes, I think you're right! Do you remember when I asked about your management style?'

I paused for a moment. 'Aha, yes. I said something like "honest, open, collaborative".'

'Yes, exactly. That almost put me off! I wanted someone a little devious, underhanded. A little manipulative. Someone who could deal with the other suppliers. I thought the suppliers would chew you up. I got that wrong!'

'WHICH WAY to Buckingham Palace Road, mate? I have an afternoon tea appointment with the Queen of England herself.'

I wasn't really going to see her. I had an interview on BPR, though not at the Palace.

The newspaper seller stopped stacking his papers and groaned. 'Mate, it's just down...' He stopped mid-flow. 'Er, it's... Head straight down this road for about 20 minutes, and you'll see it on your right.'

After a dutiful 20-minute march, I realised the chap had sent me in *precisely* the opposite direction. I graciously gave him the excuse of protecting Queen and country. I arrived at my interview 30 minutes late, but had a great story to break the ice.

I didn't get the job.

6.2 NOM DE GUERRE

You'd be surprised how many phonetic variants a four-letter name can generate. Over the years, I've heard: A-zeef, Azif, A-seef, Ahsif, 'As if he's called Asif' (obviously). I don't mind the mispronunciations, and generally appreciate the effort when people ask how to pronounce this most complex of ethnic names. It's often a precursor to a more interesting conversation on linguistics, etymology or similar. Depending on the spelling, it can mean 'sorry' or 'fiery wind'. Unsurprisingly I stress the latter. My surname always raises a few eyebrows when I mention it's a genus of frogs. I've always liked frogs. A sorry frog isn't great, mind.

Aside from the odd occasion, I've never felt the need to change my name, neither in person nor on my CV. Maybe that's because I've been luckier than most.

ON A SUNDAY AFTERNOON in late January 2006, I'm on my way to Nottingham. It's my first time in the city, and I know precious little about the place, aside from the football and cricket grounds, Robin Hood, and a reputation for gun violence. It's my first week away on a new IT programme, a short 3-month contract, or so I think. I need to live away from home during the weekdays, one of the downsides to freelance consulting. That means there's a host of logistical problems to grapple with: travel, food, exercise regime, and of course, somewhere to lay my head.

I arrive at Nottingham train station around 21:30, and catch a taxi to the hotel I'd booked a few nights before on Lastminute.com. After spending the best part of 5 hours travelling, I'm longing for a warm shower, the meal my dear wife prepared, a comfortable bed, and a good night's sleep before my first day. My Garmin watch announces 22:05 precisely as the taxi arrives at the hotel.

Awkwardly clambering out of the taxi with my luggage, I stare aghast at the hotel. *What on earth is this?* It resembled something from Oliver Twist's London. I'd paid a decent amount for the five nights, and expected more than a den. The pictures on the website looked different. Perhaps the owner dabbled with Photoshop in her spare time. Unfortunately for me, the name and address of the hotel matched.

I struggled with the sticky outside door, eventually yanking it open with force, to be welcomed by a stale smell and a dimly lit reception area. A dishevelled lady with oily, straight hair and a tired leathery face stood behind the counter. The film *Throw Momma from the Train* came to mind. Trying to avoid any comment about the stench or her remarkable similarity to Momma, I cracked a wry smile. 'Hello. I think I have a reservation for five nights.' The words crawled from my mouth. 'Though, actually, I don't think I'm at the right hotel... I'm looking for The Grand Inn. Do you know where it is?'

'Good news! You're at the right place, sir. Let me check your reservation. What's the name?'

'Azeef Rane,' I replied, thinking quickly.'

'Er, one moment. Rane, Rane... I'm sorry, I can't see anything.'

'Ah, oh well, never mind, I'm at the wrong hotel. Right, I won't keep you a moment longer.' *Phew*, I thought. *Having an exotic name does have the odd benefit.*

'One moment,' she interjected. 'Let's try again. How do you spell that?'

'Eh? Spell?'

'Your surname. How do you spell it?'

'Oh. Er, R-A-N-E.'

'Aha, yes, yes, good news, we have you, though you seem to down as R-A-N-A.'

'Oh, right... How unfortunate.'

'You're here for five nights in Room 313, one of our best rooms.

Here's your key. The lift is just over to the right. We hope you have a great stay.'

Drat. The taxi driver hadn't pulled a fast one, and this lady was a little smarter than I'd thought. At least the hotel had a lift, though. Impressive. Perhaps it was actually a little gem, just covered in a veneer of dust. I pressed the lift button and waited, while peeping back at the receptionist. *Is she chuckling to herself?*

The doors opened to reveal a grimy grey box with less cubic capacity than my fridge and certainly less technology. Risking life and limb, I squeezed inside, and managed to arrive at the third floor, despite mechanical grinding sounds emanating from all directions. *Right, Room 313, finally...*

What? Perhaps I'm hallucinating, or seeing some optical illusion? Is this Momma's doing? The room isn't level. I'm sure of it. I reckon the angle inclined at least 20 degrees from one end to the other, though I hadn't packed my protractor to validate. I paced from one end to the other and could feel the climb. *Lord, we've gone from Oliver Twist to Alice in Wonderland. Right, that's it. I'm not staying here.* I could handle the shabby interior and awful stench, but wouldn't tolerate a sloping room. I picked up my suitcase and marched back downstairs, avoiding the lift this time.

Momma was busy typing.

'Look,' I said, 'I'm sorry, but it's all been a terrible, terrible mistake. If I leave now, can I have my money back?' I placed the reservation printouts on the counter to remind her how much I'd paid.

'Sorry, sir, what's the matter? You've just arrived! You can't possibly leave now!'

As we quarrelled back and forth about acute angles, cubic capacity, and Photoshop, three thunderous bangs silenced the clamour. Now, I'm no expert, but they sounded like gunshots. Motionless, I glared at the woman. 'Er... what on earth was THAT?'

She stared back, not saying a word, before slowly lowering her gaze back to her monitor and continued typing.

I quietly collected my papers, picked up my suitcase, and trudged back to the room.

HAVING SURVIVED THE FIRST NIGHT, my next challenge involved getting to the office.

'Oh, hello, I need a taxi from the Grand Inn to Ruddington Business Park.'

'Sure, what name is that?'

'Asif,' I replied

'What name is that, please?'

'AH-SIF.'

'Eh? As if what? I just need a name, mate. Just a name.'

For goodness' sake, man. I sighed. 'Try Jon – without the H.'

'Sure, Jon, it'll be there in 10 minutes.'

6.3 UNHAPPY HOUSE HUNTING

'Room to Let – No blacks. No Irish. No dogs' read the classic sign.

Apparently, it was all the rage in the 60s and 70s. I'd seen variations scribbled on lined paper over the years, but never this specific wording. I always felt black Irish dogs had it particularly tough when room or house hunting.

Having spent around a year sampling possibly every Nottingham hotel, treading water in the vain hope we'd deliver our IT Programme, I'd finally realised it wouldn't end any time soon, and couldn't tolerate more hotel time. Perhaps even more irritated by my ongoing project, Shmaila suggested we find a suitably large house with a garden for the kids to frolic and play. She omitted any detail regarding the extra-wide parking spot for my delightful maroon Volvo.

After several weeks scouring the local area around work, I found the seemingly perfect house, only a couple of miles away from the office, and immediately arranged an appointment through the agent. My TomTom satnav directed me toward an upmarket area of Nottingham, somewhere I hadn't previously ventured. *Crikey, this really is perfect; an imposing house, manicured front garden, large bushes for privacy, and enough space to park a Challenger 2 Tank.* I parked, my Volvo looking slightly out of place next to the pristine BMW 7-Series.

The gravel path gave a cathartic crunch underfoot as I paced towards the huge front door. I raised the brass door knocker. It crashed down with an expensive clang. No answer. I knocked again. A few minutes later, a man in his sixties answered. One look and his face dropped to the polished marble floor beneath. It was the face pulled when receiving an email from the chap who wants to relinquish half his inheritance. You simply need to hand over your personal and bank details and follow a set of complex instructions.

'Oh, who on earth are you? Why are *you* disturbing me on a Thursday evening?' he grumbled.

'Oh, hello, good afternoon. I've come to see the house; I understand it's for rent?' I mustered half a smile.

'Er, house, rent, er...' He paused and continued staring, before dropping his eyes to my beard. Of course, at that point, he could have simply told me it was all a horrid mistake, that they'd decided not to embark on the world cruise after all. Or I'd just been beaten to the finish line ten minutes earlier. Either would have saved us from any further embarrassment.

'Is the house still available?' I asked, now just hoping he'd say no so I could be on my way.

'Oh, yes, yes, it is...' he mumbled, continuing to gawp like an impudent schoolchild.

'So... Can I have a look around...?'

'Look around...'

'Yes, a look around the house,' I repeated.

'Well, to be honest, I don't think you'll like it here. We don't have many of your, er, you know, your lot. You should try Beeston.'

'Who is it, Jack?' a voice came from within, before a smartly-dressed lady appeared. 'Oh. Who is this, Jack?'

'Hello,' I coughed. 'I came to look at the house for rent, but Jack was just explaining there aren't many folks like me around here, and I probably wouldn't be a great fit.'

'Oh, oh, I see...' She awkwardly looked at Jack. 'Maybe he could have a look around the house, Jack, you know. Look around?'

Jack's gaze still firmly locked on me. 'Hmmm.'

I looked over her shoulder to see two large Doberman-type dogs (they all morph into one breed above a certain size, for me). *Eh? What on earth is the woman talking about? Hang on. I think I've seen this episode of Columbo[1]. I need to get out of here.* 'Jack's quite a rude fella, isn't he? You've done well to stay with him all these years. Have you ever watched that programme, *One Foot in the Grave*? Your husband reminds me of the chap, what's his name...?'

Jack and his wife stared wide-eyed; mouths opened.

'How dare you, you, you...' Jack gave me *the look*.

'*Please* finish your sentence...' I pleaded.

With Jack's tongue now safely restrained, it was time for me to leave.

'Rightio, I think that's enough excitement for one day. Thanks for your time. Lovely house, by the way. I do like the BMW, too. Superb engineering specimen. Not a patch on my Volvo, mind.'

I jumped in my car and sped off.

Why didn't they simply scribble 'No Pakis' in the window and save everyone the aggravation?

6.4 LUNCHTIME Q&A

'I thought you were going to put a fatwa on me in the meeting, the way you glared at me!' Bob, a colleague, grabbed his tuna and cheese toasted sandwich and took an enormous mouthful, leaving pale yellow streaks dangling down his chin.

I chuckled. 'Bob, you're not important enough for a fatwa, plus you need a napkin.'

'Uh... Eh?'

'It's a good example. A word that's assumed a life of its own, thanks to the Rushdie affair. It doesn't mean what you probably think.'

'You mean like a death sentence or targeted assassination?'

'I'm afraid not. It's less exciting – an Islamic legal ruling that could relate to anything.'

'Oh...'

'A fatwa could be a ruling about fasting in very northern countries with perpetual daylight, for example.'

'I agree, that isn't as exciting.'

'Also, I can't issue a fatwa, either. It's restricted to recognised religious authorities – part of our problem in the modern Internet world. Not every Zaid, Bakr and Amr can issue a religious ruling – that's Tom, Dick and Harry in regular parlance.'

Bob gobbled another bite, before taking a swig of Coke. 'While we're on the topic, what did you think of the reaction to *The Satanic Verses*? Was it worth it?'

'No. A familiar story, unfortunately. The kerfuffle, the book burning, the vigilantism and demonstrations only popularised the book. We sold millions of copies on Rushdie's behalf. Otherwise, it would have remained an indifferent novel, as Roald Dahl described it.'

'Seems like Shariah Law in action,' he smirked.

'You're on fire today, Bob. I like it. Have you had a tough morning?'

'Er, yes, I feel annoyed. And hungry.'

'Shariah Law, eh? I knew we'd get there. Few words invoke such intravenous fear and aversion within the Western psyche as much as these.'

'Haha, yes, agreed.'

'The term 'Shariah' means a water source to which people come to drink. Legally, it refers to the entire religion, with all its commands and prohibitions, rules and regulations, derived from the Qu'ran and sayings of the Prophet Muhammad (ﷺ). If printed, the entirety would comfortably fill 20 hefty volumes, with commentary.'

'Sounds more complex than English Law.'

'There's a theory that aspects of English Common Law are based on Islamic Law[2].'

'The EDL lot wouldn't like that.'

'No. Actually, though, giving charity and protecting orphans, the poor and the needy are all aspects of Shariah Law. Indiscriminate killing and severing necks with rusty penknives aren't. In the West, the words Shariah Law have been reduced to a couple of images: a maniacal bearded man lobbing off someone's head, and a miserable, oppressed woman dressed from head to toe in a black burqa.'

'Wait one moment.' Bob rustled into his rucksack. 'You mean like this headline?'

'Bob on.'

6.5 LOST IN TRANSLATION

When asked why he never flies First Class, Sulaiman Al-Rajhi, the billionaire businessman and philanthropist, replied, 'All the classes arrive at the same time. When first-class is proportionally faster, I may consider it.'

I seldom travel other than Economy Class (unless I've got a free upgrade). That's mainly due to my frugal nature; the price differential is often far too significant to justify. Potential DVT on long haul flights can sometimes swing the decision, though, too. On occasion, when I've travelled First Class on trains, I wonder why I bothered.

I FISHED the research paper from my bag and scanned the tiny print abstract: 'A Short History of Two-Level Morphology'. *Right, let's get stuck into this.* A couple of minutes later, my eyes were already drooping — a wearisome read. My thoughts quickly wandered towards lunch, tuna paninis, maybe prawn cocktail crisps. I took another dip into my bag. Perhaps I'd be luckier this time. *Aha!* 'The Trivium: Logic, Grammar and Rhetoric'. *That's more like it.*

'Tickets, please. Can I see all tickets, please?' announced the inspector, in the usual theatrical voice. I squeezed my hand deep inside my pocket. *Now, where's that pesky ticket? Nope, not that pocket, the other one. Hmmm, not that one either... Lord.*

Like a lithe black panther stalking its prey, the ticket inspector had seemingly moved several metres in one bound and now hovered above me. *Goodness' sake, man, give me some room, at least. Why have you missed out the woman behind reading the Financial Times, anyway?*

'Can I see your ticket, sir?'

I motioned with my left hand, while I continued foraging with my right.

The inspector paused for a moment, then blurted, 'This – first – class. You – have – first – class – ticket!? FIRST CLASS!?'

I stopped rummaging and eased the book under my bag, while

staring blankly at the inspector. I clearly wasn't the first person on his ticket path. Perhaps he'd worked out a more efficient algorithm. If so, I was keen to discuss. I opened my mouth, before abruptly shutting again. The carriage appeared sufficiently empty for a little banter. Surely the situation deserved that.

'Me – no – speaking – the English – please. Me go Pres-ton. This train Pres-ton, please?' I used my best foreign accent, hand movements and all.

'Yes – this – train – Preston. But you need ticket. TICKET!' He pulled a ticket from his pocket to exhibit. 'This TICKET.'

'Ah – TEE KIT...' I repeated, in caveman speak. 'Me having TEE KIT.'

The inspector turned to the woman with the paper and shook his head. 'These people...' he sighed. 'I do apologise, we get these Muz-, err, *people* all the time trying to sneak onto trains.' The FT lady joined the condemnation. He snapped back to me. 'YOU LEAVE CARRIAGE NOW,' and thrust a finger towards the exit.

'Leaving – carriage – me – is – no. I – go – must – Preston.' Hang on, that sounded too much like Yoda.

The ticket inspector appeared to be in his mid-20s. He looked genuinely flummoxed.

Time to end the charade before he did something he would later regret. I returned to my serious, disgruntled face. 'Calm down, calm down. Here's my ticket...' I glanced at his name label. 'Craig, don't worry, I'm in the right carriage. Not that it's worth the money.'

Craig froze in horror. 'I'm so sorry, sir... I thought...'

'No point for the sorry sir bit now, Craig. Yes, I know what you thought, quite presumptuous on your part. Not to mention rude. Even if I had mistakenly wandered into the wrong carriage, it's hardly the way to speak to anyone.' I glared at the woman who had now buried herself back into the FT. 'Mr Branson wouldn't approve of this behaviour...'

'Look, I'm really sorry, let me get you a coffee or tea.'

'Well, you're young. Hopefully, a lesson learnt. I'll have a large cappuccino, please. With chocolate sprinkles. And maybe a short-bread or two.' I smiled at him and returned to my book.

6.6 NOVEL MATERIAL

During my early school years, a *Reader's Digest* Reverse Dictionary slammed onto our doorstep one January morn, a weighty yet delightful tome brimming with exotic and bizarre words like *deuter-agonist* (English: the actor next in importance to the protagonist). We're not quite sure why my father parted with £20 for the good book. Perhaps it was part of some competition, or perhaps a mistake. Whatever the motivation, it became my reading material of choice each night. I devoured the book with the same alacrity as any Sherlock Holmes adventure. Equipped with my daily dose of new words, I'd infuriate my classmates with the obscure and opaque. My English teacher's face would contort as though chewing through a wodge of Hubba Bubba bubble gum whenever I hurled new words at him, and he lost many bars of chocolate when he'd challenge us to throw a word that he couldn't define. We also had our fair share of robust discussions when I (incorrectly) used the new words in my English assignments. The hubris of youth.

Aside from the juvenile antics, this book helped foster a lifelong passion for words, language, and literature. Throughout the years, I dabbled in bouts of writing, starting half a dozen books on a wide variety of topics without ever reaching the second chapter, a prac-tice common with many great unsuccessful authors.

So, imagine my unbridled joy and excitement when I discov-ered the latest recruit to my latest IT project was a published author. Ok, not a 'Dan Brown successful' author, but published, nonetheless. Finally, I could extract tricks and tips from someone who'd already trodden that tortuous path. Finally, I could understand how to persevere beyond the first chapter. I felt like a young Kung-Fu student in the presence of a Shaolin Master.

Now, off the bat, Derek was a tad odd: seemingly devoutly religious, with earrings and covered in tattoos, dressed like a punk rocker and bald as an egg. Ok, ok, some may say that's a standard IT bod. But he was also manifestly intelligent and talented at his job. Our desks were positioned such that we could see one another across the office. On occasion, I would see him staring at me: long stares, unusual stares, cerebral stares. I would innocently smile and nod my head, a little disconcerted, though I didn't think anything sinister afoot. Sometimes, I'd give him the thumbs up. *Perhaps he's just deep in thought, perhaps looking for inspiration,* I'd reassure myself. And we all needed inspiration working on that IT project. I certainly had no complaints about his work output or ethic.

The weeks and months passed, and we eventually dragged the snarling and salivating Cerberus-like project over the finishing line. Derek left the project before me, and we exchanged pleasantries on his final day. We jested about the arduous project, and who would be first to write a 'bestseller' (hint: not me). We shook hands, and he was on his way. I never gave Derek much thought after that.

Many months later, I met a mutual friend who mentioned Derek was working on a new book. The plot centred around an MI5 agent investigating a Muslim, a devout chap, incredibly amiable, well-educated, and impeccable manners. By day, a respected member of society, embedded in the high-flying corporate IT world, suffered on the daily commute, paid copious taxes and sent his kids to school. However, by night, things were quite different. Yes, by night, this chap ran a local terrorist cell, hell-bent on launching a maniacal yet deliciously ingenious attack in the heart of London's financial district. This character reported into London HQ during the day, and the Caves of Tora Bora by night. What a superb plot!

The name of the deuteragonist? Asif. *Come on, at least change the name, man.*

Hang on... Me writing about him, writing about me... That'd be an interesting book...

6.7 SORRY, WE'RE CLOSED

It'd taken the best part of a decade, but we had finally saved enough money to buy an apartment. I needed to save half the property's value, having secured finance from a Kuwaiti bank for the remainder. Yes, that may seem an odd approach to buying a property. Why not pop down to Halifax or Nationwide and get a regular mortgage? Why bother with all this faff, and invest the money in Apple, Tesla or Bitcoin?

As a general rule, Muslims eschew interest, both receipt and payment. That makes house buying slightly more challenging than usual, particularly in the UK, where saving money to buy a home is a bit like climbing an icy hill wearing curling shoes smothered in treacle.

The moment Shmaila and I entered the showroom, the sales lady's eyes locked onto our position. We tiptoed to the farthest end of the room, quite conscious of her piercing stare. In fact, had aliens beamed into the joint and danced a jig on her table at that precise moment, the little green-headed fellows would probably have received less attention.

'Er, can I help you?' she finally questioned.

'Ah, yes, thanks, we're looking to buy a property,' I responded.

She shook her head. 'I'm afraid these properties are all *very* expensive,' she said matter-of-factly, quite sure we were shopping in the wrong store. I wasn't expecting to meet the Wicked Witch of the West. Of course, after spending the decade researching property, we were all too familiar with the prices, and were ready to buy. 'Why don't you try some of the apartments further in town? They are cheaper.'

I looked at my wife, who glared at the sales lady with a mixture of bemusement and anger. Any enthusiasm to pursue one of her properties had now completely dissipated. I walked to the lady and took a note of her name. 'Have you ever read *The Art of Closing the Sale?*' I asked.

'No, I haven't.'

'Well, I do recommend it. *Etiquette for Imbeciles* is also worth a quick read. I can send you a copy if you'd like.'

We bolted from the showroom.

That night, I wrote a furious tome to the home builder about the experience. A few days later, they sent an apologetic response offering a substantial discount on the property if we reconsidered. Unfortunately, the sales lady had soured the experience too much. However, I did recommend a bout of training for the sales lady, with my dear wife more than happy to instruct.

6.8 DANGEROUS APPAREL

The monstrous cardboard container sat patiently outside the front door as I arrived home. A long week had passed since the order, and I could barely contain my excitement. *Crikey, this is heavier than I expected.* I noisily dragged it inside the apartment before rushing into the kitchen for a pair of scissors.

The radar blazed red. Shmaila wandered over and looked down. 'And, what's in the box?'

'Oh, nothing important... Nothing to worry about.'

'Whenever it's not important, you've ordered an expensive gadget or some fitness item.'

'Well, that's a little judgemental, not to mention inaccurate. It certainly wasn't expensive. Now, if you give me a few moments, please, I have a delicate operation to perform.'

With rabbinical rigour, I made four incisions across the holding tape and pulled open the top. I peered inside. *Hmmm, that looks quite conspicuous, much bulkier than expected. I hope it's actually wearable.*

My wife, still buzzing around the box, exclaimed, 'What on earth is *that*?'

'This, my dear wife, is going to transform your husband into a super fit athlete.'

'Aha! I knew it!'

I heaved the garment from the box and lifted it over my head before gently lowering it over my torso. 'This is a 20kg 'weighted vest', used by high-performance, elite athletes.'

'That, my dear husband, is an arrest warrant hanging around your neck, and probably a hernia or slipped disc. Surely you won't go out in public wearing that? Not after recent events?'

'Oh, don't be silly, anyone can see this is just a harmless vest.' I stroked my hands over the straps, buckles and awkward, bulging protrusions. 'It couldn't possibly be mistaken for anything more sinister. It'll be fine. *Insha'Allah*' (Arabic: God willing). I grinned a broad grin, patting the vest. It made a pleasing solid, thudding sound. *What on earth have they filled this with?*

I wandered to the full-length mirror. *Hmmm. It does look more than a little suspicious. Let me try an alternative.* I reached for my workout hoodie. *This should do it.* I stared at the mirror again to see what looked like a Cardassian from *Star Trek*, or a man hiding something very suspicious under his clothes, eyeing me back warily. Either way, alien or chap with a flat-screen TV up his hoodie, quite conspicuous.

Despite the peculiar look, I couldn't wait to test its efficacy. Would it make me fitter? The next Ayódélé (Daley) Thompson?

'Right, I'm just going out for a bit...'

'Ok, I'll see you in five minutes,' my wife shouted from the lounge.

Pah, oh ye of little faith.

'Mamma, why's *Abu* (Urdu: father) wearing that strange coat?' my daughter asked.

'Don't worry, sweetie, it won't last long.'

I gulped my cod liver oil capsules, took a few long, deep breaths, and marched towards the park, around half a mile from the house — my usual running route. Less than 20 metres later, the throbbing started. The additional weight placed considerable strain around my neck and shoulders, my weight now topping 16.5 stones. Now, I had a bulky protrusion, flaying straps, contorted face and a dodgy walk. A big red button was the only item missing to complete the look. Nonetheless, I stoically continued, determined to reach the checkpoint. A few hours in the local gaol seemed preferable over the ignominy of an early return home.

An hour later, after what felt like an attempt at the 'SAS Sickener' and after multiple bizarre looks from people crossing the road to avoid my path, I crawled through the front door. No further evidence was required. That single, uncomfortable trip around the park dissuaded me from wearing the vest in public again (until COVID swept the nation, when no-one cared or noticed for a while).

I mostly restricted myself to wearing the vest in the garden and around the house. Once, I gave the Ocado delivery driver a jolly good fright when I sprinted around the side of my house, forgetting I was wearing the vest. The poor chap nearly fainted when he saw me racing towards him. Thankfully, the eggs survived.

6.9 KILL 'EM, KILL 'EM ALL

Outside of the work environment, Ed was a pleasant, intelligent, well-heeled chap from good stock (at least, that's what he told me). He'd led a sheltered life, lived in the middle of rural Surrey, had a private school education, and his range of friends and acquaintances barely covered a tiny sliver on the multi-cultural spectrum. He probably hadn't seen a non-Caucasian face until well into his teens, perhaps beyond. His life revolved around work, the local parish, the public house, and his small, leafy community, where everyone knew one another's business.

At work, Ed exemplified the nightmare consultant. Our paths crossed when providence ordained we work on the same IT project. When I say he was a nightmare, I mean most people tried to avoid him with religious zealotry. His opening position on almost all matters was, 'I'm right, and you're wrong. I know, and you don't know. I will explain to you how it is, so, listen.' Fools, rookies, experts, it didn't matter. He suffered none gladly.

On the first occasion, I found him an immediate curiosity, an oddball, an outlier. Having spent most of my life in a similar space, I could relate to him better than most. So, during the project, we took the opportunity for morning coffees, sometimes lunches, and coffees in the afternoon (ok, the project wasn't the most stressful). Our conversations were mostly jovial and benign in the early stages. Despite our very different backgrounds, we had a range of mutual interests, including computing (particularly historical computing), electronics, DIY and cars (my weathered Volvo was the instigator of many jibes). As the months rolled on, though, our conversations became increasingly edgy, political, and controversial. As an avid *Daily Mail* reader, we were soon discussing the full gambit of thorny issues: bloodthirsty Muslims, rebellion in the UK, Shariah Law, Islam's position on women, Al-Qaidah, beheadings, and amputations in Trafalgar Square.

Given our analytical backgrounds, we would take each issue and discuss in some detail, back and forth. Ed would present his understanding and perception (generally taken from the print and online media), and then I would counter with the mainstream Islamic position. We'd then discuss the differences and try to understand how the two positions deviated. The process proved cathartic for us both.

Roll on several more months, and the final day arrived on the project (sadly – I'd tried stretching as much as possible). After our final coffee, Ed announced, 'Asif, it's been really good knowing you, and *now* I realise you don't want to actually kill me.'

I paused, took a sip of coffee, and leaned back into the easy leather chair. Looking him straight in the eye, I nodded. *Eh? I didn't want to kill him?!* 'Well, I'm glad you've concluded that. I think. It's good we could clear up some of these misconceptions you've been harbouring.'

'Yes, agreed. I really appreciate your time and effort explaining,' he continued.

I smiled. Of course, Ed had it wrong. I *did* want to throttle him, but not for the reasons he thought.

6.11 BIGWIG BULLY

I spent several years working for a cancer charity organisation in London with multiple offices distributed across the city. Travel between offices became increasingly frequent as we progressed through the project. Office shuttles provided the most effective way of travelling between sites, so the company thought — no complaints from me. Securing a shuttle spot required a quick call to reception. The shuttles were clean, comfortable, and generally offered office relief, particularly if Des happened to be driving.

My laptop clock displayed 09:35, leaving five minutes to sprint downstairs and jump into the shuttle. I slammed my laptop shut and stuffed it into my bag along with my notepad, and flew down three flights of stairs in record time, nearly tumbling down the final flight.

Peering into the shuttle, something didn't seem right. *Hang on a minute...* All six seats were taken. *Aye, aye, what's going on here?*

Des was at the wheel. He grinned at me. 'Have you booked a spot on this one?'

'Actually, yes, only 10 minutes ago, but I see it's full.'

'I know you'll have booked a spot. I'm not convinced about the rest, though.' He turned to face the other passengers. 'Ok, ladies and gentlemen, has everyone booked a spot today?'

My gaze fixed on the six passengers to see who would blink first. They all nodded, some more convincingly than others.

'Right, apologies for the delay. I will have to call reception for the list.' This was the shuttle equivalent of collective detention until the guilty party 'fessed up. The threat, ordinarily sufficient to smoke out the offender, wasn't working.

Des speed-dialled reception. 'Right... Sandra, James, Janet, Bob, Alistair and... Asif'. *Phew.* 'If I haven't called your name, please leave the shuttle.'

Slowly, the bluffer, a middle-aged chap, reluctantly rose from his seat to disembark, continuing to protest, even with all cards face up. 'I'm sure I booked...'

As our eyes met, I sighed and shook my head with disappointment; much like the Panenka penalty, quite unnecessary on my part, but thoroughly pleasurable to see the ball hit the back of the net.

Fast forward 6 hours, and I'm back at base, ready for my next meeting in the belfry. Barely able to contain my excitement, I sprint up the four flights of stairs, only to find the meeting room closed. *That's odd, hardly anyone uses this meeting room.* Still breathing heavily, I knock and slowly turn the handle, to find a group of people deep in conversation.

'Er, sorry, I think this room is booked.' Always allow a little wiggle room, that's been my policy for years.

'No, it isn't, we booked it,' a man barked, a blunt, unequivocal bark.

I resisted the bait. Perhaps my foot had slipped? It happens, as with the chap in the morning. *Maybe I didn't book?*

'Oh, hang on, hang on. Sorry, sorry,' came a voice from the room. 'I don't think we booked it. Apologies. My fault!'

I stared at the man in the middle, while all other eyes were back on me. 'Just wait one minute... Didn't I see you earlier on the shuttle this morning?' Yep, it was him, Poker Dan, the annoying chap from the shuttle. 'Actually, look,' I said, 'it's no problem, take the room. It seems you need it more than I.' And, without waiting for a response, I closed the door and darted back down the stairs. *I'll just find another room. No problem.*

As I reached the bottom of the stairs, I heard vigorous panting from behind. It sounded like an incredibly unfit jogger behind me pounding the floor. Dan had followed in hot pursuit, and now glared at me with devilish venom.

'Don't you EVER embarrass me in front of my team!' he shrieked.

'Eh?' I paused, shaking my head. *Calm down, man. You'll give yourself a coronary.* 'What are you talking about?! Embarrass you? I didn't mean to embarrass you.'

'Well, you did! Do you know who I am!?'

'No, I don't. Though, does it really make a difference who you are? The booking system works much the same for everyone.'

'Right, I need the name of your manager. I'm going to report you!'

'Well, my manager's name is Lilly, so feel free to explain today's events to her, if you wish, though, to be honest, I'd keep schtum. I mean, how many blunders can a man make in a single day?'

'Right, you... ter...' His eyes bulged abnormally from their sockets, and his face swelled like a big balloon, *the look* now quite apparent on his face.

'Ter... ter...?' I repeated. 'Please go on!'

No response.

'Look. I really think you should get back to your team before you hit three blunders for the day.' He turned and stomped away angrily, shouting, 'You'll be sorry about this!'

I never was.

6.12 THE HEEDLESS BANK

'Come and talk, talk to the listening bank,' merrily sang a famous bank in the 80s. Well, it convinced me. With the catchy tune and mythical creature logo, I placed it top of the list, as I trawled the high-street banks, joining each, one by one, while collecting the freebies. Their kids' goodies were also without parallel: sturdy black school bag (ok, you needed a crocodile thick skin to dare take into school), pocket dictionary, and pencil case with mathematical set. Long before investment and savings diversification became popular, my personal wealth (around £7) lay across half a dozen high street banks.

Alas, not all banks listen so well, even in times of need, even when handling your own hard-earned money. And not a darn goody bag in sight.

'I'm so sorry, sir, we cannot transfer the money.' The junior clerk squirmed in his seat. With his odd-looking tie and baggy shirt, he looked like a schoolchild on work experience.

'I don't understand. I need to complete my apartment purchase today. So, I just need to transfer my money *today* to this account, please. It's really quite important I do this today.'

'Er, I'm sorry, I need to call my manager.'

'Yes, yes, that's a good idea. Go quickly, son.'

The clerk bolted around the side. I looked at my watch; it showed 14:10. Three hours and twenty minutes to transfer the money. *Why do they make everything so difficult?* As I wallowed in a stupor of anger and frustration, the clerk and his manager appeared.

'Hello, what seems to be the problem?'

I rolled my eyes, shaking my head. 'Well, there's really no problem. I just need to transfer *my* money from *my* account to another bank to complete the purchase of my apartment. The deadline is close of business today.' My irritation and pulsating blood vessels in my neck were now equally quite apparent.

'Ok, let me check this.' She turned and looked sternly at the computer screen, squinting her eyes. *That's not good for your eyes, you ought to see the optician. Goodness' sake lady, you're not solving the Birch and Swinnerton-Dyer conjecture[3]. Just transfer my money. Why is this taking so long?*

'Ok. I'm sorry, we cannot send such a large amount to this bank.'

Only under extreme provocation do I start shouting. Just ask my kids and the guys at work. 'THIS BANK? Why not?! What's wrong with THIS BANK.' I was shouting now, knowing exactly the problem with the bank.

'Er, funds to dubious destinations, sir,' she croaked.

'Dubious? You mean Middle Eastern? Is this bank on a terrorist watch list? I used it to purchase a property a few years ago, and I didn't have any issues at the time.'

'Well, not exactly....'

'THEN WHAT IS THE PROBLEM? THE MONEY MUST BE SENT TODAY! I don't think you're listening to what I'm saying!' My voice was becoming louder and louder, and other customers in the bank were enthusiastically watching the drama.

'We understand sir, but, unfortunately, we have rules, and we *cannot* send this money.'

I took hold of myself. *Ok, calm down, just calm right down. A few deep breaths...* Back to calm waters and monotone voice. 'Ok, this is disgraceful. You are quite happy to use my money for your own gains, but I cannot withdraw my own money! I shall be sending a full report, and your bank will reimburse every penny that I am charged as a result. Of that, I promise!'

Enraged, without waiting for a response, I stormed out of the bank. My heart was pounding as though I'd just run a sub twenty minute 5K. I couldn't complete the purchase of my apartment with my own money! What an utterly preposterous situation.

As I paced back home, the consequences of not completing the purchase before the deadline raced through my mind. *Lord, how will I extract the money, and how will I explain to the other bank?* I replayed the events over and over in my mind, my irritation only increasing with each replay.

Ten minutes later, I'd approached my apartment, mentally prepared to explain what had transpired to my wife. We wouldn't be completing the purchase today, thanks to the bank that doesn't listen. I had no idea even if we could complete at all now. I'd been with the bank for more than 20 years, but I couldn't wait to close all my accounts, ASAP.

I pushed the front gate when, my phone rang.

'YES!' I barked.

'Hello, is that Mr Rana?'

'Yes! Speaking!'

'Hello – this is Miss Jones from the bank. I've just spoken with my senior manager, and your funds will be released in a few hours.'

Phew. 'Well? Do you expect me to thank you for transferring my money?' I demanded.

'Well, er, er...' she spluttered.

'I'll still be sending a full report to your bosses,' and, with that, I slammed my thumb on the phone screen, knocking the device clean from my hand.

By 17:30, I'd completed the purchase of the apartment and a new phone screen.

6.13 PADDINGTON-SWANSEA 18:52

It's an icy December night in 2009. Heavy rain, to boot. I'd left the office rather later than I'd hoped, and managed to forget my umbrella in the process, so arrived at Paddington station drenched, rain dripping from my beard and new briefcase, making puddles on the hard floor. The entire day had been squandered working through a collection of obscure problems. And it didn't help when the grown-ups demanded updates every hour, that's for sure. My head throbbed as though metronomically struck by a large blunt instrument. I needed a double dose of co-codamol in boiling water. That'd set me right.

As I arrived on the Paddington concourse, the synthesised voice blared, 'The next train to depart from Platform 2 will be the Golden Hind 18:52 to Swansea. Please board the train if you intend to travel.' *Personalising the train with some grandiose name hasn't improved this service one jot,* I thought. A man of Brunel's erudition would have known that. The train, typically heaving, mostly ran late, the carriages resembled Fagin's den, and yet the prices increased as though governed by the precise movement of a finely tuned Swiss timepiece.

I glanced at my own shiny new Garmin sports watch, delivered that same day at work. I'd learnt this work delivery hack a few years earlier. As a general strategy, it successfully circumvented trouble-some queries at home. *Right, only five minutes before train departure.* Now seemed an opportune moment to test my watch's capability. Momentarily forgetting the image of a sizeable brown bearded man racing through a train station, I clicked the 'Run' feature, and sprinted towards the ticket barrier with a surprising degree of gusto, given the torturous day. I forced my card through the turnstile, and of course, on this day, the turnstile had joined the conspiring cabal.

'Calm down, son, you'll get on the train,' the guard groaned in a whimsical drone.

'Look', I blurted, 'I do need to get on this train, and I'm already late.'

'Yes, yes, *everyone* wants to get on the train,' he snapped. The guard was the top banana here. He ambled from his pedestal and examined my ticket. 'Right, seems to be in order.' He gave a nod of approval, and opened the gate. Now, with less than two minutes before train departure, I sprinted down the platform with my last morsels of energy, and finally crawled onto the train.

Panting heavily, I knew the chances of finding a seat were remote, despite the XL train size, and I wasn't about to burn more glucose traipsing up and down like a wandering nomad. *Let me just settle into a space between carriages. No one will disturb me there.* The train doors locked with an audible and reassuring click. I leaned against the wall advertisement and door, trying to make myself as comfortable as one can on the 18:52 to Swansea. My laptop briefcase carefully rested between my legs, considerately out of the way.

Now, where's my HTC HD2[4] *smartphone?* I rummaged in my bag. *Great, ten new work-related emails already. Good grief, it's 18:52, and I'm still being bombarded. Leave me alone!* The battery icon turned red while I glanced at the top of the phone. *Wonderful. It won't survive the journey home. No plug socket here, either. Hmmm.* As I mulled through the limited options, a mysterious grey apparition appeared in front of me and leaned on the wall opposite. *Goodness, it's quite tight here. Was it really necessary to increase occupancy in this particular 3 square feet of train space? Can you please stand somewhere else?* I gave a disapproving, irritated look at the formless body. Not waiting for any response, I lowered my gaze back to the phone.

My head still ached, but the pain seemed to soften as I caressed a few droplets of rain from my watch's face. It sparkled. Even under this wretched train lighting, it sparkled. The face broadcast an array of cryptic metrics that I didn't understand, yet were no doubt vital to my general well-being.

Right, back to work. Unfortunately, the watch won't help solve these astronomical computational queries. How can we reduce processing time from days to minutes or even seconds? Perhaps we try running more threads in parallel? That requires more hardware. Maybe we start afresh? Though that means we lift our shirt and expose our midriff. Lord, do we start afresh? I could already feel the opprobrious crosshairs swaying across my torso.

Back to the phone. 3% battery charge.

With my eyes wholly absorbed in the tiny screen pixels, I unexpectedly transport myself back in time, recalling a piece of advice from my father... Back to our tiny, terraced house in Burnley, 30 years earlier. The smell of fresh *aloo parathas* sizzling on the pan wafting throughout the house... Mmmm... The Six O'Clock News, with its catchy opening tune, on the TV, and my father marvelling at the vividness of the new colour picture... Me wailing, 'Oh, no, I need more batteries. I can't test my experiment!' My father looking over the mesh of wires, bulbs and other components sprawled over the carpet, saying, 'Look... try this...' Him taking two of my AA batteries and rolling them vigorously in his hands, then handing them back to me... Me holding the batteries, surprisingly hot in my hand... 'They should work a *little* longer,' him saying, smiling.

Back to the present, I smiled, too. I could almost taste the crispy paratha coating. I eased the back cover from the phone, placed the flat chunky battery between my palms, and started to rub, faster and faster. I felt the battery getting warmer and warmer. *Yes, it's working, it's working!*

'*WHAT* are you doing, man?! STOP! STOP! Are you trying to blow up this train?!'

I sluggishly raised my head. The fuzzy grey shapeless form slowly came into focus. I stared at the man, and noticed clumps of perspiration strewn across his puffy, pink brow. Still in a hazy stupor, I could parse the man's words, but struggled to process them in any meaningful way. *Perhaps he covets my new watch? Or maybe my laptop? Why is he talking to me, anyway? Let's start there. Doesn't he know the rule about strangers talking on a train? Firmly taboo.* Moments later, the second processing cycle began. *Hang on... Did he just use the phrase 'blow up this train'?!*

Now the words landed with the full force of a Roy Jones Junior body punch. My gaze back in complete focus, I eyed the man glaring at me. His face was contorted with anxiety, uncontrollably flinching from side to side, with his eyes flicking between mine and the battery.

'Er, no, no! Obviously not!' I spluttered. 'What on earth are you talking about?!'

'Well, what are you doing with that thing?' he demanded, pointing his still trembling finger.

'Eh? Er, actually, I'm trying to excite the electrons within the battery. Hopefully, that will give a few more percent, enough for me to get home. You see, when I was younger, my father...' I stopped. Still petrified, the sweat continued to drip from the man's forehead. He clearly didn't want a physics lesson.

'Battery. Battery.' He shook his head and breathed, probably for the first time in several minutes.

'What on earth is wrong with you, man?' I asked.

He paused and sighed. 'You know, I was a split-second away from pulling the train cord and stopping this entire train. I was absolutely convinced you were about to detonate your briefcase.'

Good grief. I put the phone back into my pocket, trying to digest his words. 'That's, that's... amazing. It's ok. It's just a regular battery and phone. I only have a laptop in the briefcase. Look...'

He breathed a visible sigh of relief, a sigh of a man saved from the guillotine with the blade in transit. He momentarily closed his eyes and mopped his brow, breathing heavily against the back wall.

'Look, I'm really sorry. You see, I used to work in Iraq, and, well, we were trained to be on the lookout. I'm afraid you ticked all the boxes: big, brown, bearded, suspicious activity. I'm very sorry.'

I continued to stare in bemusement. Both of us were now gripped with an embarrassing silence. A couple of minutes passed before I punctured. 'Are you interested in physics?'

'Sure...'

We spent the rest of the journey discussing electrons and terrorism. Unfortunately, we didn't have too long before we reached my stop. We exchanged pleasantries, and I disembarked.

Later that evening, I replayed the events. A retrospective, as we say at work. *That guy really did think I was about to blow up the train. Lord, we have work to do.*

During my morning call with the team the next day, I described the previous day's events. They remained silent, shocked, until one chap quipped, 'Asif, I thought you were going to say at the end that you dropped the briefcase, and it exploded as you jumped from the train!'

I roared with laughter. 'Only in the film version.'

7. WORKPLACE GYMNASTICS

*'To be yourself in a world that is constantly trying to
make you something else is the greatest accom-
plishment.'*

— RALPH WALDO EMERSON

Working as a freelance IT consultant in the UK, I've
sampled many new offices, some spectacular (with
onsite Olympic-sized swimming pools and Feng shui
certified gushing streams), and some downright dodgy (fear of
litigation prevents elaboration). I've also experienced quite a few
first days. Aside from the discomfort of unfamiliar surroundings,
there's the office tour, shaking lots of hands (not so much, post
COVID), failing to remember a multitude of names, health and
safety briefing, and the all-important introduction to the coffee/tea
area. I once experienced a health and safety tour lasting more than
2 hours, including a lengthy trek to a distant fire evacuation point
through a lively part of town. I felt the whole ordeal perilous to my
own personal health and safety.

Negotiating the modern-day workplace can be a challenging affair for anyone: backstabbing, gossiping, harassment, trying managers, jostling for promotion, and the like. But for Muslims, there are a few layers of additional obstacles, often requiring gymnastic agility to negotiate. Aside from some unfavourable industries, we have to accommodate the daily prayers and ritual ablutions that fall within the working day, Friday prayers at the mosque (once a week on, er, Fridays), Ramadan and Eid holidays, scouring for Halal food in the canteen. And, of course, there's dodging alcoholic shindigs. A ringing phone in the middle of a minute's silence for the latest atrocity can be tricky, too, particularly when you're the only brown face in the office, as one friend narrated. Goodness' sake, these Muslims!

7.1 INTOXICATING ADVENTURES

If I had a penny for every time I'd been invited to the pub for an after-work drink, lunchtime drink, leaving drink, joining drink, project success drink, project failure drink (*not* my projects), team-bonding drink, or team-breaking drink, I'd have enough pennies to fill a 200-gallon tun. Possibly two.

'Why don't you ever come with us to the pub after work?' one of my managers asked me, early in my career.

'Well, I don't drink alcohol.'

'You don't need to drink alcohol.'

'Sure, but I don't actually feel comfortable in the environment. I also like to get home early and get on with other stuff. I have an active social portfolio after work.'

'Oh, ok... Well, that's fine.' My manager paused. 'You do realise this *perceived* lack of socialising will hamper you? You don't want to appear aloof. Lots of important decisions are made after work in the pub.'

What on earth is he talking about? How can my non-attendance at the public house after work affect my career? Surely I just need to be great at my job? Well, I did say this was early on in my career, when I enjoyed youth and naivety in abundance.

Sure enough, my lack of attendance resulted in comments such as 'unsociable' and 'aloof' in my end of year appraisals. 'Works great, but as sociable as a leper,' quipped another manager.

I hadn't considered myself aloof, and was happy to join social activities that didn't involve gushing rivers of alcohol. Though, during my working life, I discovered that those social activities were as common as the Transit of Venus.

Several years into my career, realising the paucity of sober activities, I started the social organising myself: indoor cricket, darts, go-karting, softball, a whole range of sporty events, with fabulous feedback, by comparison, though possibly because many of the alcoholic events couldn't be remembered so well.

7.2 BATHROOM ANTICS

Ablution. It's an unusual word, from the Latin *ab-* (away) *luere* (wash). It's a term seldom used outside of a religious context. Muslims ritually ablute (that's the first time I've ever conjugated that verb) before each prayer. Though they're not alone. Orthodox Christians, Jews, Hindus and Buddhists all enjoy some form of ritual ablution. For Muslims, two or three prayer times can coincide with the working day, so ablution can present a watery challenge, especially when washing the hands, face, arms and (sometimes) feet.

Some particularly trailblazing workplaces have dedicated washing facilities for their Muslim workforce, although this is uncommon. I was pleasantly surprised to see the full, sit-down works, accompanied with cloth towel dispenser, at Royal Mail. The facilities surpassed those found in many mosques I've frequented.

I'm not sure Henry VIII[1] would have given his seal of approval, though.

'Asif, I've just walked into the Gents to see Armad washing his feet in the sink, making a right mess on the floor. I thought he was going to climb in and do the whole thing at one point. I did the British thing and tried my best to ignore him,' my manager announced, crimson faced.

I grinned before roaring with laughter at the thought.

'What's he up to?' he asked.

'I wouldn't worry. He's not plotting anything, and he's not brushing up on waterboarding techniques. I suspect the cleaner will be seething, though. He's washing himself before prayer, though he may not realise he can simply wipe over his socks or shoes. I'll have a chat with him.'

The wiping over socks and shoes is a handy alternative at work, particularly for those without dedicated washing facilities. Next time you see someone dangling their feet in the sink, try, 'You know, according to many Islamic scholars, ancient and modern, you can simply wipe over your shoes and/or socks...' It'll impress, if nothing else.

'While I've got your attention...' he continued, 'and we're having this slightly taboo conversation right in the middle of the office with everyone eavesdropping... What's the deal with the empty cups and bottles in the toilets?'

'Aha, yes, you've noticed those, have you?' I nodded my head. 'Well, think of an early version of a bidet, perhaps vo.2. It may not be sophisticated, but it does the job. Small shower taps are common in the Middle East, Asia, and some parts of Europe. They aid cleanliness.'

'Right, gotcha... How's that project plan coming along?'

7.3 HAPPY EID MUBARAK

Muslims have two major festivals each year, one at the end of *Ramadan,* and the second crowning the *Hajj.* Congratulating a Muslim on these occasions is quite straightforward, even for the hardest northern palette. There's a single monosyllabic word to remember, and it applies to both festivals: Eid. So, just remember that three-letter word, and add an appropriate adjective.

So, that's the easy bit. Unless I've managed to negotiate the whole of Ramadan off (which happens with increasing frequency these days), I'll typically have the following conversation with my manager:

'Ramadan is coming to an end soon, so I'll need to take a day off for Eid.'

'That's great. Which day?'

'It'll be either Wednesday or Thursday.'

'So, which day?'

'Well, I can't tell you just yet. We need someone to spot the moon.'

'Eh? The man in the moon is going to tell you?'

'Not quite. You see, we use the lunar calendar to determine the start and end of months. And even though we've known how to calculate the birth of the new moon for millennia, we still have a tradition whereby someone needs to spot the new moon crescent. A universally simple method.'

'This sounds complicated. Can't you have a fixed date as we have for Christmas?'

'Er, no, that wouldn't work. Changing from the lunar to solar calendar at this point – 1400 years on – would be complex.'

'Asif, just take off whatever days you need.'

'Sure, thanks.'

'Oh, Asif, Happy Eid Mubarak!'

'Eid Mubarak or Happy Eid is just fine.'

7.4 FLAMIN' GREGGS PASTIE

'Right, I'm just nipping out for some lunch.'

'Eh? Are you sure you have enough time? We have a meeting with Chris in 10 minutes.'

'I'm not about to trek across the Gobi, I'll be back before you know it. I can't function too well at the moment; glucose levels are low.'

'Right, ok. Don't be late!'

I grabbed my coat and strolled towards the exit. Chris wielded power with an iron fist. He reminded me of a high priest sitting on his throne, surrounded by willing subjects. I never played the obsequious, servile card very well. Hence our frosty relationship.

No sooner had I exited *Greggs* on the high street, than...

'Son, accept Jesus Christ as your salvation or be damned forever! Do you hear me?!' a booming, thick Irish accent reverberated. I turned around amidst a group of busy shoppers. He'd obviously taken a shine to me, and why wouldn't he? Clutching his well-thumbed, note-strewn black Bible in one hand and his walking stick in the other, he screamed, 'Gehenna awaits! The unquenchable fire! You'll burn in the fires forever!' He now felt the need to point directly towards me.

I suppose, on the one hand, I admired his honesty and passion. But, on the other, greeting me with glad tidings of *Gehenna* (Greek: abode of the damned in the afterlife) straight off the bat appeared an unusual strategy. Surely, he should have a word first? Get to know me a little?

I've always attracted a decent amount of interest from the preacher fraternity, perhaps due to my Mosaic beard, perhaps my affable nature, or more likely due to my willingness to make eye contact. There's an honour amongst us lot, you know. It's impolite to ignore. In any case, anyone who's willing to stand all day in the middle of the high street on a freezing day in January is worthy of some attention.

I stopped and turned towards the preacher, his staff still accusatively erect in my direction. I *really* didn't want to stop. I wanted to walk on, admittedly mainly out of fear for my hot pastie, not the promised doom. I also had my meeting. However, his piercing stare and seemingly magnetic stick altered my course.

He stopped his exhortation and clambered from his step-stool, seemingly confident he'd secured a catch for the day. The small poster he'd printed on the stool read: 'Work for God, the pay isn't much, but the pension plan's out of this world.' *Well, at least that's quite witty.*

Up close, the preacher looked like death warmed up. Think Reverend Kane from *Poltergeist II*: sunken eyes, flaky withered skin. The weather hadn't been kind to him over the years. Dressed head to foot in black with wild, wispy white hair. He also proudly displayed a weighty crucifix around his neck. It distracted my eye. I couldn't help but wonder how much it weighed. It reminded me of Mr T's cross (though that was golden and diamond studded). An offensively thick stench of body odour enveloped him and completed the look. *Well, this preaching isn't easy.*

'Son, do you know where you'll be in the next life? Do you?' he breathed, his accent even more pronounced at this short range.

'Er, no, we'd say judgement is for God alone.'

'Well, I'll tell you son; you'll be in the Fire, and I will be in Heaven sitting in the company of the Lord.'

'That's quite presumptuous, if you don't mind me saying. You're sending me to the blazing fire, but you don't know anything about me yet. I may be a standout guy with many good works to my name.'

'Son, do you accept Jesus Christ as your Lord and Saviour?' The heavens suddenly opened, and the rain hammered around us, soaking his leaflets on the table.

'Look, I don't have much time, I'm afraid, but, no, I don't accept Jesus Christ as my saviour. A great prophet, yes. The Messiah, yes. My saviour, no. He won't be able to help himself, let alone you or me.'

'Jesus says, "I am the way, the truth, and the life: no man comes unto the Father but by me. You cannot achieve salvation except through Jesus Christ. It's impossible."' He seemed to be suffering with one of his legs, perhaps a maritime injury.

'We believe only God is the redeemer of our sins, not Christ. Have you read the Book of Daniel? Chapter 9-9, I think: "The Lord our God is merciful and forgiving, even though we have rebelled against him." I've always found Christian theology complex. Our's is very simple in comparison.'

'Eh? Er, are you a Saracen[2]?'

'Look, I do need to go. But not many people use that term these days. I'm a Muslim. And I've studied comparative religion for a few years.'

'A Muslim! Mohammad was a false prophet, preaching a false religion. The increase of Muslims is only a sign of the end times, paving the way for the return of our Lord. He will raise an army to fight the Anti-Christ and his followers, and "You will see the Son of Man (Jesus) coming on the clouds of the sky, with power and great glory."'

'Well, that's quite negative. Do you mean us, the Saracens?'

'If you're not with us, you're against us.'

'Yes, that's what George Bush said. It seems everyone is waiting for the Messiah: Muslims, Christians, Jews... Let's try and get on until that time, eh? Sorry, what's your name?'

'Brian,' he said.

'My name is AH SIF. Would you like half a pastie, Brian?' I split my now cold, drenched cheese pastie and offered him half.

'Er, thank you, but I don't want to take your lunch, son.'

'Well, if two loaves and a few fishes can satisfy the five thousand, I'm sure this will suffice the two of us.'

The preacher chuckled, snatched the half pastie, trailing strands of cheese, and swallowed it in one swift movement.

'I may have erred, though,' I said. 'Was it the five thousand or the four thousand, two loaves or five?'

'Eh? Er, five thousand. No, four thousand... No four...'

'Yes, I understand the difficulty. The numbers depend which Gospel you read. Aside from the unknown authors, the Gospels differ in many details, as I'm sure you're aware, some trivial, involving fishes and loaves, some quite significant. We don't have this problem in Islam, not with the Qur'an. There's just one version. Look, I need to get back to work. I only came out to grab some lunch, and now I'm late for my meeting. Anyway, it's been good chatting to you...'

'Ok. And thanks for the cheese pastie.' Then, 'Be damned. Gehenna awaits. The unquenchable fire...' he muttered, before clambering back onto his step-stool.

My cheese pastie clearly wasn't enough of an offering. *Right, back to the other high priest.*

7.5 LUNCHEON IN THE SKY

I've always encouraged dialogue and discussion within the workplace – particularly amongst my teams and peers. Yet one traumatic side effect of our politically correct age is that we're constantly fearful. Fearful of offending. Fearful of saying something that may be misconstrued or misinterpreted. Fearful of that dreaded call from HR. So, when confronted with the option of pulling a tantalising thread or sitting in cloistral silence, people most often choose the latter. But the workplace represents a unique intersection for people from different backgrounds, cultures, creeds and persuasions who'd ordinarily never meet.

I worked on a tortuous project (yes, there's a theme with IT projects), involving painful travel and a drab location. We eventually delivered the project around two years after the first planned date. After all that effort, the organisation fell afoul of regulators, and our efforts evaporated, though that's a different story for another book. On the bright side, we had an excellent management team, and the canteen offered a decent food selection, so lunchtime provided a welcome escape from the incessant project toil and grind. My team comprised a dozen hardened IT professionals – skilled, intelligent, mostly older and more experienced. We took the opportunity to lunch together.

Our conversations were mostly cordial: football in the winter, cricket in the summer, a splattering of politics, a drizzle of current affairs, military medium, nothing controversial — all very pleasant. Within the canteen, a substantial flat-screen television perched prominently on one wall, covering a large area, and it blared Sky News around the clock. We tried changing to Sky Sports during the football season, but to no avail. Each morning it dutifully returned to the news.

Every so often, the latest headline provoked a jolt of merriment and a talking point for the team. We'd laugh and jest amongst ourselves, and dissect more serious issues, arguing back and forth. However, on occasion, some headlines prompted a deathly, prolonged silence, a silence broken by nothing save the clatter of knives and forks on white porcelain. The headlines provoking such ear-shattering silence? Bad news Muslim stories. Stories involving a protagonist who happened to be a Muslim. Miscreants committing unsavoury deeds who happened to be Muslims. During such news stories, or often breaking headlines with the dramatic accompanying music, we'd collectively gaze at the television, while munching on chips and cheese pie. Every so often, I'd scan the team, expecting *someone* to comment. Nope, nothing. Not a peep. Quieter than a monastery of Trappist monks. But not only that, I would also miraculously be instantiated with Medusa, gaze-avoiding qualities.

This continued for weeks until I could no longer hold back the waters. I felt compelled to puncture the silence and confront the team. During the next lunch, after another bad news story, I gently placed my cutlery on a napkin and asked, 'Tell me, why do we never discuss these stories? Why has no-one ever asked me about them?!'

The team, though quite used to the most ludicrous project demands (typically on Thursday afternoons) and wacky innovation ideas, were ill-prepared for this comment. After another lengthy pause, one chap awkwardly responded, 'Well, we don't want to offend you.' I shook my head and replied, 'Come on, you all know me better than that. We've worked together for months now. What a great opportunity for us to discuss what's going on. Seize the opportunity!'

That one statement spectacularly shattered the fetters and manacles. Liberated, like starlings soaring into the skies, our lunchtime conversations became livelier than ever. We discussed terrorism, the 7/7 bombings, Islamic theology, Middle East turmoil, and countless other previously taboo topics. We took no subject off the agenda. Of course, we didn't always agree. But we created a safe place for the team to ask questions and raise genuine concerns. The team appreciated the opportunity and took advantage. It gave me an ear to the ground, and the team an opportunity to ask the horse (who became increasingly hoarse with all the questions). Ear and eye-opening on both sides.

Adopting this open approach throughout most of my working life, I've only been reported to HR on a handful of occasions, all of them in Riyadh, ironically, except once, when a lady complained that I likened her to Tyson Fury.

7.6 TAKING A KNEE

> '*Sittings in both Houses of Parliament begin with prayers. These follow the Christian faith, and there is currently no multi-faith element. Attendance is voluntary.*'

I stumbled across this little gem while watching Parliament TV. No, I'm not a glutton for tedium and punishment. It's the only occasion I've ever watched PTV live, and there was a fair amount of self-interest involved on that occasion. The prayer read:

> 'Lord, the God of righteousness and truth, grant to
> our Queen and her government, to Members of
> Parliament and all in positions of responsibility,
> the guidance of your Spirit. May they never
> lead the nation wrongly through love of power,
> desire to please, or unworthy ideals, but, laying
> aside all private interests and prejudices, keep
> in mind their responsibility to seek to improve
> the condition of all mankind; so may your
> kingdom come and your name be hallowed.
> Amen.'

That's quite a prayer. I wonder if Tony B, a man of devout faith, recited this before launching attacks in the Middle East?

Muslims also pray daily, five times, no less: before dawn, after noon, late afternoon, after sunset and post twilight. Generally, one or two (sometimes three in winter months) prayers fall inside the working day. As some people find comfort taking a cigarette break, others gossiping around the water dispenser, I find a few minutes away from my desk in prayer helps settle and recalibrate my mind. I don't see it as problematic or taboo to tell colleagues I'm going for a 'prayer break', even if it still appears a little alien to most eyes, and anachronistic in the sophisticated world of TikTok, Snap Chat, and Instagram. It's usually followed by a wise-crack – typically, 'Asif, please pray for this project,' or, 'Say one for us, mate,' and so forth.

However, some less wizened colleagues are quite embarrassed discussing the issue.

'Er, Asif, should we go...' followed by pointing of the eyes.

'Go where?'

'You know, go... It's time to go... You know...'

'Eh? Aha, you mean to pray? Sure, let's go.'

These youngsters, honestly...

Finding a place to take a knee at work is often a challenge, and, over the past twenty years while working in the UK, I've prayed in some weird and wacky locations: broom cupboards, medical rooms, carparks, meeting rooms, chilly data centres. Some truly *Twilight Zone* moments have ensued as a result. For example, the shower room provided a thoroughly soggy but refreshing experience (now I know how baptism in cold water feels). Although, I thought calling the security guards was a tad excessive.

I GLANCED THROUGH THE WINDOW. *Great, the room's empty.* I slid the occupancy tag to the engaged position and strolled into the medical room. Whisking out my prayer mat from the cupboard, I laid it neatly on the ground facing Makkah, and removed my shoes. My watch not only measured VO2 Max and blood oxygen levels, but also pointed me in the right prayer direction. Moments later, I'd been transported to a different realm, deep in prayer.

A few minutes passed, and suddenly I heard the door creaking behind me. At this point, I happened to be prostrate on the floor. *Drat,* I thought, *please go away. Please close the door and go away.* A few more seconds passed; no such luck. I could sense the penetrating stare, the look of bewilderment, and what was about to happen.

'Oh, my God, Asif!' my colleague screamed. 'Asif, are you alright?!'

I raised my hand to motion I was still alive, if not kicking; a conversation, even briefly, in the middle of prayer isn't allowed.

She ran from the room, but I could still hear her shouting. 'Someone call an ambulance, for God's sake! Asif's keeled over in the medical room! I think he's had a heart attack! Quick, quick, call the ambulance!'

Lord... I stopped my prayer and sprang to my feet. Still in socks, I sprinted out of the room and down the corridor to see my colleagues gathered in a huddle, with one on the blower to 999. 'I'm ok, I'm ok, I'm just praying!' I yelled animatedly, waving my hands.

My colleague, now with her head in her hands, feeling quite embarrassed, sighed, 'Oh, my God... I'm so sorry for that.' The call ended abruptly.

On a positive note, it was heartening to know they weren't going to let me die a death in the medical room. I limped back to complete my prayer.

If you do see one of your Muslim colleagues prostrate in the medical room, give it a few minutes before you call the emergency services.

7.7 FRIDAY AFTERNOONS

It's unusual for a desk, laptop, and login id (that works) to all materialise on a first day. Rarer than hen's teeth, in fact. When I finally negotiate the laptop login screen, my opening project contribution involves blocking a recurring Friday afternoon calendar slot. That's the only non-negotiable hour in my week. I can attend meetings at any time – pre 07:00 (and we've had them), post 22:00 (and we've had them), but I *can't* attend at this particular hour on a Friday. So, no matter how hard people try to wedge a meeting into that slot, I decline.

So, what's so special about the Friday afternoon hour? That's Friday prayer hour, which usually involves travelling to a local mosque, or the in house 'multi-faith' room. One location I worked boasted a Muslim Room, Sikh Room, Hindu Room, Jewish Room and Christian Room. It resembled a gargantuan 60s school, so I suspect the Agnostics and Atheists were also afforded a small space to contemplate the mysteries of the universe (I just hadn't walked around the whole building).

The Friday prayer comprises a short sermon followed by prayer, and typically lasts 20 to 30 minutes. I've attended Friday prayers in some curious locations, including the basement of the Barclays Tower in Canary Wharf and the 30th floor of the HSBC Tower (every time I looked outside the window, I could see planes flying towards me – *I've got to get out of here,* I thought).

On one occasion, while leaving for Friday prayers, a colleague rushed over, grabbed my arm, and asked with eyes wide in anticipation, 'Asif, what exactly goes on down there in that room? I've walked past it a few times and heard strange noises and chanting, but never gone inside. Some kind of hoodoo voodoo stuff?'

I paused for a moment. He'd thrown a meatball, and in a moment of regrettable mischievousness, I couldn't resist an almighty swing. 'Right, follow me.' I escorted him to my locker and carefully removed a small, crimson and ivory woollen prayer mat and unfolded it on the table. 'You see this prayer mat?'

'Yes...'

'It's a very special prayer mat.' My voice tapered to a barely audible whisper. For some reason, I'd switched into Willy Wonka mode. I stroked the smooth, finely woven fibres from side to side several times, straightening the tassels on either side. 'See how wonderfully silky this feels....' I invited him to caress the mat.

'Yes, that's amazingly soft. Where did you get it?'

'This is from a small market in the heart of Fes, Morocco. Off the beaten tourist track, though. It takes hours to reach this market.'

'Right... So that makes it so special?' he asked, eyes glinting.

'Well...' I whispered, edging closer to him, 'when the knobs and dials are tweaked just right, in the depths of the night, middle of a lunar month while the moon shines brightest, this carpet begins to rise. It rises above the ground maybe a foot, maybe more, and it hovers in that position... Have you seen Aladdin?'

'Yes, yes. You mean it flies...? Like the carpet in Aladdin?' My colleague, a man of considerable intellect, acumen and standing within the team and local community, awaited my response. He had the look and attentiveness of a man about to learn the secrets of gold transmutation from the Chief Alchemist Officer himself.

I shook my head. 'Well, if I'd worked out how to apply anti-gravity and propulsion techniques to a Moroccan rug, I probably wouldn't be working here. I'm afraid there are neither flying carpets nor any other hoodoo voodoo shenanigans inside that room. It's just a small prayer room. Why don't you come and have a look? '

He paused, before roaring with laughter. I neatly folded the rug, tucked it under my arm, and strolled to Friday prayers.

OF COURSE, by attending Friday prayers, I miss the other, ubiquitous gathering: the gathering in the local pub. It's the most important meeting of the week, so explained one of my early managers. He strongly encouraged my attendance. I politely declined. As a junior IT ranch hand, it took me a while to work out why some of my colleagues were a little giddy on Friday afternoons, and why everyone avoided work-related afternoon meetings.

A friend related an amusing incident whereby his colleagues organised 'Friday joining drinks' – an innovative variation on the 'leaving drinks' theme. 'Unfortunately, I can't attend due to Friday prayers, but have a great time without me,' he quipped.

An hour or so later, all parties returned to the office, thoroughly satisfied.

7.8 DIVERSITY, INCLUSION, BAME

There are possibly few things in life as blood-sappingly deathly as mandatory Computer Based Training (CBT) courses at work: Code of Conduct, Fair Competition, Data Protection, and the like. There's usually a torturous set of slides followed by a 'quiz.' To add further misery, the test isn't marked complete unless the entire feedback form is also answered, which involves several 'this is how I will *immediately* apply what I've learnt from the course' type questions.

I recently took a CBT, though only under considerable duress and after multiple threatening emails. Apparently, the UK MD for a large IT consulting organisation took a personal interest whether I completed the course, so the threatening email said. The topic? Diversity and Inclusion in the Workplace. As I clicked on the link, my endorphin levels dropped like a bowling bowl on Jupiter. *Lord, slide 1 of 75... For goodness' sake, this will take hours.* After a full twenty-five minutes of prevarication and procrastination, including several cups of water and a stroll around the garden, I bit the bullet. *Right, let's get into this, it's not going anywhere.*

I doubt Marcus Aurelias could have matched my level of stoicism in that first section, as I diligently read each slide. Around twenty minutes into the course, possibly around slide 30, my energy levels further sagged. There was only one course of action possible. I needed to take matters into my own hands and adopt the old 'next, next, next' approach. *I'm sure I can wing this test. Well, I'm from an ethnic group, after all, Muslim to boot, experienced all manner of prejudice and abuse, so surely I'm overqualified? If I can't pass, who can?*

Roll on ten minutes, and I'd failed the test by a furlong or more. Devasted, I immediately retook the test. *Perhaps the computer erred when marking my script.* Perhaps a bug in the code? *It happens.* Nope. I failed again. *Crikey, this Diversity & Inclusion is more complex than I thought.*

THE SHIFT in the modern workplace demonstrated by the elaborate CBTs, ubiquitous office posters and badges, and the Black Asian Minority Ethnic (BAME) movement, all show that Diversity & Inclusion is quite trendy these days. There's an entire industry around it, offering impressive career paths to match any traditional occupation. I often see 'Head of Diversity' roles pop up on my LinkedIn feed, which never fails to fascinate. I attend anything BAME-related at work to keep abreast of the latest thinking (plus they're more interesting than my regular meetings, and nobody ever questions my attendance). It's often amusing to see the reaction of colleagues when I tell them; I can see the desperation on their faces as they withhold a quip or two.

But, long before diversity became fashionable, and certainly not to tick boxes or curry favour with any particular group, I recognised the benefits of building diverse project teams – first while studying at university, which wasn't difficult given the high percentage of international students, then within a work context. My highest performing teams have been socially, culturally, educationally, and religiously diverse. I remarked to one Partner from a Global Consultancy, 'Everyone here seems very similar – white, well educated, middle-class, privileged background... Great bunch, mind.' The comment left him a little winded. He could hardly refute the evidence, mind.

Though building and working with diverse teams isn't all full of frolics and fiddle-de-dees. There are plenty of potential pitfalls and problems, with communication at the forefront. Cultural/religious friction is another, albeit rare, as people generally avoid taboo or potentially controversial topics. But it can rear its head from time to time.

On one project, a couple of Indian chaps joined my team, unbeknown to me, from two different Hindu castes, one high and one low. I noticed a level of friction and hostility between the two, but couldn't explain it; one seemed relatively mild-mannered, the other bristly. I dismissed it as personality differences. Frankly, I had many other problems to grapple with at the time.

But the friction grew progressively worse over several months, until, one exploded. 'You can't tell me to do that, you filthy dog!' he screamed with fist raised and clenched. The other poor fellow was left startled, speechless and embarrassed. Unfortunately, the incident occurred right in the middle of my morning team meeting. In a powerful and moving address, I explained whatever our differences, we had a greater purpose during that time and had to deliver the project. The team left emotional, some in tears, and the pair shook hands. We experienced no trouble after that.

On another occasion, a colleague called me to join him in a meeting room, PDQ. I sprinted down the stairs and flung the door open, to be greeted by two senior (and well-respected) members of the team, both with enflamed, irate faces, panting, and within an inch of fisticuffs. One was making references to the turban on the other's head. 'I cannot work with this man!' he screamed. 'He's a complete imbecile! He should be working in the fields!' So much for my diversification strategy. We managed to talk them down. Eventually.

∼

ARRANGING team lunch or dinners is also fraught with pitfalls. Social events have never been my strong suit (unless they are outdoors, in a large park). Nonetheless, after some significant milestone or success, I do try.

'Oh, hello... Is that Paccino's Restaurant?'

'Yes, how can I help?'

'I need a table for ten, next Thursday, between 12:00 and 14:00.'

'Ok, that's fine. Any specific requirements?'

'Aha, yes, I'm glad you asked. I just need some halal, kosher, lacto-vegetarian food, and can you ensure it's prepared on the day, hasn't grown underground, and that no insects have been harmed in the process?'

'Eh...?'

Yes, organising lunches for some teams has proven more complex than the actual project delivery. Muslim, Jain, Hindu, Sikh, Christian (Catholic), Mormon and Jew – try arranging lunch or dinner for that little lot. I think we dined on water and insipid lentils that day.

MINORITIES, blacks, coloured, people/citizens of colour, non-white, off-white, olive, brown – just a few names that have been used over the years to describe us non-Caucasian folk. FA Chairman Glen Clarke had to resign after using the phrase 'high-profile coloured footballers' (that wasn't his only misdemeanour), yet, in the not-so-distant past, 'coloured' was preferred over 'black'. In the bizarre and cyclical acceptability merry-go-round, 'people of colour' is now making a comeback (has its roots in the 18th century).

'What's the ethnic makeup in your Scottish locality?' I asked one young chap during one of the many tangential team meeting topics.

'Well, we don't have many black people where we live, but I'd feel uncomfortable saying that to people I don't know. Is that acceptable? Is 'black' the right term?'

'Er, I'm not sure. Genuinely.'

I don't blame him for feeling uncomfortable. It's challenging to keep track, even for those on the 'inside'.

'In that case, I'd rather not say anything!' he continued.

'That's disappointing, though understandable,' I replied. 'People are terrified to say anything!'

'Person of colour' might be back in fashion now, but I would never use that term to describe myself, or anyone else. A colourful person, yes. A 'person of colour'? No.

7.9 PIGS IN BLANKETS

'Three swordsmen sat down at a table in a crowded Japanese inn and began to make loud comments about their neighbour, hoping to goad him into a duel. The master Musashi (the greatest samurai in all Japan) seemed to take no notice of them, but when their remarks became ruder and more pointed, he raised his chopsticks and, in quick snips, effortlessly caught four flies on the wing. As he slowly laid down the chopsticks, the three swordsmen hurriedly left the inn[3].'

Another of my first days in the office, and before I had a chance to utter a single word, she took an *immediate* dislike. Think *The Omen*, specifically *Omen II*, a *look* worthy of Damien Thorn's troubled teenage countenance. And what had I done to elicit such a reaction? Nothing, yet. I'd merely waltzed through the door, with my naturally cheery disposition and flowing beard. She simply saw me as an orthodox Muslim, and presumed I was about to rain down fire and brimstone on her impious being. I might as well have been wearing sandals, sporting a full robe, and clutching tablets of stone.

Sure, there were fires (infernos, no less), but only on this damned, eighteen months overshot, £20m overspent, forsaken project. I'd only been sent to extinguish the flames and steer it back to safety.

Jessamine (Jas) led another area on the programme, but, more importantly, she also wore the Chief Social Officer badge. That involved organising a fair number of outings – mostly to local pubs and restaurants. With my teetotal outlook on life and general aversion to entering public houses, things between us were always going to be a little fruity.

A few weeks into the project, I noticed Jas having breakfast as I wandered into the restaurant. *Aha, this is my chance to have a word.* I grabbed my boiled eggs, marmalade, toast, and cappuccino, and headed towards her.

'Hello, do you mind if I sit down?'

Jas looked up, bleary-eyed, and squinted. 'Er, er, ok, if you want.' She pushed her tray and jug of water to one side.

I began surgically slicing my eggs into quarters, before taking a sip of coffee. 'That's quite a large breakfast you've got there,' I opened. 'You must be hungry. Those look interesting, what are they?'

'These? They're called pigs in blankets,' she replied, matter-of-factly.

'Right. That's quite a novel name.'

'Yes, streaky bacon wrapped around pork sausages. They're quite tasty. You should try some. You may find them liberating.'

Liberating?!

Now, pork is the last bastion of the non-practising Muslim. I know Muslims who drink alcohol, take cocaine, (wo)manise, eat non-halal meat, but you'll never catch them with a bacon butty. They'd rather starve.

I smiled. 'Aha, pork on pork, a bit like pork squared. No, I don't eat pork for religious reasons.'

'Yes, I figured that. I gave up all that religious nonsense years ago.' She stared at me, poised, waiting for the fire and brimstone.

'That bacon looks really fatty,' I squinted. 'About half of the fat is saturated. You're increasing your risk of heart disease and stroke, eating that. Not to mention the general risk associated with processed meat and cancer.'

'Eh?'

'Well, I can heartily recommend these eggs, they're great.' I gobbled another quarter. 'So, on to matters mundane, I'm afraid. I'm leading all the technical areas of the project implementation. I'll need to discuss a few items with you. Ensure our areas align.'

She foraged into her bag and removed a packet of paracetamol. 'We have a social event later this week. Will you be coming?'

'Is it softball in the park?'

'No, it's drinking in the local bar. Probably vodka shots.'

'Oh, in that case, no. I don't drink. How many calories are in one of those shots?'

Jas glared at me. 'What? Who cares?! Look. I really don't like your sort.' She took out three tablets and quickly swallowed them with a gulp of water.

'Yes, I was beginning to sense a little animosity. You seem upset about something, like I've offended your mother. Perhaps we can thrash it out?'

'We have enough religious nutters back home,' she scowled. 'They stopped all education for girls, at one point. That's why we left.'

'Aha, I see. That *is* unfortunate.' I spread a thick layer of marmalade on my toast and took a bite. 'Hmmm. That's delicious. You should try the marmalade. My daughters aren't sure what they want to study at university. Maybe engineering or physics. What do you think? Any advice?'

'Uh... Er...' She looked baffled. 'I've got a splitting headache.'

'Yes, you do look peaky. You should try giving up the alcohol. Imagine – no hangovers. You may find it liberating.'

Jas stood, leaving most of the blankets tightly wrapped. 'I need to get to my 09:00 meeting.'

'It's only 08:49. When can we discuss the plaaa...?'

7.10 PARTNER LAND

For many young, fresh-faced consultants in the corporate world, the Land of Partnership is the end goal, the Utopia. It's the final abode of salvation, after many years of dedication, service, and sacrifice. It's also the promised land of riches. Riches, no doubt, commensurate with the religious levels of servility and propitiation required to navigate its tortuous path. I genuinely marvelled at those pilgrims.

I met one such young, idealistic consultant working on an IT Programme many years ago – Ahmad. Sharply dressed, clean-cut, intelligent – he appeared destined for Partnership. I warned him early on, as a practising Muslim, his path would be laden with even greater trials and tribulations. Running a marathon is tough, but try running it in a seven-foot gingerbread-man costume. Not impossible, but certainly trickier.

Being slightly older, I took him under my wing, imparting what little wisdom I'd gleaned along the way. And, sure enough, our relationship came under the spotlight, when I was labelled a 'negative and distracting influence'. How preposterous! As if I could possibly negatively distract anyone! When he started to grow stubble, one of his senior managers encouraged him to crack open the Gillette gel, and suggested his increasing devotion would likely prevent him from progressing within the firm. He suffered jibes of, 'Look, there's Al-Qaidah Ahmad in the (military) tank!' on fun away days. Ahmad, still relatively young at the time and unable to find any support within the organisation, eventually yielded to the demands, and remained schtum about the jibes. He didn't want to cause a kerfuffle or be perceived negatively, as is often the case.

A few years later, he left the company, realising he couldn't break through the granite ceiling. But he didn't let his earlier experiences deter him — no, far, from it. I'm pleased to say he is now a partner in a different organisation. And, of course, he now realises, Partnership isn't the promised Shangri-La.

8. CULTURAL AND RELIGIOUS NUANCE

*'If we're going to be damned, let's be damned for
what we really are.'*

— CAPTAIN JEAN-LUC PICARD

Muslims of Indo-Pak extraction living in the West seemingly exhibit some weird and wacky outward practices. No, I don't mean anything involving backpacks or sharp objects.

'You come to our country, wrap your women up in bin bags, and make strange noises in the morning. Who do you think you are?!' one comment I overheard. The strange noises presumably referred to the morning call to prayer.

There's also a range of more subtle practices, not immediately evident to the casual observer. For example, as a general rule, Muslim men don't use urinals. We're keen to avoid the dreaded splashback (not to be confused with cashback, which is usually welcome), and uphold general chivalry and modesty. Admittedly it's not always possible. Even after all these years, I find the sight of men lined at urinals, in full flow, in full conversation, highly disconcerting. Now, unless the great armies have started to gather on the plains of Megiddo[1], or you're planning some covert black op, I'm reckoning the urinal conversation can wait a few minutes.

'So, Asif, I hear rumblings we're not going to hit the project deadlines. There's a lot of chatter from above...' a voice echoed from behind me.

Washing my hands with the focus and rigour of a brain surgeon about to enter theatre, I was far too engrossed to pay any attention. My colleague, who stood at the urinal, decided he needed a project update right at that moment. I ignored him and continued scrubbing my hands halfway to my elbow.

'Asif...'

No response.

'ASIF...!'

'WHAT?!' I finally exploded. 'What do you want?!'

Deathly silence.

I yanked a handful of paper towels, nearly breaking the dispenser in the process, and darted outside to wait for my colleague.

He looked worried. My ordinarily mild disposition transformed. 'Look, Tom,' I said, quickly regaining my composure, 'when I'm in there, I just want to use the facilities and leave. I really don't want any detailed conversations about work, or anything else. Now, what was your question?'

'Er, sorry, it's not that important. It can wait for the next project meeting.'

'Right...'

8.1 MISUNDERSTANDINGS

In 1625, Francis Bacon, the Viscount of St. Alban, penned the most famous saying about the Prophet Muhammad (ﷺ) known in the West:

> 'Mahomet cald the Hill to come to him. And when the Hill stood still, he was neuer a whit abashed, but said: "If the Hill will not come to Mahomet, Mahomet wil go to the hil."'

We're not sure where Francis took this saying; it's not mentioned in any Islamic sources.

Around two billion people, a quarter of the world's population, identify as Muslims and more than fifty countries have Muslim majority populations. That's a fair slew of people, languages, hues and cultures. Yet, by unanimous consent, Muslims have done a miserable job to quash misconceptions about Islam. On the contrary, we're mostly headlining the news bolstering them. In one of those infernal 'recent YouGov UK polls', 58% of the 2182 adults surveyed linked Islam with extremism, while 69% believed it encouraged women's repression, and about half associated Islam with terrorism. Frankly, that would suggest an awful lot of British Muslim terrorists, given the three million Muslims living within these Isles.

'If I visited your house, I'd probably see all this weird and wacky voodoo stuff,' a colleague once said. 'You're probably a completely different person at home to what we see at work!' Hmmm. What did he mean? What would he classify as weird and wacky? He'd see woo-doo, yes (ablution). But voo-doo? No. I suppose the 'different person' comment disappointed a little, playing into the narrative that Muslims all lead some clandestine alternate life, maybe as a card-carrying member of some divisive group.

At one point, in the late 2000s, on the back of swollen support post 7/7, Burnley enjoyed half a dozen BNP councillors. That was fun. Interestingly, the BNP member list found itself on the Internet a few years later. In a curious twist, Dave, a friend and ex-colleague (top-notch IT bod, too), appeared on the list. Someone mentioned it to me. Dave and I had always enjoyed a good relationship, so this revelation surprised and disappointed. Had I misjudged him, all those years? When questioned, Dave assured me he'd only joined in 'protest against the mainstream parties'. I believed him, too. Well, misunderstandings can happen.

8.2 THE LAND OF RAMADAM

'Why don't you lot just go back to Ramadam?!' a rugged youngster of perhaps twenty years once shouted in my direction.

'Hmmm, that's an intriguing question,' I responded.

Ramadan is the 9th month of the Islamic lunar calendar, which is around ten days shorter than the Gregorian solar calendar, resulting in months shifting backwards through the year. For example, within the UK, Ramadan may fall in December, with very short fasting days, but, fifteen years later, it will have shifted to mid-summer, with very long days. If you can handle the spiders, migration to Australia for the month is an option at this point. Whatever their location, during Ramadan, Muslims abstain from food, drink, and sexual relations from dawn until sunset. Aside from the significance of fasting, Muslims also believe God revealed the Qur'an through the Archangel Gabriel in the month of Ramadan.

Though the youngster didn't appear in the mood for explanation on this occasion. He'd successfully confused and merged a couple of concepts: a physical land, and a month associated with a specific practice. Receptive or not, I felt compelled to respond. 'You see, you can't actually go to Ramada...' I began.

'I don't care! I can kick your 'ead in!' he interrupted.

We'd somehow gone from geography and austere religious practice to fisticuffs in one swift movement. 'That's highly unlikely,' I replied, 'but a scuffle here would look much better on your CV than mine.'

∼

EVERY YEAR, just before the start of Ramadan, my wife asks what I'd like for *iftar* (Arabic: the feast after the fast). Without fail, I'll respond, 'Please, nothing fried! No samosas, no pakoras, no spring rolls, no chicken nuggets.' Shmaila always raises her eyebrows in scepticism. I'm going to be healthy this year,' I'll continue. 'Maybe a light salad. Graphene light iftar followed by a simple meal. I want to ensure I'm still exercising each night. I'm not getting any younger, you know! Not so easy to digest all that oily food these days.'

'Right, ok, we'll see...'

Fast forward to the first day of fasting. The hunger pangs are severe. The emaciated body is craving high calorific foods, the oilier the better, the sweeter the better. The family gathers around the kitchen table like a pack of slightly docile hyenas encircling a wounded wildebeest. Every so often, eyes twitch towards the digital microwave clock, lips slowly murmuring with prescribed supplications. I'll scan the kitchen table. All I'll see are dates, water, lettuce, cucumber, carrots, tomatoes...

'Where are the samosas?! Where are the pakoras?!' I wail, with head in hands. 'I need samosas! I need pakoras!' I then remember my previous foolish comments. *Will my wife let me down?*

Not a chance. As the moment arrives, she'll suddenly conjure a plate of piping hot fried food.

'Phew... But I'm definitely starting that lettuce and cress diet next Ramadan.'

THE TEAM SAT in monastic silence, gazing at the pendulum clock on the wall of the restaurant. They'd ordered a lavish spread, with far more food than we could possibly eat in two sittings, let alone an hour. From the group of twenty or so, I was the only fasting person present. Yet, all graciously withheld from eating until the clock finally ticked over to 19:16. Keeping with tradition, I took a single date and sip of water to break my fast. By 19:17, the hounds had been unleashed.

As we cracked and dunked the poppadoms into the mango chutney (this combo never materialises at home), I asked if anyone knew the meaning of the restaurant name.

'Madi-hah?' They shrugged. 'What language is that?'

'*Maa-i-dah* is Arabic, often translated as 'dining table laden with food'.' A reference in the Qur'an to a meal Jesus shared with his disciples (some say the Last Supper).

'That's quite an appropriate name, given the size of this feast. But I don't know how you fast for 30 days!? You can't even have water?! I couldn't do it!'

'Yes, I noticed you were getting quite restless as we waited the last few minutes.'

'So, you must be an expert on all this food? What exactly is the difference between balti, dopiaza, karahi? What do those names mean?'

'I've no idea, mate. I just speak a few words of mixed Punjabi-Urdu to the waiter to order spicy chicken. I think all the names are for your benefit, and occupy space on the menu.'

RUNNING in a fasted state isn't advised, unless you're a pro athlete. I tried it once. Never again. Badminton wasn't much easier. As a fitness aficionado, that presents a problem. How do I run or generally exercise during Ramadan – particularly during the summer months when the window between sunset and dawn can be as little as four hours? After a few experiments, I realised 01:00 hit the sweet spot, giving me enough time to get back from the mosque and fully digest my meal (which is quite significant, after a full day fasting), whilst also allowing enough time to sleep a little before waking at 03:00 for the pre-dawn meal.

Now, being out and about at 01:00 is not without problems. Vagabonds and unsavoury types lurk in the shadows. Though, frankly, if you're running around at 01:00 in a hoodie (sometimes) through the pouring rain, you're probably a bigger crackpot than most.

Alternatively, I'll switch on the garden lights around that time. While dodging the foxes and hedgehogs, I'll start swinging kettle-bells, mountain climbing, battling with the rope or pull upping. My neighbours' blinds will begin to twitch. *Lord, what on earth is he doing now?*

8.3 AWKWARD HOUSE VISITS

It's not *always* obvious, with all the bombs, explosions and whatnot, but we Muslims are actually a hospitable, sociable bunch. We're normally happy to help neighbours and get involved in the community. But there are a few things you should know, before you pop round to Mr Khan's at Number 87.

'Sorry, boss, do you mind taking off your boots,' I shouted in my best workman's accent. *What on earth am I saying? When have I ever previously called anyone 'boss'?'* I looked down at Mike's mud-encrusted boots, while picturing Shmaila's face as he trekked across our new beige carpet.

'I was expecting that when I saw you,' Mike replied.

'Ok, right.'

'Health and safety, sir.' He spoke like an older Vinnie Jones. He puffed his cheeks and pulled out two grubby elasticated blue shoe covers, probably teeming with every virus known to man. *Can I change my mind about the muddy boots?* He managed to put the covers on without giving himself a hernia, though it looked dodgy while he precariously balanced on one leg. 'Right, then... Let's have a look at this boiler.'

An hour of clattering pipes and clanging hammers later, I popped my head around the corner with a cup of tea, plate of biscuits and some freshly made spicy mincemeat samosas.

'Ah, thanks mate... I was just about to take a breather.' Mike put down his spanner, wiped his grimy hands on his overalls, and took a samosa bite. 'Jeez, these are spicy, mate.' He rapidly took another bite, before devouring the last piece. 'I do love an onion bhaji. Can I have some water? These are hot!'

'Sure, give me a few minutes.' I returned with a large glass of cold water from the fridge.

He gulped the entire contents in one swig. 'Right, I'm just about done, mate. Can I just get your autograph here and here?'

I squiggled a few random shapes on the paper.

'Right, let me clean up. Oh, and can I quickly use your lav?'

For a second, I froze. 'Er, sure, one moment...' I scrambled downstairs and into the kitchen before gently closing the door. 'He wants to use the bathroom! What should I do?!' I whispered in a state of panic.

Shmaila's eyes widened, and I saw the blood draining from her dear countenance. In the words of Dickens, she 'turned very pale and gazed in stupefied astonishment for some seconds and then clung for support to the copper.' There was no copper in sight, but the kitchen pedestal offered a suitable substitute.

'Don't worry, don't worry, I'll explain,' I said, animatedly waving my hands.

She squinted her eyes. 'Ok, make sure you do that!'

I gingerly returned upstairs, rehearsing the lines in my head, while dearly wishing Zeno had it right all along and I'd never make it.

'Right, mate,' said Mike. 'Just the bathroom, and I'll be on my way.'

'Sure, you can use this one, but just one thing, Mike...'

He smiled and patted me on the shoulder. 'Don't worry, mate. I've been to many Muslim houses. I always sit down.'

Mike, my boiler repairman, I salute you.

But NOT ALL tradesmen perform with such merit. 'Do you know the meaning of DIVINE RETRIBUTION?!' I screamed down the phone.

'Er... er... Mate, is there a problem?'

'WELL, DO YOU?!'

'No, I don't think so. Divine what? Retro. Is that a new type of cooker?'

'Look it up in a dictionary. You can't just get away with this criminality. There WILL BE retribution, in this life or the next. You can be sure of that!'

'I can see I've upset you, and you're beginning to upset me, too, so let's leave it here, eh?'

'Fine!' I slammed down the phone.

That'll teach him for trying to hoodwink me with a dodgy oven element and charging me £130 + VAT. Did he really think I wouldn't find out?! Zero-star review on Trustatrader.com, too.

8.4 TRYING RELATIVES

When you're born, live and work in the UK, there's a perception from relatives 'back home' that life is all tickety-boo and tranquil, without a cloud in the blue sky. Not only do we lead a trouble-free life, but vast wealth is under our direct control. We cultivate trees sprouting sterling notes, and fertile crops yielding coinage. Profitable and diverse investments abound, with multiple bank accounts to harvest and store these funds. There's an expectation money can be transferred whenever requested, no matter how frequently. A bottomless pit of cash exists. After all, any casual scan of the newspaper or currency websites will reveal a single pound is worth a couple of hundred Pakistani Rupees. *So, what's the problem, send the money now!*

Cash aside, a second expectation exists, around holidays, sponsorship, and immigration, that somehow, we have a Batman-like hotline to UK Immigration and Visas, or even Priti Patel herself, and we can 'sort it' for anyone who fancies hopping over for a short or permanent stay. Nearly sixty years on, we still field these requests with annoying regularity.

A friend described how his father built a house back in an Indian village and left his brother in charge to manage the development, a house with four storeys, seven bedrooms and bathrooms, and land covering more than an acre, all enclosed in a brick, plastered wall – delightful. Soon after completion, the brother moved in, and decided the property was his. The local police, after some monetary persuasion, agreed with the brother that he was the rightful owner. My friend's father still hasn't recovered his property.

Being taken hostage by gun-toting vagrants is also a genuine threat when visiting Pakistan. We've heard many stories of people being taken hostage, with others merely being stripped of all cash and jewellery en-route from the airport. Hostage-taking is a low-cost lucrative endeavour. Alas, many of the attempts can be traced back to relatives of the victims.

One family, who, in good faith, sent relatives tens of thousands of pounds over the years, thinking they were helping build a family business, received a call early in the morning (UK time) to say that an unsavoury group had 'come to collect', and threatened physical harm unless a further £15,000 was immediately despatched.

'I suggest you speak with the gang boss, just to make sure,' I offered.

～

'I CAN ONLY DREAM of a wedding like this,' sighed Wasim, shaking his head in despair. 'I hope one day I'll have one just like it.' He looked at me with sorrowful, glazed eyes. I glanced towards him, before returning to watch my cousins dancing from afar, a truly baffling and uncomfortable sight. Pakistanis do enjoy a traditional wedding. It lasts for days and days, with all manner of customs and components, far exceeding tolerance levels for most British born Pakistanis. Well, certainly me.

I'd only met Wasim once, for about five minutes the day before, yet he now treated me like his long-lost twin brother. He was actually a friend of my cousin in Lahore. 'You must come to my house tomorrow for tea to meet my mother,' he said, his glaze now replaced with a glint, 'and I won't take no for an answer!'

'Sure, ok...' I reluctantly answered.

With the help of my cousin, and an awkward, bumpy ride on his borrowed 50cc Honda moped, I arrived after noon the next day. Wasim lived in a densely populated nearby town. Once I'd managed to negotiate the cattle and speeding rickshaws on the dusty road, I knocked and waited outside. He greeted me with customary enthusiasm, and ushered me inside. I unsuccessfully ducked, trying to avoid the top of the door frame, slightly catching my head, resulting in a painful scrape. Not a great start.

Wasim lived in a modest abode, but he'd done his best to tidy the place. We sat in what appeared to be his bedroom and living room combined. He'd managed to amass an impressive collection of

VHS cassettes of pirated Hollywood movies, which almost encircled the entire room. The Lipton tea in a silver pot and biscuits were neatly prepared for my arrival. We began talking about his work and ambitions in life.

As we munched through the digestive biscuits, laughing and joking at my Punjabi attempts, his mother appeared. A woman of perhaps sixty years, she stared at me through squinted eyes, and croaked in Punjabi, 'Is this the boy from England you spoke about?'

'Yes, mother, this is him,' Wasim replied in full deference.

Lord, I've been set up again. I should know the drill by now.

'So, can you take Wasim to England or not?' Her withered face now even sterner.

I don't mind direct questions, but this was taking things a little far. I didn't know Wasim's surname, for a start, required for all the paperwork.

'Er, Auntie...' I mumbled in dysfunctional Punjabi, 'it's not that simple. I can't just take Wasim to England in my suitcase.'

'Ley! Not so simple! *Nakama!*' (Punjabi: useless fool), she scowled and left the room.

I glanced at Wasim, who'd lowered his head in disappointment or shame. I sipped the rest of my tea in silence.

But we're not the only ones with trying relatives. The word pundit originates from the Sanskrit *payndita,* meaning 'learned man'. Some bright spark decided we should give ex-footballers and commentators such a grandiose title.

A friend (we'll call him Mo) travels around the country to watch Liverpool play. Nay, he travels around the world for his beloved Liverpool. On one occasion, he jumped on an early flight to Russia to watch an evening game with Spartak Moscow. As soon as the referee blew the final whistle, he hopped into a taxi back to the airport, round trip time just over 24 hours. Now, there's misguided commitment. Liverpool only managed a draw, too.

As a bearded brown chap travelling around the world amongst the football supporter fraternity, he's seen a fair number of lively incidents. However, the most memorable didn't occur at the hands of a regular football fan – no menacing skinhead sporting the aforesaid, knee-length, *Dr Martens* black boots, clutching a broken bottle and hurling abuse. Nor did it involve walking past a Spartan wall of opposition supporters, fingers raised, advising he should be somewhere else. No, it involved a very well-known football pundit.

Mo happened to be sitting in a Basel hotel, a few hours before the Europa League Final kick-off, along with other fans and some well-known 'celebrities' and football pundits. Now, even more curiously, Mo enjoys having his photo taken with pundits and footballers. He's got hundreds in his collection, which he shows me every time my guard slips. One pundit (we'll call him Gary – no, not that one) was busy taking snaps with his elderly father, generally mingling and enjoying himself with the supporters. Eager to add Gary into his collection, Mo darted towards him and asked for a picture, already busy fiddling with his iPhone camera settings for the best shot.

'Sure, no problem...' Gary replied (I won't try and mimic the accent).

As the two of them adjusted their posture for the selfie, Gary's father screamed from behind, 'But he's a Paki! You can't have your picture taken with a Paki!'

'Dad, you can't say that!' cried Gary.

Click, click, click...

The startled look on their faces, particularly Gary's, produced a genuinely notable selfie – Mo's favourite to date. He sent me a copy, too.

8.5 HOSPITAL VISITS

My younger brother, Amer, spent a few nights in hospital after breaking his right fibula while playing seven-a-side football. We visited him on the first day, packing the mandatory homemade spicy curry to facilitate recuperation (hospital food wasn't going to fuse his bone back together, that's for sure).

As we entered the hospital ward, he lay forlorn, leg hoisted in the air by some elaborate contraption, delirious on morphine. All eyes immediately turned towards us. A few of the patients had a single visitor, most had none: Amer had six members of the family, including my parents. We drew the curtain around his bed and grabbed whatever seating we could find, pilfering where necessary.

My father looked at Amer, stretched on the bed and shook his head. His first comment? *How are you, son? How did it happen? Are you in pain? Don't worry, it'll soon heal?* Nope, none of the above. My father fumed the Punjabi equivalent of, 'And, who told you to play football?' My father always played the percentages game. If you play football, your chances of breaking a leg increase. So why play? If you skydive, your chances of splatting on the ground increase. So why skydive? It's a sound mathematical argument

Once we'd moved beyond the what, who and why, and the role of the human intellect in determining which sports to leave well alone, Amer tucked into the lamb curry, and the discussion moved on. We stayed until the last moments of visiting time.

With an elevated leg, Amer got to know most of the other patients in the ward. Edna, an 80-year-old, lay adjacent, hospitalised following a botched hip replacement. 'Oh, you're very lucky,' she gushed. 'That smells very good! I hardly get a single visitor, let alone any food!' A few of the patients managed to sample spicy curry for the first time during those few days. They were thoroughly disappointed to see him leave.

8.6 DOGS AND DNA

According to Wikipedia, Frederick the Great of Prussia supposedly coined the phrase 'man's best friend'. Whether Fred said it or not, the furry creatures are certainly not best friends to all men (and women).

For a long time, I thought the uneasy Pakistani-Canine relationship could only be explained at the molecular level. After all, I didn't know a single Pakistani who owned or liked dogs. Most were also anxious, if not scared, around dogs, at odds with the general British populace. Yet, when I completed a recent DNA test, I discovered Finnish and Siberian ancestry, asparagus odour detection characteristics, but no genetic traits for dog aversion. Dogs are considered impure in Islam, specifically their saliva, which no doubt contributes to the troubled relationship. Though, it's acceptable to keep guard dogs outside the house, or as hunting dogs, which are popular in some Arab countries (for instance, the Saluki).

Looking back, I remember a gang of feral dogs patrolling the streets of Burnley. Supposedly, dogs have eyesight inferior to humans when distinguishing colours, but they had no issues identifying Pakistanis from a crowd. Maybe the curry smell helped. One black terrier with a white stripe, who responded to the appellation 'Skip', terrorised the local Pakistani community. He could run at terrific pace, and his nasty bark matched the bite.

A school chum kept two large Labradors in his house, Romulus and Remus, one golden and the other pristine, jet black. Every time I visited his house, they would pounce. I'd race upstairs and scramble onto his bunk bed, while they would continuously jump and bark, as though possessed with some demonic spirit. I always wondered how he lived with the pair in the house. Aside from their enormous appetites, and the masses of dog hair they scattered throughout, they appeared to defecate with impunity. A bewildering arrangement for a Pakistani.

We're generally not huge fans of other pets either, though that may be related to our frugal immigrant roots, where every shilling mattered. The first wave certainly wouldn't spend (burn) money on vet's bills, pet food, and necessary accessories. Mind, a 'Gen Z' colleague of Pakistani extraction, recently bought an exotic cross-breed American Bully dog. He tells me its grandfather is some superstar in the Bully world. Whatever his lineage, the dog eats like a horse, making his poor father wince each time he returns from the butcher's. He only eats halal, too.

8.7 REVOLVING NEON SIGN

Walk through the town centre of any major city, and you're likely to bump into the homeless, beggars, buskers, preachers and Scottish Power salespeople, all vying for your attention and hard cash. As a visibly brown Muslim, there's another category of people whom I regularly meet.

'Brother, I need to get to Scotland, and I've lost my wallet.'

'Brother, I've run out of petrol and my credit card, wallet, and phone are all at home.'

'Brother, I need just another £4.65 for my train ticket home.'

'Brother, I'm selling these items for this charity.'

In fact, a few days seldom pass without me meeting someone with a similar story. It's particularly embarrassing for the petrol-money guys, who don't keep records of turf covered, when I remind them how we previously met. I never forget a face or a con artist.

Shmaila, seen as a friendlier, more malleable target, attracts more requests, and is often the first point of contact when we're together. On one occasion, while parked outside a Costa drive-through, a dishevelled chap knocked on the window. In a moment of misplaced generosity, she handed over a £5 note. I shook my head in disbelief.

Later the same day...

'Oh, look, there's the chap you gave that £5 note. He's holding a bottle of cheap cider and pack of cigarettes, look. Just over there. How strange.'

'He hasn't bought that with the £5 I gave him,' Shmaila retorted. 'Obviously, he's bought that with other money he had!'

～

'BHAI,' came a voice in Punjabi, 'can you help me? I need some money to get back home.'

I rolled my eyes and glanced at my friend, who looked even less interested than me. 'Brother, I've stopped giving to people. I've been let down too many times. Let me tell you a little story....'

'No, no, I don't want to hear your story. I just need some money. Can you give me some money to get home? God will be pleased with you!'

I clear my throat, and in my very best Punjabi, I begin narrating an incident from university:

'Assalaamu alaikum, brother, you're not going to believe this... I feel so embarrassed, I don't even want to say.' Any excuse to miss my next Linear Algebra lecture, I stopped and eyed the balding, white-haired man closely.

'Look,' he said, 'I really need to get home, but I'm £20 short. Can you help me out?'

As a student, I operated on a razor-sharp budget, and I certainly didn't carry that amount of cash around. 'Walaikum salaam...' I replied awkwardly, staring at him, trying to determine whether he was a fruitcake or a charlatan. With his sleeves rolled up and beads of sweat glistening around his forehead, he looked primed for a brawl. He'd obviously been canvassing hard. 'Sorry, brother, I'm a student.' Reaching inside my pocket, I removed a few coins. 'I've got, er, £3.43 here, if that helps.' I limply pushed the money towards him.

'Oh, come on! That's not enough, it won't get me home, brother, back to London. I really need to get home to my family.'

'That's all I have, I'm sorry.'

'Look, son, let's do this properly. If you don't have the money, let's go to a cash machine.'

Cash machine?! What's he talking about? This is a highly unusual move. Does he really think I'm going to do that?! I wasn't born yesterday. 'Er, brother, I'm late for a very important lecture. I really do need to go.'

He became silent, and slowly lowered his head.

Sure enough, minutes later, I found myself plodding to the nearest cash machine, muttering to myself, 'This guy is genuine, he's definitely genuine, I hope he's genuine...' I withdrew a crisp £20 note and gently fondled before handing it over. Quite a novelty; it'd been a while since I'd withdrawn more than £10.

He thanked me profusely, and I continued towards my Linear Algebra lecture.

A week later, I'd completely forgotten about the incident. While walking in town, I glanced inside HMV to see the same man jovially browsing the latest VHS movies. Perhaps the time is right for that brawl, I thought. Perhaps he'd returned from London for a few days? *Right, I'm going in there. No, no, let him enjoy himself with his new movie. I gave the money in good faith.*

'That's the story. You see, brother, too many times!'

'Bhai, you've really hurt my feelings with that story. I'm very upset you're questioning my motives. I'm going to leave now.'

JOHNNY WAS AN UNUSUAL CHARACTER, dark-skinned, sunken eyes, seemingly of no fixed abode. Not a typical raucous beggar. He wouldn't hurl obscenities at people for not giving money. Not that I saw. Instead, he'd sit *sukhasana* (Sanskrit: cross-legged, meditative pose), barefoot for hours on end outside KFC, perched on a rollable blue exercise mat, an enviable feat for any Yogi. His flip-flops would sit neatly to one side, always perfectly aligned, while his entire worldly possessions lay folded in a durable, black Sports Direct bag. He wore a long beard, but not the wild beard of a homeless man.

I'd become accustomed to the boisterous homeless crowd in town, so his unusual poise caught my eye. My eyes tarried towards him for some time, but I sensed he didn't want to reciprocate. The same happened again a few days later, but, after a third rejection, I decided to make the first move.

'Hello, can I get you something to eat? Or a coffee, perhaps?'

'Oh, that's so very kind, thank you,' he whispered, with a gentle smile.

I returned a few minutes later with cheese sandwiches and a large latte coffee. He lowered his head and graciously accepted the gifts.

'You remind me of Diogenes the Cynic[2], minus the wooden tub, and the bad habits, I hope.'

'Haha, I'm not that wise, unfortunately,' he replied. Somehow his knowledge of the ascetic didn't surprise me. 'Are you a Muslim?'

'Yes.'

'Ah, I often get Muslims stopping and offering help.'

We spent the next thirty minutes discussing how he'd arrived in this sticky position. He explained his background – he was from a wealthy Indian family, had received a decent education, and worked in finance, but, after some internal family problems, they abandoned him. I felt he skipped a few critical details. Now he found himself begging for money and sleeping rough.

I didn't push him on the incoherence. 'Look, I know people who work in the Council. I'll ask what options you have. You shouldn't have to sleep rough.'

Johnny smiled and nodded his head. 'Sure, any help would be appreciated.'

Oddly, Johnny disappeared for a few weeks after that, until I saw him in his flip-flops and shorts sitting outside the disbanded Debenhams. 'Hey Johnny, I haven't seen you for a while. How are you?'

'Not great. Look, can you spare any cash? I'm really desperate at the moment.'

Here we go again. 'I'm sorry, I've stopped giving money in that way. I've been burnt too many times. Give a man a fish, and he'll eat for a day[3]...'

Johnny lowered his gaze. 'Yes, yes, I know – teach a man how to fish...'

'Though I do have some good news to share!' I exclaimed, hoping to recover the situation. 'I've investigated how you can get a council place and some council benefits. Isn't that great?!'

Johnny wasn't yoga-flipping with excitement. He sighed. 'Oh, I've tried all that. They ask too many questions. The process takes forever! I just need some cash. Just give me some cash!' He'd started bellowing, suddenly, for some reason. *Goodness sake', calm down, man.* 'You Muslims! You're all the same!' he shrieked.

'I can see you're upset. Maybe we'll speak when you've calmed down.'

In the following weeks, him I'd call from the other side of the street, 'JOHNNY!' and raise my hand. No response. 'Hey JOHNNY! It's me.' No response.

Johnny had dropped me like a bad habit. It took a few more weeks to recover from that betrayal. He's still giving me the cold shoulder.

～

BUT MY ADVICE isn't always rejected, at least not outright to my face.

'Brother, please, can you spare a cigarette?'

I wiped the sweat from my brow, and carefully lowered my fence brush. I needed a break, and a spurt of enthusiasm. 'Sorry, I don't smoke, and neither should you.'

'Come on, bro... I've given up everything else! No alcohol, no weed, no cocaine. I'm clean!

Surely I can have the odd cigarette.'

'I see. What's your name?'

'Jatinder. People call me Jat.'

'Well, Jat, first let me congratulate on your excellent work so far. You're well on your way. But what if I gave you something that would make you fly higher than a kite? Something available on tap that won't cost you a penny? Plus, it will make you healthy, not kill you. Would that be worth something to you?'

He paused, allowing this amazing revelation to sink in. 'Yes! What is it, bro? Tell me!'

'Grab your trainers, go for a run, preferably in the rain, maybe when it's slightly dark. Make sure you run hard, so your heart beats quickly. Run for twenty minutes, at least, even if you have to stop every few paces. I guarantee you'll never go back.'

Jat wasn't expecting that type of stimulant. 'Thank you so much, bro... I'm definitely going to try that.'

'Yes, finally!' I picked up my brush and continued painting with renewed vigour.

8.8 INTERESTING TIMES

'Happy the man who, far from schemes of business, like the early generations of mankind, ploughs and ploughs again his ancestral land with oxen of his own breeding, with no yoke of usury on his neck.'

My Nokia 6210 phone blinked luscious luminous green: 'Thanks for livening up my weekend. I don't receive many Horace[4] quotes.'

My very first week at University and I enter a well-known high street bank to deposit a cheque Amjad had given me the night before. As I complete the deposit slip and wait in line, I notice an unusual, shoddy white cardboard box on the counter, with a hand-written label displaying 'Interest'. It looked completely out of place with the rest of the plush interior.

'Just a deposit, please.' Handing over my cheque, I turned to the box and nudged it slightly to gauge the contents. 'What's this box?'

'Oh, that's for Muslims,' the teller replied, nonchalantly.

'For Muslims? Really? How so?'

'Well, Muslims don't take interest on their savings, so we offer this facility to take it off their hands, so to speak.'

'Aha, right... In this box?' I peered inside. Remarkably, it contained wads of notes and coins.

'Yes.'

'And once you've relieved the offensive notes from the Muslims, what do you do with the money?'

'Er... I'm not sure... Right, that's all done for you. Anything else?'

'No, that's all, thanks.'

How thoughtful of the bank. Though, I don't think I'll be contributing to the Friday afternoon pub fund.

'You MEAN to say you don't pocket interest from your bank?' my work colleague said, hands waving, eyes bulging, in disbelief.

'Er, no, I don't.'

'Are you completely bereft, man?! Why wouldn't you do that?'

'Well, interest isn't allowed in Islam.'

'Why, man? Why?'

'Well, oppression, subjugation of the poor, reinforcing the status quo for the rich, money without effort – a whole hatful of reasons, really.'

My work colleague remained silent.

In Islam, interest in all its manifestations is forbidden, irrespective of the rate. The traditional term for interest at exorbitant rates is 'usury' (covering the 4000% APR charged by popular payday loan companies). Similar prohibitions exist in other religions, though with less fervour. Hindu and Buddhist scriptures criticise the practice. The Old Testament condemns 'charging interest on a poor person, because a loan should be an act of compassion and taking care of one's neighbours' [Exodus: 22:25-27]. Curiously, the prohibition is lifted for foreigners: 'You shall not charge interest on loans to your brother; you may charge a foreigner interest' [Deuteronomy: 23:19-20].

Jesus famously ejected the money changers, presumably usurers from the Temple, while in Matthew [25:14-30], he gives an unusual parable apparently legitimising interest. However, theologians debate the meaning of the parable. The great Christian Councils of Nicea, Laodicea and Lateran all inveighed against usury.

Shakespeare (*Sheikh Sbeare*, according to my Libyan friends) graphically refers to the practice in *The Merchant of Venice*, when Shylock demands 'a measured quantity of muscle from Antonio's chest' when he defaults on a payment (the origin of the phrase 'a pound of flesh').

∾

A FEW YEARS after my arrival back in the UK, while working as a freelance consultant, I religiously submitted tax returns and the other documentation, hoping to stay onside. Though, as expected, I shone on the HMRC radar like a UFO performing outrageous manoeuvres. A couple of months later, I received a letter about 'missing tax years', questioning why I hadn't paid any income tax or declared interest from savings accounts — quite an accusative letter.

In a lengthy response, I explained I'd been out of the country for several straight years, and no relevant UK income tax applied. But explaining why I hadn't paid interest on savings required a little more effort. In truth, I had given all the money away in charity payments (not to the bank pub fund) with no audit trail. The matter would no doubt become incredibly messy, and I fully anticipated a backdated tax bill with, ironically, dollops of added interest.

I patiently awaited my fate and the accompanying tax bill. One week, no response. Two weeks, no response. When I'd almost forgotten about the matter, HMRC sent a wonderfully understanding letter without any stapled bills.

Who said they're an unreasonable bunch?

GIVEN the Islamic prohibition on interest, payday and short-term loans have never been popular in the Muslim community, not historically, anyway. For a long time, there wasn't ever a need. We had a community-based lending system: the *kamitee* (Punjabi: committee).

Its exact origins are unknown, though I'm sure similar concepts exist in other cultures. The general idea is quite simple: a pool of members (generally around twenty) from the community each contribute a set amount (say, £100) each month. Then, each month, one member of the committee takes the money (and doesn't abscond to Marbella). Monthly contributions continue until everyone has taken the pot. A fair amount of trust is required for the process to work, though: trustworthy members, and a person of impeccable character collecting and recording the contributions. No wonder the system is rapidly joining the passenger pigeon.

8.9 STUNNING HALAL

'You Muslims are a barbaric lot! Using a razor-sharp knife straight to the neck! What you should be doing is stunning cattle by firing a bolt through its brain so it explodes. Or piping electricity directly into the brain, so it's frazzled like a piece of toast after ten minutes under the grill. Or hanging chickens upside down on metal shackles and electrocuting them in a water bath, before chopping off their head! You have it all wrong! That's the humane way of doing it!'

From all the negative, bad news and misunderstood aspects around Islam, halal food (specifically meat) is probably Top 5, and there's *tremendous* competition at the top of that list. The word *halal* comes from an Arabic root meaning 'something permissible', and therefore has broad application, not specifically to just food or meat. Helping a granny across the road is considered halal, whereas robbing a bank (in a burqa or otherwise) wouldn't be considered halal (the opposite of halal is *haram*). Most Muslims try and eat halal-only food, but it's not always easy, particularly when eating out, when ingredients aren't obvious. Deciphering esoteric E numbers on the backs of food packets can also be a challenge. Meat must be slaughtered correctly to be considered halal, whereas general food mustn't contain any specifically prohibited ingredients, such as pork. In addition, particular classes of animals with talons (like eagles) or claws (like crocodiles) are also prohibited – in case anyone fancies roast croc.

Seldom do a few weeks pass without a bad news story about a rogue halal abattoir or butcher somewhere in the country. Or some dodgy halal takeaway harbouring illegal immigrants that's failed a health and safety inspection. Or, of course, some snippet about how halal slaughter is barbaric and archaic, 'designed to inflict maximum pain on the animal', as I heard one well-known speaker comment. Brigitte Bardot picked up the anti-halal flag back in the 90s. Her remarks provoked amusement when I first read them. Yes, Ms Bardot had suddenly become an expert on Islamic Law and halal meat. More recently, she wrote an open letter in several French newspapers calling for an outright ban on halal and kosher meat.

The process of Islamic animal slaughter is quite straightforward; there's no hoodoo voodoo involved. After beginning with *Bismillah* (Arabic: In the name of God), the slaughterman (or woman) uses a surgically sharp knife to cut the animal's throat and windpipe, and the blood vessels around its neck. The animal's blood is then allowed to drain from the body. That's about the whole process. Contrary to widespread belief, the halal method is designed to inflict the *minimum* pain on the animal: consider the knife's sharpness, the swift movement, the lack of herding beforehand to avoid animals witnessing slaughter. Even sharpening the knife in front of the animal is prohibited.

According to most Islamic scholars, the case of stunning animals before slaughter is not an issue, if the animal doesn't die as a result, and, ironically, if it can be proven the stunning doesn't cause the animal any additional pain. But if the animal dies from the stunning, it becomes carrion, and impermissible for Muslims to eat.

~

'Don't these fish cakes taste a little, er, smoky?' I announced, while lunching with the team.

'You didn't get the fish cakes, did you?' my colleague wailed, looking genuinely mortified.

'Well, it's Friday, and in the absence of any haddock, I opted for the fish cakes, potato wedges and mushy peas. I wasn't expecting this smoky taste, though.'

'No!' he shrieked, causing a fair amount of commotion in the canteen. 'That's pancetta!'

'Pan-what? I wondered what was written next to the fish cakes.'

'Pancetta is pork belly meat!'

'Eh?!' I exclaimed, taking a napkin and unceremoniously emptying the contents of my mouth. At this point, most of the canteen had turned around to watch the show. I reached for my water bottle and gulped the entire contents. Regular, run of the mill pork felt unpleasant enough, the belly bit just added to the horridness. 'Phew, that was close to my gullet! Thanks for letting me know. I really ought to have asked about the pancetta. It's put me right off the wedges and peas now, too.' I pushed the plate to one side.

Once things had settled, my colleague remarked, 'I notice you didn't actually have any type of reaction, you know, allergic, or something?'

'Allergic? I don't think I'm allergic to pork.'

'What about eating meat that isn't halal?'

I chuckled. 'Do you know what the difference is between halal and non-halal meat?'

'Er, no...'

'Well, physically, none. A chicken leg is a chicken leg; a cutlet of lamb, a cutlet of lamb. What makes a chicken halal is the mention of God's name and specific method of slaughter. So, for example, the Jewish method of slaughter is acceptable to Muslims. Pork is a separate category that Muslims don't eat; it can't be made halal under normal circumstances. Not even by wrapping it in cosy blankets.'

≈

DURING A LIVELY PROJECT for a well-known auction house, I had the dubious privilege of managing the Go-Live operation with a colleague. We managed to secure our own room at the back of the large open plan office, decorated with whiteboards, plans and activity schedules. It provided an excellent interrogation space for individuals and areas deviating from the plan, and a welcome space away from the clamour and crowd. Somehow, most people entering the room were quite amenable with the 'Brothers of Doom' giving orders.

The overall Go-Live plan included changes to dozens of IT systems, involving teams across New York, London and Hong Kong. It required months of scrupulous planning and rehearsals, with the actual event spanning a wearying five days (24/7).

As part of the deal, we had to ensure workers were fed and watered, specifically with the entire team present on the final day. We obviously didn't want anyone passing out while on duty; they had important work to do. But, crucially, that meant we could control the menu. After canvassing opinion, we ordered the orthodox, straight-bat choice for the fifty workers outside: a range of sandwiches, catering for everyone on the food spectrum, vegetables with dips, and soft drinks and mineral water. Top quality sandwiches, too, from a local delicatessen, not run-of-the-mill M&S variety. My colleague and I fancied something a little different, something more filling. We were famished on this final day, having run the operation for nearly a week, an incredibly stressful and brain-sapping endeavour. He abdicated order responsibility to me. And, after a quick online search of central London eateries, I ordered our meal, and replaced the desk phone handset with the contentment of a man who'd just secured a lucrative deal. 'Don't worry, you'll enjoy this.'

An hour later, the taxi arrived with our special order. I wandered through the office to collect it, grinning, high-fiving and giving the thumbs-up to one and all for a successful project implementation. They looked content to me, nibbling on their sandwiches, dipping their carrots, and sipping Perrier. Outside, the taxi driver handed me the bill. *Crikey that is expensive, better keep the receipt.* Moments later, I trekked back through the office, trying to look inconspicuous while heaving two white bags bulging with containers.

Once back inside our room, I silently closed the door. It felt like a grand heist, as we spread the food on the project table, using old A3 printed plans and PowerPoint sheets as a tablecloth. While the team ate cheese and pickle sandwiches, we gobbled roast chicken, lamb curry, kebabs, chicken wings and biryani rice. I even bought cookie dough and chocolate chip ice cream for dessert, and a gallon of Diet Coke.

Unbeknown to us, Jim, the Head of IT, and clearly no mug, realised something was afoot, as he eyed us through the small door window. He knocked and prised open the door. 'You two have ordered for yourself, I see.'

'Er, yes... Yes, we have quite specific dietary requirements,' I mumbled, with half a spicy chicken wing poking out of my mouth.

He ogled the table of half-open containers, naan bread and spilt rice. 'Yes, I can see that. I like your dietary requirements. Do you mind if I join you?' He walked in a trance-like state towards the table.

Well, we were expensing all the food back to him, so it seemed rude to turn him away. 'Sure, grab a seat.'

Jim hadn't previously sampled any Pakistani cuisine, let alone curry with TNT levels of spice. But, as the sweat poured from his pasty brow, he couldn't resist one mouthful after another, determined to sample everything on offer, gulping Coke and belching every ten seconds. Yes, Jim, a devout Christian from the heart of Alabama, became a fully-fledged halal convert on that great day of the feast.

8.10 NINJAS & MARAUDING LETTERBOXES

Since the early jiujitsu seed in Burnley, my fascination with all things martial arts remained into adulthood, particularly the East Asian flavours: Kung Fu, Karate, Taekwondo, and their variants. Perhaps due to the discipline, rigour, honour and dedication they required. Or, more likely, Bruce Lee single-handedly defeating twenty armed assailants ingrained in my memory from *Enter the Dragon*. Yes, long before MMA, Bruce Lee and Chuck Norris films were compulsory viewing.

So, imagine my surprise and delight when I heard screams of 'Ninjaaaaa!' while walking down Nottingham High Street. My happiness quickly dissipated as I turned to see a group of young-sters sniggering and pointing. How odd? The little grey cells were clearly parched that day. Once the cogs started moving, I realised the lads were referring to Shmaila. She'd cottoned on immediately and initiated her default protocol: ignore the comments and walk on. I followed no such protocol. I looked at her. Yes, thinking more about it, she did look a little like a ninja. Yet, despite my interest in ninjas, I'd somehow missed the connection. How disappointing. Her shoes were all wrong. Of course, at that point, I advised the obvious next step: an intensive course of martial arts. Perhaps the next time the situation occurred, she could demonstrate ninja flips and roundhouse kicks and maybe throw a few shuriken stars. That'd surely impress the little blighters.

A FEW YEARS AGO, some creative chap invented the 'Punish a Muslim Day', a single action-packed day collecting points for feats of nastiness against Muslims: 10 points for abusing a Muslim, 100 for 'beating up a Muslim', all the way up to 2500 for 'Nuking Mecca'. I'm not sure he'd given the points system too much thought.

Whatever the case, attacks spiked, and he received twelve and a half years for his efforts.

A few months later, with characteristic buffoonery, Boris de Pfeffel Johnson, the then backbench Conservative MP, quipped in an article for *The Telegraph*, 'It is absolutely ridiculous that people should choose to go around looking like letter boxes.' That would be the Royal Mail special edition kind, no doubt. Though, after the mockery, Boris did defend the right of Muslim women to wear the burqa: 'Denmark has got it wrong. Yes, the burqa is oppressive and ridiculous, but that's still no reason to ban it.' Some may consider Boris's golden mop oppressive and ridiculous, too. With his qualifier or not, the damage had been done. Again, attacks on Muslim women rocketed in the following weeks, according to 'Tell MAMA[5]'.

The following year, post Boris's miraculous ascension to Prime Minister, Tan Dhesi, the first turbaned Sikh MP, countered, in the House of Commons, 'For those of us who from a young age have had to endure and face up to being called names such as towelhead, or Taliban, or coming from bongo-bongo land, we can fully appreciate the hurt and pain of already vulnerable Muslim women when they are described as looking like bank robbers and letterboxes.'

I hadn't heard 'bongo-bongo land' in some 35 years. One of the more creative kids at school penned a bongo-bongo ditty based on the ad for the drink Um Bongo, which they drank in the Congo (do YouTube the advert). Boris looked genuinely flummoxed, before burping his own Muslim heritage[6] and, in true political style, retorted with some random accusations of his own.

'You're in England now- take that bin bag off!'

'Aren't you hot in that, love?'

'Why are you wearing that awful thing?'

'You must be a right ugly witch!'

'You poor, oppressed woman!' Just a sample of comments Shmaila has received over the years. Far from being oppressed, my wife, like most Muslim women (certainly in the West), chooses to wear the hijab and/or niqab. The non-Muslim families of convert women are certainly not forcing the attire, I'm sure most would concede.

A personal favourite comment, 'God, your husband must be a *right bastard* to make you wear that!' The speaker's rage screaming from her face like steam from a boiling kettle. It's astonishing just how the hijab and niqab can incite such hatred. Just try swimming across the channel in a burkini and ask for Monsieur Macron.

Then we have the stares, the spitting, the *looks*. Oh, the *looks* of absolute, unbridled disgust. A friend described an incident with his wife while out shopping. As she compared Braeburn and Gala apples, a young man took particular offence to her niqab and spat squarely into her face (thank goodness for the covering), while yelling obscenities suggesting she ought to return home. My friend, choosing kids' toothpaste with his two daughters in a nearby aisle, sprinted around when he heard the commotion. A solid right hook later, the young guy was reeling on the ground in a pool of blood and with a likely broken nose. He hadn't accounted for the possibility she might not be alone. Bloody fool.

8.11 BARBAROUS PRIESTHOOD

Growing up, the probability my father would shell out £1 per haircut for each of his boys approached zero. Instead, he invested in a roll of industrial orange plastic sheeting, sharp scissors, and a hefty hair clipper. Every few months, we'd await the dreaded lines, 'Look at that hair! You all need a good haircut!' One by one, we'd then strip down to our underwear and sit cross-legged on the plastic. It became sticky and very uncomfortable after a few minutes.

Post a quick splatter of icy water, my father would administer a 'Number 1' all over, adding a few finishing touches with the scissors. Flinching would often result in a painful nip. Like a fine oil painter, once finished, my father would sit back and admire his work. 'Now, which barber can cut better than that?!' We didn't argue. But the shameful trudge into school the next day, amidst a cacophony of jibes, eclipsed any other trauma. 'Asif, who did that?! Your dad?! Haha! That's crap!'

As we grew older, we couldn't wait to pay for a decent haircut. 'If you can make money like you grow hair, you'll be very wealthy,' quipped my first real barber during my early teenage years.

'Er, let's hope so.'

My barber, who sported tremendous white sideburns himself, was never short of a witty, if not always welcome, comment. Alas, he didn't live long enough to see me wearing a beard. He'd have thought I'd found rhodium deposits in my garden.

But the barber experience is quite personal, even when fully dressed. Not many people are allowed to occupy such personal space. Consequently, I've always chosen my barber with the sharpest pencil. When I move to a new town, it's one of the first items on my to-do list. As a general rule, I try and avoid Asian or Arab barbers, most of whom seem to have attended the same hairdressing school as my father.

~

HMMM, this looks like an Italian barber, different from my usual.

I peered inside the window to see four seats and two barbers busy snipping away. *Right... here goes...* I took a few deep breaths, walked in, and uneasily sat down on one of the red padded chairs. A familiar odour of talcum powder and unwashed hair wafted through the shop. The older, grey, balding barber briefly looked up and nodded his head in approval before returning to his snipping.

To my right, a mound of well-worn magazines and newspapers cluttered a high table. Nothing appealed.

Ahead, I noticed a Rubik's snake puzzle on display. I hadn't seen one in twenty years. *I wonder if I can still make the ball...*

'Anda nexta gentlemana, please...' called the older barber, in a thick Italian-English accent.

I grudgingly rose, slipped off my jacket, and sat down in the seat.

'And what can I do for, sir?'

'Er, just a number three at the back and a trim on top.' As he wrapped the apron around my neck, I noticed a mound of razors on the cabinet. 'Oh, and can, can you also use a new blade for my neck, please?' I really didn't need a bout of Hep B.

'Ok, no problema... Sit back, please. Just relax, you seem a little tense.' He tightened the apron around my neck and began with the hair clipper. 'Your hair is very tough. Like steel wool. You won't go bald like me.' He chuckled. I glared at him in the mirror. *Please just cut the hair, no commentary needed.* 'And what shall I do with this beard? All off?' He moved the clippers towards my chin.

I flinched as though dodging a sniper's bullet. 'Just the top of my head, please. Just focus on the top,' I snapped.

'No problema. No problema at all. You live local? I haven't seen you before.'

'Yes, I just moved into the area. This is my first haircut here.'

'Si, Si. So, you must be a bishop or priest or...?'

My irritated face now on full display. I looked into the mirror again as he momentarily paused before opening his razor. He took out a new blade from its wrapping and inserted into the holder. His hands trembled as he performed the delicate operation.

'Er, a priest? What do you mean?'

He gestured towards his chin.

'Ah... I think you mean Imam or Mullah?'

'Ah, yes, Mullah, you must be a Mullah?'

'No, I've just got a beard. I am a Muslim, though...' I stopped abruptly. Perhaps that was too much information at this delicate time. *Why is he asking me these questions, anyway?*

'Si, si, musalmano. You musalmano. We have musalmano in Italy!' The barber raised the instrument to the light and closed one eye. 'Look, I've put new blade in for you.'

I nodded sheepishly.

He started with long, deliberate strokes to my neck, up and down, round my right ear, then my left. *Just finish this part,* I thought. *Really don't need a slip here.*

'I am like musalmano butcher... Halal – you cut the neck of animal, right...?' He motioned the blade close to my neck. I swallowed hard. How had I chosen this comedic Italian Sweeny Todd? He chuckled again.

I needed to change subject, sharpish. 'So, are you, er, Catholic?'

'Catholic! Me, no! Why should I give the Pope my hard-earned money! They have enough money. Right, just a trim on top, you say?'

'Yes, just a little. Well, I suppose that's a fair point about the Catholic Church. I heard Ol' Blue Eyes paid $50 million for Papal Services. Who knows?'

'Eh? Blue eye? Papa?'

I shook my head. 'Never mind.'

'Do you go to confession? You know, little box?' he continued.

'Yes, I know about confession, but in Islam, there's no need for confession. God can hear us directly. We don't need to confess to the priest.'

'Si, si, capito, capito. What's your name?'

'My name is Ah sif, Ah sif.'

'Eh...? Your name, what is your name? Nome, nome.' He put his hand to his ear.

'Jon...JON,' I shouted.

'Si, si, Giovanni.'

'Yes, er, Giovanni.' I nodded in approval as he completed the final few snips. He brushed the loose hair from around my shoulders and took the mirror to demonstrate his work.

'My name is Luigi.'

'Yes, I see that from the name of your shop, 'Super Mario Brothers': I never cared for it.' I stood and brushed myself down. 'Thanks, here's the money, keep the change.'

'Grazie, grazie, Signore.'

So impressed, I stayed with Luigi for nearly 20 years. He passed on to the next realm, almost clutching his clippers – poor chap.

8.12 SUSPICIOUS FOLLICLE ACTIVITY

Ah, the beard, the beard. What a long and fine tradition, and an equally long line of proponents. Just look at the list, it's a who's who of history: Confucius, Socrates, Aurelius, Da Vinci, Shakespeare, Darwen, Dickens, Lincoln, Marx, Grace (WG), the wrestler Braun Strowman, to name a few.

I grew my beard in 1993, during my first year at university, much to my parents' distress. They argued my visible show of religiosity would create another excuse for prejudice and present obstacles for me while living in the UK. They may have been on to something. But the warning wasn't enough for me to reach for the BIC razor.

The beard has wandered in and out of fashion over recent years; frankly, it's challenging to keep track. Given the bewildering number of male beard products currently on the market at present, I reckon it's now in vogue. Beard care used to be trivial in the 90s and 00s – a quick shampoo and comb and on your way. I recall being off work for a couple of weeks, and returning to see a new chap, Dave, with a huge yet immaculate dark brown beard. He started to explain about the different products he kept in his bathroom cupboard, but I felt compelled to stop him mid-conversation. He made me look like a whippersnapper in short trousers.

In many traditions, the beard is considered a praiseworthy addition to the male arsenal: Eastern Christianity (not so much Western, these days), Judaism, Sikhism, Hindu Mysticism and the Amish have all been keen advocates. The stoic philosopher Epictetus[7] preferred losing his head before reaching for the razor:

'Come now, Epictetus, take off your beard.'
- If I am a philosopher, I answer, I will not take it off.
'Then I will take off your head.'
- If that will do you any good, take it!

Muslim males are encouraged to grow their beards as a sign of maturity and in emulation of the Prophet (ﷺ). In the current climate, though, the beard has become a symbol of dread and horror on a young, brown Muslim (or white convert) – dread no doubt reinforced by the constant stream of bearded reprobates splashed across the news. Thank goodness for Moeen Ali.

Rogue imagery aside, the beard can create a myriad of general problems, vocational or otherwise. Off the bat, eating spaghetti or a bowl of soup can be troublesome. Some years ago, the Territorial Army refused entry to a friend until he sheared his beard (I think the policy has now changed). I've known bearded doctors and (male) nurses receive considerable pressure to shave, and friends working for high profile consultancies encouraged to look sheen and shorn.

Slightly further afield, in Tajikistan, police shaved the beards of 13,000 men to prevent 'radicalisation'. Similar episodes were reported in Uzbekistan. Other countries have cut the problem at root. The Chinese Government, for example, often leading the way, banned the beard amongst the beleaguered and persecuted

Uighur population. What would Hongwu[8] think? Who'd have thought follicle activity could create such a palaver?

SLIGHTLY BEFORE THE days of 'right, I'm going to report this to your boss, or someone senior, or someone who might be more politically correct', a friend, Imran, had an usually candid conversation with a recruitment consultant during an initial screening interviewing. Keen to ensure success and receive his commission, the recruitment chap gave Imran a few pointers on his CV, before moving to more personal matters.

'Well, if you make those adjustments, your CV is absolutely ideal. You've got all the right credentials.'

'That's great. So you think I've got a good chance of getting this job?' Imran asked.

'For sure, for sure. There is one thing. Look... I love the hair, I really do...' he gestured with his hand.

'Aha, thanks for the compliment. Appreciated.'

The consultant comically raised his thumbs, 'Love the glasses, too! They look great!'

'Right, ok...' Imran sensed this wasn't going in the right direction.

'But can we do something about this beard? The company has a young, dynamic image. I'm not sure you're going to fit in with that!'

The comment left Imran momentarily dazed, like he'd just been hit by a stinging jab to the nose. 'Oh. That's disappointing. I'm quite keen on it.' Imran paused. 'You know, I don't like the wig on your head either, but I'm sure you're great at your job. My beard hasn't caused problems at work so far. I suggest you put me forward for the role, and we'll see what happens.'

The consultant, now slightly embarrassed at his absurd comment, chuckled. The cogs whirred at the possibility of losing his 15% commission. 'Hmmm, ok. That's fair enough. We'll arrange the first interview.'

A couple of weeks on, Imran landed the role, beard and all.

'Asif, two questions for you....'

'Sure,' I responded, with a glint in my eye, hoping this would liven up my chaotic day that I'd spent in planning sessions. My head was spinning like a Catherine wheel.

'How long have you been growing that, and, as a follow on, does anything live inside?' The first question appeared genuine, at least.

'Fifteen years, and probably nothing larger than a few micrometres,' I responded. 'There are no chameleons nesting inside, if that's what you're worried about.' It's good to ask questions about stuff you don't understand or potentially fear, even something mundane like a beard. 'Any other hirsutal questions?' I asked.

'One more, if you don't mind. Is it for fashion or religious reasons?'

'Well, does it look fashionable?'

'I'd say so. You wear it well.'

'Thanks. However, it's for religious reasons. Quite benign, really.' I stroked my beard. 'You know, I do some of my best thinking like this. Many problems I've solved while in this state. A bit like Holmes smoking his pipe with a tobacco opium mix.'

'I'm pleased to hear that. Please continue, and how can we expedite delivery of this project?'

9. THE ALGORITHM OF CHAOS

'A fool may throw a stone into well, which a hundred wise men cannot remove.'

— GEORGE HERBERT

It's an algorithm that is depressingly all too familiar, all too well-trodden, an algorithm that brings misery to Muslims and non-Muslims alike. In fact, it brings a double dollop of misery for Muslims. The first bout is administered at the time of the atrocity: the bomb, the explosion, or the diving plane – the projectiles don't discriminate on the grounds of faith. The second materialises in the form of a baseball bat to the young hijab-wearing girl, or the knife through the heart of the elderly man walking to the mosque for morning prayers, or the bomb from the unmanned drone flying at 30,000 feet. It's a lose-lose situation for the overwhelming majority of Muslims.

With apologies to al-Khwarizmi[1], the following snippet describes the general algorithm:

REPEAT

Media: News of atrocity

Media: It's probably those pesky Muslims again

Muslims: Let's hope none of them has a Muslim sounding name

Muslims: Open condemnation: 'It's nothing to do with Islam'

Knuckleheads: Increase attacks on Muslims

Twitter: Pray for #victim

Of course, It's reasonable to say that the Muslim community has its share of morons; there's a decent amount of empirical evidence to substantiate the claim. In any given population, there's a percentage of psychopaths, or people displaying psychopathic tendencies, and general sociopaths, as well as others who simply demonstrate undesirable tendencies. Add a combination of youth, foolish dreams and a sprinkling of religious catechism into the mix, and it's a recipe for a particularly dangerous group. With around two billion Muslims across the globe, the statistical population is larger than most.

Mainly through our own handiwork, Muslims enjoy a unique position in the sun during this time. Just ask George Alagiah and Jon Snow. Almost every misdemeanour or atrocity committed by a Muslim seems to be performed in the name of the faith, when reported. Sometimes we'll hear, *'There's no evidence this was an act of terrorism'* (Translated: no involvement from anyone with a Muslim sounding name). The connection between faith and atrocity isn't usually made with any other religion – it's just a crackpot or lunatic with a beef, wielding an automatic gun (generally in America). After all, who else would commit such an outrage? When it comes to Islam and Muslims, any flimsy connection and 'it's those troublesome Muslims again'.

But what if the person claims his (or her) heinous action in the name of Islam? So what? Does the mere claim give legitimacy? As the Arab poet says:

*Everyone claims love for Layla, but Layla doesn't
care for any of them!*

. Irrespective of motive, the entire Muslim Universe must then condemn the atrocity each time. Yes, it's unacceptable to hack someone in the high street. Yes, it's wrong to attack monks and nuns in a church. Yes, it's unacceptable to detonate a bomb on a bus. Yes, it's wrong to throw litter on the streets. And so forth. No, Islam doesn't sanction such crimes.

9.1 FUNDAMENTAL NOMENCLATURE

Depressingly, the words 'terrorism' and 'suicide bombing' have become synonymous with Islam since 9/11. For most, Islam has now a monopoly on both. Yet, neither suicide nor terrorism has any real precedent in 1400 years of Islamic history. On the contrary, the idea of suicide directly opposes the clear Qur'anic injunction: 'Do not kill yourselves (or others), for surely God is merciful to you' [Qur'an 4:29].

The idea of suicide missions appears to have been popularised in the 20th century by *Kamikaze* (Japanese: Divine Wind) pilots during World War II, where defeat or surrender was unthinkable. The Luftwaffe undertook similar one-way missions in *Selbstopfere-insatz* (German: self-sacrifice) missions. Some Muslim groups swallowed this idea of weaponising oneself in the 1980s, and 9/11 later provided the main focal point. Novel names were coined to circumvent the clear prohibition on suicide. Despite the camouflage, the overwhelming majority of Islamic scholars rejected the concept, and continue to do so.

A virulent, extremist strain has existed within Islam since the very early days[2]. In fact, the father of the group is said to have directly confronted the Prophet Muhammad (ﷺ). The group later fought and killed many of the Prophet's Companions (disciples).

Recent extremism and terrorism perpetrated by Muslims have taken on new, ugly guises. Though, admittedly, it's tricky to nail down an agreed definition of 'terrorism'. The Oxford English Dictionary defines it as: 'The unlawful use of violence and intimidation, especially against civilians, in the pursuit of political aims'. But who decides what is lawful and what isn't? A single individual strapped with Semtex driving into a wedding party in Afghanistan is considered terrorism. That's rightfully unlawful. But a B52 bombing campaign, pouring iron and fire from the skies, destroying acres of villages and land, and the same wedding party is not considered terrorism. That appears to be lawful when 'spreading democracy', and any civilians killed are collateral damage. Moreover, there are no marble-etched memorials, no eulogies, no recital of names for those killed. Nobody even knows their names.

Whatever the definitions, there is no history of vigilante-type terrorism in Islamic history against civilian populations as a political tactic. Again, the direct targeting of civilians is expressly prohibited – even in cases of clear warfare.

So, why do people attribute these acts to Islam? Why do people think they are performing these acts 'In the name of Islam?' Does simply yelling *Allahu Akbar* (Arabic: God is Great) give all actions legitimacy? Can I take a swig of vodka if I shout something Islamic beforehand? Yes, clearly preposterous. As we have seen throughout history, people have found creative means of justifying whatever action in the name of religion (or irreligion). The famous preacher and cult leader Jim Jones, managed to convince 918 men, women, and children to drink Flavor Aid laced with cyanide. Would the Buddha give his seal of approval to atrocities in Rohingya? Is the usurping and occupation of another people's land really in conformity with the Torah? Pope Urban II declared before the First Crusade in 1095:

'Advance boldly, as knights of Christ, and rush as quickly as you can to the defence of the Eastern Church. For she it is from whom the joys of your whole salvation have come forth, who poured into your mouths the milk of divine wisdom, who set before you the holy teachings of the gospel.'

He gave his blessing with the famous cry, 'Deus vult!' or 'God wills it!' What would Jesus have done?

9.2 MURDER ON SNAKE PASS

As Jeremy Clarkson (or his scriptwriter) would probably describe: Snake Pass is a beautiful, yet chastening ribbon of asphalt draped over a section of the Peak District, sandwiched between Manchester and Sheffield. Architected by the great Thomas Telford in the early 19th century, it's known as one of the most dangerous roads in the UK due to its many serpentine-like bends. It's also the fastest route between the two cities. That's a lethal cocktail. On a bright summer's day, in a high-performance sports car with Nigel Mansell at the wheel, it can be a wondrous experience. On an overcast Thursday morning, torrential rain, in a decrepit white transit van laden with odd bits of furniture bouncing around, and a petrified driver, it's quite the opposite. Though it's an ideal place to dispose of a cadaver, should the need arise.

Amer and I were on our way to collect furniture from Sajad's flat, part of relocation activities away from the Sheffield area. We found Rob in the local directory, under 'Man with a Van', a cheap and cheerful service for a £100 round trip fee, cash in hand, no questions asked. Surely, we couldn't go wrong.

'So, is it just you comin'?' Rob stared, while pausing his rearrangement of grubby sheets and random cupboard parts in the van. *What's the point of the sheets? They look grimier than the rest of the van.* I cracked a smile, a feeble smile, all I could offer at 07:05 on an empty stomach. In his enthusiasm, Rob had actually arrived on time. He was a short chap, 5' 6', maybe half an inch more, and enjoyed a robust northern accent and a military-grade crewcut.

'No, my younger brother will also be coming. He'll be here in a moment. I think he's trying to gobble some breakfast.'

'Ah, ok'. He returned to his grimy sheets.

Five minutes later, Amer arrived and stood behind the van. Rob peered up again, this time at my younger yet taller brother.

'Er, ok... Rightio... Let's be getting off. Long way to go. You two can sit in the front, unless you fancy sitting on these old mattresses in the back.'

Hmmm, is there a third option? 'Er, we'll go in the front, thanks, Rob,' I eventually mustered.

Rob perched high at the wheel, Amer and I squashed into the front seat, amongst the cigarette butts, old letters, and various DIY catalogues. A gelatinous odour of hard work, cigarettes and old furniture hung in the air.

Ashamedly, I played the elder brother card and sat near the window, with Amer sandwiched in the middle. I glanced at him. *Lord, several hours of this.* 'Rob, do you mind if I open a window?'

'Er, no, just wind that handle down. Be caref...'

'Sorry... I haven't used one of these in years. I'll put this back on in no time.'

As I fiddled with the handle, Rob announced he needed petrol and some items from the shop. 'Right, I'm just stopping here. Won't be long.' He stepped out and started filling the van. A few minutes later, he was busy selecting items from the shop.

'Why's he staring at us in there. Look at him!' Amer asked.

'Eh? Yes, he looks dazed. He's buying cigarettes too. Didn't even ask if we wanted anything. Never mind, as long as he can get us to Sheffield and back.'

Rob returned, carrying his cigarettes and a copy of *The Sun* newspaper. He eyed us shiftily, before folding his paper and placing it on the dashboard.

The rain lashed down from the moment we left Burnley and continued on the motorway. I could barely see through the windscreen, and the wobbly wipers hardly shifted any water. *How on earth is he going to drive through The Pass?* I wondered.

Another thirty minutes, and we sped past the Snake Pass sign. 'I'm going to stop here for a quick smoke,' Rob announced.

I looked at Amer then my watch. The rain continued to lash down. It's *a little odd to be having a cigarette out here in the middle of nowhere.* But, not wishing to be impolite, I replied, 'Sure, we're doing well for time.'

Rob pulled over into a lay-by. He stood, huddled against the rain, hands trembling as he struggled to light the cigarette and place it to his lips. He stared into the empty space ahead of him, wide-eyed, in a hypnotic state.

We both continued to eye Rob from the van. 'He seems a bit nervous, doesn't he?' I said, turning towards Amer.

'Yes, what's wrong with him?'

'He looks dazed, a little lost. I hope he's not under any narcotic influence. This road is dangerous enough with a sober driver.'

Rob continued to puff his cigarette, as though the chair awaited him beyond the curtain, and the rain continued to thrash on his head. He took his time, taking full extended, deep puffs, slowly inhaling, then exhaling. He looked like a man with the weight of the world on his shoulders. We simply needed safe passage to Sheffield and back. This wasn't a particularly dangerous mission.

Ten minutes later, he crawled back into the van, dripping wet, and we were off again.

'Lads, you know, I'm ex-Army, tours of Afghanistan and Iraq. I learnt hand-to-hand combat for many years. I can kill a man with my bare hands. Look, just look at all these marks on my hands.

That's from army training, that is. You don't want to mess with me, lads. Believe me...'

I glanced at Amer, who reciprocated with an equally quizzical look. *What on earth is he blabbering on about now? Why's he telling us this? Just drive, man!*

His bizarre comments bounced in the restricted van airspace for a good while. 'Thanks, Rob, we'll bear that in mind. But can you just focus on driving?' He looked even more menacing now, straining his eyes while his hands continued to tremble on the wheel. We decided against prodding him any further.

An hour later, and we had arrived. 'Right,' I said, 'finally, we're here. Just take that left and park. His flat is just over there.' We fell out of the van, lungs desperately in need of fresh oxygen, and marched towards the block of flats.

Sajad arrived a few minutes later in a grey t-shirt drenched in sweat. He'd obviously started the packing and moving. 'Oh my god...' Rob exclaimed on seeing him. 'I cannot believe this. What is going on?!' He smacked his forehead in theatrical style and paced away.

'Eh? What's wrong with him?' Sajad asked.

'No idea. He's been acting strange since we left Burnley. He'll be alright. Let's get this lot loaded.'

Around two hours later, we'd managed to creatively pack all Sajad's belongings into the back of the van, including several oddly-shaped items. Rob's army background finally proved useful on a couple of fronts.

'That's the lot. Let's get back to Burnley.' I rubbed my hands with satisfaction.

'Well, ok, but we can go back the motorway route this time, it's better,' Rob blurted.

'No, no, back through Snake Pass, it's much quicker,' I responded firmly. 'I don't want to spend an extra 45 minutes in the van. Sajad can follow in his car.'

For a moment, Rob remained silent. 'Right, I need another bloody cig.'

I rolled my eyes. 'Ok, then we'll get something to eat.'

'Yes, good idea,' interrupted Sajad. 'I'm famished. There's a burger place nearby. Follow me.'

We jumped into his car, not needing further prompting. Rob followed alone in his van. A short ride later, we'd arrived outside the burger joint. Rob grabbed his newspaper and joined us inside.

Around five hours from our departure, we *finally* sat down to eat. 'I could eat a couple of these chicken burgers. And these spiral chips are tasty. What do you think, Rob?' I looked at him, hoping for a smile or some reaction. He still hadn't said a word. 'Rob!'

'Eh, what? Sorry, miles away.'

'Rob, if you don't mind me saying, you've been on edge all day. Is there something wrong?'

He grimaced, and slowly lifted his newspaper to show the front page: *'The murder of Lee Rigby'*.

Good grief...

Like the backend of a *Columbo* episode, the chain of events gradually started to make sense: the treacherous weather, the insistence to take the short route through Snake Pass, the two sizeable, bearded Muslim brothers joined by an even bigger third brother, Rob's army background, his Herculean tales of slaying men with his bare hands, the large objects now in the back of his white transit van, all against the backdrop of Drummer Lee Rigby's grisly murder a few days earlier, on the 22nd May 2013.

Rob had concluded three bearded brothers would commit another grisly murder on that rainy Thursday afternoon through Snake Pass.

Alas, Rob was no Columbo.

9.3 KICKING OFF AGAIN

'Is that your lot kicking off again?'

A wet Tuesday morning arriving at the office, and I wasn't expecting that greeting. John always had a way with words, and was quite forthright and bullish with his views, which I appreciated, most of the time. He'd caught me off-guard. My thoughts were preoccupied with other matters, the runaway project, for one, United taking a thrashing the night before, a second.

'John... Good morning to you, too. Let me just pop my coat off, and I'll be right with you.' I hurried past him to my desk. *Lord, what's happened now.*

I wandered over to look at his screen – there'd been a church attack in France. The headline read: '*Islamic Terrorists Attack Church and Kill Priest*'.

I sighed and shook my head. 'These headlines! Terrorism is *never* Islamic! Muslims engaged in acts of terrorism – that is quite different.'

'But they are your boys,' he continued. 'One of them looks like you: long beard, sizable schnozzle...'

'That's where the similarities end,' I interjected. 'I wouldn't say they were my boys, either. Looks like they're the same profile as many of the other attackers, though – young, foolish, ignorant, with probably only a veneer of Islamic teaching and understanding.'

'How do you know that?'

'Well, off the bat, there's randomly attacking innocent people. No sane person does that. Also, we have several inviolables in the tradition – even in a time of declared, unambiguous war, let alone on a wet morning in Paris. Attacking women, children, the elderly, places of worship, and their inhabitants are all in that category. Strictly prohibited.'

'They haven't read that bit of the Koran, then?'

'I'd be surprised if they had read or studied anything. There's a very long list of miscreants, but what do all these people have in common?'

'Psychological problems?'

'Possibly. What else?'

'Converts?'

'Hmmm, sometimes... What else?'

He shook his head, 'I don't know.'

'Did these people spend their lives studying the Qur'an, Islamic theology and jurisprudence? Did their epiphanies descend after years of study and learning at the hands of devout and learned scholars? Did, after a lifetime of study, they think: 'Aha, yes, everything is clear now! I need to blow up a bus! Yes, that's the answer!' Or, 'I need to cook some homemade potion and pour into the heels of my shoes to try and bomb a plane full of people?'

'I've no idea, but you're going to tell me they didn't.'

'Yes, I am, with some conviction, too.'

John paused. 'This isn't your jihad', then.'

'Attacking a church or school full of children isn't jihad, except in the twisted mind of the individual perpetrating the act. It's terrorism. Carpet bombing countries with bunker-buster bombs and other weapons of mass destruction isn't jihad either.'

'Agreed on that last point.'

'Well, that's a start.'

'Right, well, er, ok. You probably have a busy day ahead; I won't keep you a moment longer.'

'Thanks John. Team meeting in five.'

9.4 PENCILS AND CARTOONS

'Asif, brace yourself...'

My technical project lead, often the harbinger of doom and gloom, was no doubt ready to deliver more bad news, more delays, more problems. I thought I'd had my quota for that week. 'Right,' I sighed, 'I'm fully braced. What's gone wrong now? Give me your Irish best.'

'Do you find *this* offensive?' He lifted his A4 notepad to reveal a glossy magazine underneath. I looked down to see an image depicting a cartoon of a turbaned, bearded man with a hidden bomb. Not the news I expected.

Aha, this is one of the Danish cartoons. I hadn't previously seen any of these cartoons in the flesh. They were first published in 2006, and later reproduced by the French *Charlie Hebdo* magazine. Extremists attacked the magazine offices in 2015, leading to the deaths of 12 people.

'That's a good question.' I stared again at the crude cartoon. 'I suspect no other cartoons in history have created so much commotion. They *are* offensive, dangerous, unhelpful in the current context, where so much uneasiness between communities exists. What's the point of deliberately offending so many? They're not building bridges with these.'

'No, agreed. But why do they create so much turmoil in the Muslim world to the point of mass demonstrations, even teachers being killed in France?'

'Of course, killing a teacher because he shows them in a French RE lesson is unacceptable.'

'Well, I didn't think you'd agree with that.'

'No. For Muslims, there is no imagery, no depiction of the Prophet (ﷺ). Nothing has been created in the last 1400 years, aside from the odd aberration. It's very different to Christians, for example, and their depictions of Christ – think the Sistine Chapel. So, creating an image in the first place is troublesome. Then to mock and satirise is simply pouring fuel on a fire.'

'So, Muslims cannot accept criticism of Islam?'

'People have been criticising Islam since its birth. It's the mockery and ridicule that creates a problem nowadays. The mockery easily morphs into hatred. We'd find cartoons of Jesus or

Moses equally reprehensible. People will react in different ways. You didn't seem to worry I'd throw a right-hook when you showed me this.'

'Er, no, good point. I ought to have considered that.'

'I'm against the demonstrations, effigy burning, and chaos in the streets. It doesn't achieve anything. The cartoons became popular due to the Muslim reaction towards them. Otherwise, they'd have remained buried in that obscure Danish magazine.'

'Quite.'

'The cartoons aren't even funny,' I continued. 'I mean, not like *Dastardly and Muttley* funny. They're simply designed to offend. Do you find them funny?'

'Actually, not really.'

'Islam is far above this pettiness and nonsense. Muslims, alas, are not.'

'Right, I've got some terrible project news for you, Asif. Brace yourself...'

9.5 COUNTERTERRORISM

We enjoyed a disproportionate number of quiet, cerebral types at university, the 'Axis of Evil' well represented (minus North Korea), and a fair number from other Muslim countries, too: Libya, Egypt, Syria, Morocco, Saudi, Malaysia. Of course, what better location for our prayer room than the depths of the main building, three flights down. It felt like 'going down t'pit', a location where few dared to tread. Hardly surprising that rumours circulated that secret service spies were in our midst. I wasn't convinced. Having served on the 'Leadership Team' for a few years, I knew we had nothing to hide; organising prayers, meals during Ramadan, academic support and the odd, sodden camping trip were the high points.

Living in a student house with a dozen others felt like a game of

Cluedo, but not due to the presence of secret service agents. Me, one of the few Brits in house, always willing to engage in controversial, political topics, would throw snippets to the group, snippets often met with gloomy silence, much to my annoyance. When questioned, a couple of housemates expressed concerns about espousing any type of political views for fear of spies within the house and possible repercussions back home. In truth, astronomical electricity bills concerned me more than Middle Eastern revolution. Their collective abuse of high kilowatt electric heaters morn, noon, and night was the only genuinely fanatical trait I witnessed.

Fast forward 20 years... In 2013, the FBI assigned a secret agent to infiltrate a mosque in Southern California, a supposed hotbed of extremist activity. The agent regularly attended, until he'd gained the trust of other members within the mosque. At this point, he became more vociferous with his 'radical views', hoping to curry favour with the other attendees. To his surprise, calls to 'kill the infidels' weren't met with chants of, 'God wills it! God wills it!' No. In a strange twist, the other mosque attendees reported him, ironically to the FBI, out of concern he may be a terrorist. An embarrassing event for the FBI that ended in the courts.

A few years later, I found myself working close to the spectacular MI6 building on the River Thames. A little like Willy Wonka's Chocolate Factory, nobody entered, nobody exited. Instinctively I would hold my breath and dip my head when walking past. Surely that would make all the difference. Ironically, our dungeon-like office at the time resembled an Iraqi torture cell (from what I'm told). Just the right setup to deliver our project, mind.

'I BET some right dodgy things are going on in these mosques. I don't trust them,' Joe whispered over a fish, chips, and beans lunch.

'What, you mean like special bomb-making how-to sessions after morning prayers? Or creating a Wiki page on joining ISIS?'

'Yeah... Something like that, All this preaching for GEE-HAD', he replied.

'GEE-HAD?'

'Yes, these people are crazy. You're, ok though. I think.'

'I wouldn't bank on it,' I batted with my sternest poker face.

'Eh?!'

'What do you think GEE-HAD means?'

'Kill all the infidels?'

'If it meant that, there wouldn't be many people walking around.'

'Kill some infidels?'

'You're not getting warmer. It means to struggle or exert effort, and has wide application.'

'Including kill all the infidels?'

'It can be used in a military or a combative sense. If someone breaks into my home and tries to assault my family, I can fight back, yes?'

'Er, yes...'

'Sure, the term is used and abused for all types of unacceptable activities these days.'

'You're not wrong about that.'

'Seriously, you should pop down to your local mosque one evening and have a look for yourself.'

Joe threw down his cutlery. I could see the blood rushing to his face. 'Look at those three girls who left the UK to join ISIS. Why would anyone do that? The mosques are responsible!'

'Well, I think they were groomed over the Internet, not in any mosque. Told a pack of grandiose lies and distortions. So, if you want to blame anyone, have a chat with Tim Berners-Lee. Naïve, yes. Foolish, yes. Ignorant, yes. But, at fifteen years of age, if they were groomed for anything else, they'd be considered victims. To quote one MP, 'more sinn'd against than sinning³'.

IN 2019, we had a visit from local counterterrorism at our local mosque. Surprisingly, there was no attempt at subterfuge.

'Hello, I'm Richard from local counterterrorism.'

Eh? Well, you're not very good at this undercover stuff, are you, Richard? I dampened my instinctive response and vigorously nodded my head. 'Oh, ok... Welcome to our humble mosque. How can we help you today?'

'Well, I've come to see what goes on inside this mosque. Standard practice. We're doing the same with all the mosques in the area.'

'Rightio. Have you got any ID?' He flashed a card, which could have been his bus pass. 'Well, that seems all in order. You'd better come right in. Just pop your shoes off here.'

Richard awkwardly removed one shoe, almost keeling over and hitting his head on the shoe racks. *I hope you've done your homework and worn clean socks, Richard.* I glanced at the gaping hole in his left sock, as he tried to cover it. *Evidently not.*

'Ok,' I said, 'let's keep this hush-hush so you can see what really goes on. Follow me. If you keep quiet, everyone will just think you're a new convert, ready to be radicalised. The ginger hair will help. Quite popular with converts, don't you know.'

'Eh?'

'Never mind. Just joking. Oh, do you have a hidden camera or mic? Will we see this later on YouTube?'

'Er, no.'

Richard followed me into the main hall, miserably failing to blend in with the brothers at the back. I left him to chew over the Friday sermon. Thirty minutes later, I caught him fiddling with his shoes. 'Don't worry, you'll get the hang of it. You'll be doing it blindfolded, under a dripping wet rag soon. Anything to report?'

'Eh? It was an interesting talk, actually. I'll be back.'

'Any nefarious activities?'

'None, sir.'

'Just one, mo. A little gift.' I grabbed a couple of leaflets on terrorism and ISIS. I handed them to Richard; leaflets refuting terrorism and ISIS, that is.

'Oh, thanks, I'll read these tonight.'

'Sure Rich, pop in any time. We're open 365 days a year, even on Christmas Day.' I waved as he disappeared down the street.

10. BACK HOME

To nawihte ne hopað, se to hame ne higeð.
'He hopes for nothing, who does not think about home.'

— DURHAM PROVERBS

I've been hearing, 'Why don't you go back home, we don't want your lot round 'ere' – with slight variations – for the best part of forty years. Such calls were direct and industrial in the early days growing up in Burnley, but they're much more subtle these days. Being told 'go back home' as a 6-year-old is confusing. What did it mean? Go back home to my house? Go back to Burnley? *Well, I am already home, you buffoons!* But it isn't a great time to ask for clarification or additional detail when surrounded by a pack of snarling, salivating youths.

'Jig, why don't you go back to Wogga Wogga Land?' Wogga Wogga Land wasn't in our Junior World Atlas (1980 edition). Amjad soon enlightened me on their intent.

'This is our country – you've fuckin' come over here, stealing our jobs. You should all be sent on a boat back home. I'd pay for it myself.' One comment I received from a teenage girl travelling into London, while advising her about putting her muddy trainers on the seats. After allowing her words a few moments to marinate, I smiled and responded, 'I think we're on different paths at present. Though there's always hope. Also, I don't think we compete for the same jobs, either.' That bamboozled her sufficiently to remain silent for the rest of the journey.

There was talk of 'voluntary repatriation' back in the 70s. The voluntary part no doubt involved a group of lively youths knocking on the door at 03:00. I reckon we'd need a smidgeon more than the £1000/head on offer. I don't think the girl was offering even that.

The events of 9/11 and 7/7 certainly complicated matters. Sending one ethnic group home sounded eminently doable, but asking adherents of a particular religion, comprising perhaps 30 ethnicities, to go back home is a tad trickier. And all the more difficult when large numbers of those adherents trace their lineage back to these Isles.

So where is home?

10.1 BURNLEY FC

In his *Meditations* treatise, Marcus Aurelius penned some wonderful snippets he'd learned from his family, teachers and mentors. For a start, he'd cleverly worked out which football team to support, or rather which not to support, long before the game was invented.

'(I learnt from my tutor) not to become a Green or a Blue supporter at the races, or side with the Lights or the Heavies in the amphitheatre; to tolerate pain and feel few needs; to work with my own hands and mind my own business; to be deaf to malicious gossip.'

If only we'd listened. It seems Marcus would have handled the tabloids and Twitter abuse well, too.

IT'S A WELL-TRODDEN SCRIPT.

'Where on earth is that accent from?! Sounds odd...'

'A small town in the north of England, near Manchester – Burnley – though the pure accent has been polluted over the years with travels to the Middle East, London and, er, Swindon.' I always anchor with Manchester. Who hasn't heard of Manchester United?

'Barley?'

'BURN–LEY. Famous football team. Ever heard of it?'

'Er, no, don't think I have.'

'You know, Burnley used to be one of the most affluent areas in the world,' I gush. 'During the height of the industrial revolution, it was a powerhouse. Have you heard of the Weavers' Triangle?'

'Er, no.' Eye glaze is forming at this point.

'Well, that's in BURN–LEY.'

'So, you must go and watch the football often, then? Hang on, though, just one minute. Don't you support Manchester United? You're not one of these glory supporters, are you? That's disappointing! I expected better from you, Asif!'

'That's a tricky one,' I finally say, mustering a squeak.

'LOOK, our next trip to visit Burnley coincides with the home game against Man United!' my daughter squealed with excitement.

I pause. 'Aha, yes, seems you're right.'

'Where should we sit? Which stand? I'd like somewhere up high for the view!'

Stony silence.

'Eh, Dad? Dad? What's wrong?! We must go!'

THIRTY-FIVE YEARS earlier in the school playground:

I raced past the first stodgy defender, deftly round another, and, through on goal, slotted the ball beyond the keeper. It bounced hard off the brick wall. Raising my hands, as though I'd just scored the last-minute winner in the European Cup final, I raced back to my teammates, arms hoisted in jubilation.

'Oi, Paki... What football team do you s'port?' asked Andy. He was a brute of a boy, dissolute in his habits, who sported fierce red hair and a menacing freckled scowl. He was a couple of years older, and regularly terrorised the playground, without a crumb of discrimination. He didn't care. *Hang on, how did we even end up on the same team?*

I wasn't an avid football supporter at eight, although I had a passing interest. Perhaps demonstrating a lack of interest would antagonise him further. After all, we were playing on the same team.

His glare still firmly fixed, I felt compelled to respond. After a few quick calculations, I barked, 'Burnley, of course. My home team. What team would I support!?' I even surprised myself with the response.

I didn't think it possible, but his scowl morphed into an even more gruesome look. 'You don't s'port Burnley, you dirty little Paki! If you say that again, I'll kick your fuckin' 'ead in! We don't want Pakis s'portin' Burnley! There are no Pakis at Turf Moor! No black bastards! Stay out!'

Ok, ok, calm down. He knew how to take the shine off an occasion. Maybe it was a predictable response. As we stood in the middle of the playground, with the rest of the boys smirking and giggling, I felt a little disenchanted with the game. Though perhaps most disappointing, my maths had also failed me.

Andy helped with our decision-making process. One thing was clear: we needed another club. Around the same time, Amjad's interest in football had peaked. He decided Manchester United would be our team. I suggested Liverpool as a better alternative, given their success in the 70s and early 80s. He made it quite clear the matter wasn't for further discussion – Manchester United it was. It would take another ten years for us to agree with him.

I'm yet to watch a game at Turf Moor. Even in 2021, the view from the famous Burnley terraces seems a little too uncomfortable. Perhaps one day.

10.2 SIBERIAN FINNISH PUNJABI INTEGRATION

A full six feet and half an inch; lightly tanned hue; nondescript accent (with an occasional northern sounding diphthong); a sprinkling of bizarre Punjabi tones. It's not easy to guess where I'm 'from'. The question would feature highly in my FAQ. I *never* take offence to the question, as it's almost always well-intentioned (plus, I'm guilty of asking it myself). Unsurprisingly, when someone asks, they want to know about the origins of my parents/ancestors. When I'm feeling particularly uncommunicative or curt and respond with Burnley, I'll receive the mandatory, 'No, no, where are you *really* from?' Let's face it, an ancestral tale of poverty in pre-partition India, a perilous migration to Pakistan, followed by an equally hazardous journey to the UK via umpteen other countries, all in a dilapidated Toyota, is more interesting than 'Burnley' as a stock answer.

'Asif, can I ask you a question?' Pete looked bored.

'Er, is it about my beard?'

'No...'

'Ok, shoot...'

'Are you British, English, Pakistani, or something else? Do you feel part of this society? Er, well integrated?'

His question transported me back to primary school again:

'Who can tell me how many countries we have in the UK?'

My hand shoots into the air. 'Miss... England, Scotland, Wales and Northern Ireland.'

'Yes, very good, Asif. So, do we have any Scots in the class?' Isla raised her hand.

'Any Welsh?' Silence.

'Any Irish?' Silence.

'Ok, and how many English?'

The remainder of the class raises their hand, including me.

'Oi, Asif, you're not English – you're a Paki,' screamed Gary. The class erupted.

Genetically, my school chum's argument appeared sound at the time. How could I possibly be English?

'That's a good question,' I finally respond to Pete, 'but it may take some time to explain.'

'Excellent. I've only got boring meetings this afternoon. Let me get you a coffee.'

Pete's question is more tortuous than it first appears. Firstly, we have to suspend our faculties of science, reasoning and logic for a moment, otherwise, we'll get bogged down in a gooey, boggy swamp of sticky questions. For instance, is English an actual ethnicity, or is Anglo-Saxon heritage an ethnicity? Didn't the Angles and Saxon Germanic tribes migrate here in the first place? What about those pesky invading Romans who didn't fancy going 'back home'? Did someone say migrants and invaders? In that case, maybe it's all down to skin colour? What about the white-skinned people who've lived in England for generations, but have Irish or Welsh ancestry? Are they English?

I'm going to sneakily sidestep the historical and scientific questions, which are clearly beyond the scope of this work. Instead, I'm going to focus on the lived experience. From the time I could fathom the question until I left university, I would never have described myself as English or even British. Even through my early career, I'd wonder how best to respond. This, despite the fact I was born in Burnley, had a British passport, a strong northern accent, loved fish and chips, and could queue with the best of them. The only exception materialised during team meetings, when I'd sometimes impishly remark, 'We English...' and see the muted, raised eyebrow reactions. 'We used to rule the world,' I'd continue, while shaking my head. 'Now look at us! Oh, how we've fallen!' Head in hands.

Growing up, we considered the terms 'British' and 'English' too loaded. We'd been hard-wired from a very early age, weaned on Enoch, the National Front, British National Party, and skinheads swinging the Union Jack and St George's Cross. The flags were part of their iconography, embossed in our memory as racist symbols. If England played any other team, we supported the other team by default. That covered all sports without prejudice. When England played Cameroon in the 1990 World Cup, we supported Cameroon (who can forget the great Roger Milla?). When the West Indies played England at cricket, we supported the West Indies (and what a joy, with their four pace bowlers and Viv). When England played the All Blacks at rugger, we were all black. Why would we support the country that we felt had rejected us and pushed us to the periphery of society?

This position did gradually change as we grew older and became more comfortable with our identity. I certainly took advantage of my nationality when working abroad. Travelling to different parts of the world, it helped to define our identity and character as British. When we travelled to Pakistan, we were clearly British Muslims, a slightly different breed. Mind, we'd still fail Norman Tebbit's cunning integration cricket test.

But questions around integration are notoriously difficult. I studied calculus and complex integration for rather more years than I had hoped at college and university. Oddly enough, I haven't felt the need to dust off my textbooks or perform a differential equation since. I reckon questions around social and cultural integration are equally, if not more, complex. What do these terms mean? How do immigrant communities integrate into the wider society? What's the difference between integration and assimilation? Tough questions.

'The Muslim community cannot integrate into Western societies.' It's an oft-repeated phrase. Popping down to the local for a swift half? Eating a pork sarnie? Altering my name, so it's easier to pronounce? Wearing three lions on the shirt? Jettisoning my faith? Are these examples of successful integration or assimilation?

On the other hand, David Cameron, former Prime Minister, famously uttered: 'Integration is a two-way street.' I presume he was enjoying a spicy onion bhaji or samosa at the time.

Admittedly, some countries have found the 'two-way' part more troublesome than others. Look at the French model, for example, the model of *liberté, égalité, fraternité*, the French tripartite motto: demonising all things Islamic, halal meat, women wearing the hijab and niqab, even the rather bizarre burkini. What manner of liberty, egality and fraternity is this? What on earth would Jean-Luc Picard think?

Today, I still wouldn't say I was English. British, yes; Pakistani, yes; with a smattering of Finnish and Siberian ancestry thrown in for good measure.

10.3 A PENITENT DELIVERY

It's a quiet Friday evening, and the intercom buzzer blared three times in quick succession. *Goodness' sake, have you seen the Four Horsemen galloping across the horizon?* I rushed to the intercom handset. 'Hello?!'

'Yes, hello. Sainsbury's delivery.'

'Oh, that's disappointing. Come through the gate on the right.'

'It's not opening, mate. I keep pushin' it.'

'Not the big gate, the small gate on the right.'

'Eh? There's only a big gate.'

'ON THE RIGHT!'

'Oh, yes, now I see it. It's bloody murder trying to find this house.' *This guy has an odd accent*, I thought.

A few moments later, I see the man, lugging six heavy bags round the path, walking towards the front door. 'Right, where do you want this lot?'

'Just here's fine, thanks. Sorry, just a moment. We don't want any substitutes...' I knelt down to rummage in the bags, pulling out a box of Persil, a Kingsmill loaf... I glanced back up at him and froze in position. 'You look familiar...' I said. 'I'm getting deja-vu... Hang on, you're Carl? Carl ... Thompson?'

'Er, yes. Who are you?' His Burnley accent was now quite apparent.

'We went to primary school together. You were a year older.'

Carl screwed his eyes and stared.

'Yes,' I said, 'I remember you. Quite well, actually. You used to terrorise us in the playground! I only recognised you from down here! You thumped me once, left me spluttering, kneeling on the ground.'

'Uh, er, no, I think you've got the wrong person, mate. Look, I need to get on with my deliveries.'

I stood up, staring at Carl. 'Smelly niggers, you called us. Said we should all go back home. I never forget a name or a face.'

He grabbed the Kingsmill from my hand. 'Right, mate, I'll be off.'

'Not so fast... Don't worry. We all did silly things when we were young. Hopefully we grow out of the silliness. So, what have you been up to since we left school?'

'Well, for a while I played for Burnley reserves, but they dropped me.'

'For what, racist abuse? Assault?'

'No, no! I kept missing' training. Turnin' up late, an' that.'

I shook my head. 'What a wasted opportunity!'

'Yeah.'

'So, do you regret how you behaved in those days?'

'Look mate, I'm sorry for all that abuse. We were young and stupid. I remember you, now – you're Asif, right?

'Yes, that's me.'

'We were jealous of the Asian kids, so we picked on them.'

'Jealous of what?!'

'Doing well at school, an' that. I wish I tried harder, got some qualifications behind me. When I got kicked out of the football team, I didn't have anything else to do. I couldn't find another team to take me on, and then started on a building site. Then I got injured, and now I do deliveries.' He bent down and picked up the Persil.

'You can still get qualifications. Still learn.'

'Yeah, maybe.'

'Well, now you know where I live. And, our preferred washing powder... You should come round for tea and biscuits. Though, please spare the windows...'

'Eh? Right... Thanks, mate. See you around. I may take you up on that offer.'

He did, too.

10.4 TWO SPORTS BAGS

I've travelled around the world but always savour returning to Burnley: the famous Towneley Hall, the boating lake in Thompson Park, the sentinel-like wind turbines perched across the glorious countryside; the generally slower pace of life. When I feel the cool chill, strolling along the Leeds-Liverpool canal beside our old house, I think, *Yes, now, I'm home.* I seldom pass anyone on my morning walks without getting a nod and a 'how do'. That reaction is startling for someone who's lived the last twenty-five years around London when a 'how (are) (you) do(ing)' to a stranger will result in a quizzical look at the least and possibly a physical altercation.

Time softens the jaggiest edges. Walking around our old streets feels like a pilgrimage, minus the sandals and garb. Unfortunately, a new estate occupies the Rec area, and the school is also buried under housing, though they managed to keep aspects of it, including the glass roof. Thankfully, I do feel the place has changed for the better. It's less biting, less hostile, than when I clambered off the coach all those years ago.

Ironically, as I wander through the streets of my current town, I feel a discomfort: a discomfort when I see groups of Eastern European immigrants huddled on street corners, seemingly passing the whole day without purpose; a discomfort when I see immigrant youths creating mischief, domineering the pavement, harassing passers-by (one young lad even threatened to slit my throat); a discomfort when I see youths skipping school. But, also a *guilty* discomfort that perhaps I shouldn't feel the discomfort as a son of immigrants.

This is how we, too, were viewed and are still viewed. Looking back, I can understand elements of the prejudice we faced in the early years: a fear and ignorance of a new community, alien habits, different dress, food, language, and customs. A fear of the other.

Is there less racism generally around? Alas, not according to the 'statistics'. If you're black, just try missing a penalty for England, or having a poor game for a Premier League team. I wouldn't say that's quite the 'whip hand' predicted by Enoch in 1968. The introduction of modern media has shifted a good proportion of abuse online, too. At least in days bygone, the deuteragonist required a degree of old-fashioned boldness to abuse someone to their face. Now it can be done with a few clicks in the comfort of one's own reclining chair, and distributed across the world in a few nanoseconds. That's just not cricket.

Anti-Muslim sentiment (I've only used the word Islamophobia once) still chugs along nicely, too, twenty years on from 9/11, cresting with every new misdemeanour committed by a Muslim somehow acting in the name of the entire two billion, worldwide. As I often repeat, shouting *Allahu Akbar* before bashing an old granny with a cosh doesn't legitimise the act. The utterance neither legitimises granny bashing, nor legitimises indiscriminate killing. It's simply a criminal act.

The 'you look a bit like a terrorist' attitude is still prevalent, along with a decent amount of presumed guilt. Could be worse, mind. Much worse. *Sans citer de nom.* No, no, it's not all doom and gloom. A greater knowledge and awareness between communities does exist. There's an increasing level of Asian and Muslim representation in many spheres of modern life. And Britain is still one of the friendlier European places for a Muslim.

But there's still much work to do on all sides (as a 2021 MI5 report on failed plots highlighted). We need ongoing discussion and dialogue, at all levels, around the luncheon table and elsewhere. For ignorance, fear, and extremism can only be extinguished with knowledge and understanding.

ALHAMDULILLAH, my siblings and I still gather with Ma and Pa in Burnley, sip tea and munch biscuits. Amidst the clamour, we still set the world aright, and discuss the 'good old days' growing up in Burnley. The elder kids momentarily look up in bemusement, as we weave our yarns, before returning to whatever electronic device they have at hand.

My father, now in his eighties, suffers from all manner of ailments, including arthritis and back problems traceable to his days at Michelin. But, even in dotage, he's still evidently the patriarch; father of seven, grandfather of fourteen, the image of the fifteen stone, 6' 3" Cassius, forever entrenched in my memory.

We're also still blessed to enjoy my mother's roast chicken, *mullee* (Punjabi: radish) *paratha* and sage advice. Her vision of the future wasn't quite realised verbatim, however we all graduated from university with various degrees: law, medicine, optometry, maths, computer science, and journalism (there's always one). I can't attend to my mother's teeth when visiting, but at least I can fix the home computer and calculate bills on an Excel spreadsheet

As I finish writing, peering out of the window, with my son keepy-uppying in the garden, I am left to wonder: which rickety bus will he mount with his two sports bags?

NOTES

1. IN THE BEGINNING

1. Enoch is revered in Judeo-Christian tradition and Islam. He's known as Idris in Islamic literature.
2. Aeneid, Latin epic poem written from about 30 to 19 BC by the Roman poet Virgil. Composed in hexameters, about 60 lines of which were left unfinished at his death, the Aeneid incorporates the various legends of Aeneas and makes him the founder of Roman greatness.' [brittanica.com]
3. Slang for Britain, from the Hindi/Urdu meaning 'foreign', originally from Arabic meaning 'state/province' [etymonline.com].
4. The charges of dirty, smelly, unwashed, often follow immigrant communities and we were no exception. We found general insults often prefixed by one of these descriptors.
5. Unfortunately, Ali went on to fight once more against Trevor Berbick in 1981. No US State would sanction the fight, so it was moved to Nassau, Bahamas- 'The Drama in the Bahamas'.
6. Two main branches of the language exist, one spoken in Indian Punjab and one in Pakistani Punjab. The spoken language is quite similar between the two countries. I sometimes attempt to speak Punjabi with Indian colleagues at work, and hilarity aside, they generally understand. The written script differs considerably between the two. Gurmukhi is used in India and Shahmukhi in Pakistan.

2. TEENAGE TRAINING

1. Amin came to power in Uganda in 1971, when he overthrew the elected government and declared himself president. In a ruthless eight years an estimated 300,000 people were massacred, with Indian and Pakistani nationals expelled in 1972.
2. Mechanics aside, a critical credal difference exists between the two accounts. According to the Qur'an, the two made a mistake and God forgave them (also Adam doesn't try to blame Eve). Consequently, the concept of 'hereditary sin' doesn't exist within Islam. This important variance defines the differing nature of Jesus within Christian and Islamic traditions.
3. 'To understand how it emerged, it is essential to unite Einstein's theory with quantum theory. The best candidate is 'string theory', which views the basic building blocks of reality as tiny strings of mass-energy vibrating in 10-dimensional space-time.' [sciencefocus.com] *Well, that's obvious.*

4. The experience put me off further graduation ceremonies at university, one of which was held at the Royal Albert Hall. My mother still reminds me today,
5. Referring to Imran Khan, the former Pakistani cricketer and now President.
6. Meaning 'openness and transparency'. Popularised by Mikhail Gorbachev as a political slogan for increased government transparency in the Soviet Union.
7. The restructure of the Soviet political and economic system.

3. A FEW ACADEMIC MATTERS

1. An international Crime Tribunal finally convicted the Bosnian Serb General, Ratko Mladić in 2017 of genocide, crimes against humanity and war crimes. He was sentenced to life imprisonment. The presiding judge said Mladić's crimes ranked 'amongst the most heinous known to humankind'. His partner, Radovan Karadžić, was also convicted of genocide a year earlier.
2. Lieutenant Commander Worf 'Star Trek: Next Generation – The Emissary'
3. Other-Race Effect (ORE) is the tendency to recognise and remember faces of one's own race more readily than those of other races.
4. Orthodox Jews generally don't write the names of God.
5. Said to be descendants of Noah's eldest son, Shem. 'Member of any of a number of peoples from ancient southwestern Asia including Akkadians, Phoenicians, Hebrews and Arabs' [Merriam-Webster]. Interestingly, I could follow portions of *The Passion of the Christ*, spoken in Aramaic, albeit while looking away from the screen – a brutally gory film, but fascinating from a linguistic perspective.
6. A prayer of blessings said by Muslims after mentioning the name of the Prophet.
7. Moses ben Maimon [1138-1204 CE] medieval Jewish philosopher and scholar, known as Maimonides. Born in Cordoba and served as personal physician of the famous Muslim leader Salah ad-Din Ayyub [1137-1193 CE]. He wrote his famous work 'Guide for the Perplexed' in Classical Arabic using the Hebrew alphabet.
8. Often referred to as 'Jewish penicillin'. A cure for 'asthma, weight gain, and leprosy' amongst other ailments, according to Maimonides.
9. 'It was under the influence of the Arab and Moor revival of culture, and not in the 15th century; a real renaissance took place. Spain, not Italy, was the cradle of the rebirth of Europe.' [The Making of Humanity, Robert Briffault]

4. ROAD TO EXIT

1. Ironically, the word alcohol (as with many words beginning with 'al*') is derived from the Arabic word *al-kuhul* meaning a type of metallic powder (similar to antimony), a by-product of the distillation process. Perhaps more interesting, though less clear, is the origin of the word 'spirit' in relation to strong alcohol. One theory suggests a connection with the Arabic word *ghoul* (which became ghoul in English)- an evil spirit! The Qur'an [37:47] references the word in rela-

tion to a delicious wine the inhabitants of paradise shall drink, without experiencing any ill effects.

2. If still in doubt about the harm, Paul Merson's book 'Hooked' is worth a read.

3. Adam, Noah and Abraham are all revered prophets in Islam, as are Abraham's sons Ishmael and Isaac.

4. It never ceases to amaze how many individual words Punjabi/Urdu exist to describe specific relations. For example, *Salehar* is my wife's brother's wife and *Puppo* my father's elder (not younger) sister. A generic 'Uncle and Auntie' are a lot easier.

5. See Qur'an [10:91-92] for an interesting reference in relation to the preservation of his body.

5. EASTWARD MIGRATION

1. A common phrase in Islamic and Arab tradition: the 'Baab (chapter) of such and such'.

2. As You Like It: Act 4 Scene 1

3. Five logical arguments for the existence of God summarised by the Catholic philosopher and theologian St. Thomas Aquinas [1225-1274 CE]

4. When the Danish footballer Christian Eriksen collapsed on-field during the Euro 2020 tournament, the footballing world stopped and prayed. Suddenly football didn't matter one jot. Not to the fans in the stadium (a Nordic, Finnish / Danish derby, too), or the fans at home, or the pundits on the BBC covering the game, all of whom emotionally said as much. Yes, the footballing world stopped and prayed for Christian. That's the same programming, the same underlying code, praying for Christian.

5. An MI5 report published shortly after 7/7 based on hundreds of case studies identified two repeating themes: vulnerability and 'lack of religious literacy'.

6. Did I mention I got married during my time abroad? Though this endnote is far too narrow to contain that saga.

7. *Qahwah al-bun* – literally 'wine of the bean'. The word coffee entered the English language via Dutch *koffie*, borrowed from the Turkish *kahve*, borrowed from the Arabic *qahwah* [etymonline.com].

6. BACK TO BLIGHTY

1. Columbo: How to Dial a Murder – a masterful episode.

2. See the 'Islamic Origins of Common Law' http://scholarship.law.unc.edu/cgi/viewcontent.cgi?article=3823&context=nclr for an interesting discussion on the topic.

3. One of the seven Millennium Prize Problems from the Clay Mathematics Institute. An award of $1,000,000 awaits the clever person(s) who can solve.

4. A superbly crafted phone, only ruined by the awful Microsoft Windows Mobile operating system.

7. WORKPLACE GYMNASTICS

1. Henry VIII established a 'Master of the Posts' in 1516, a position renamed 'Postmaster General' in 1710.
2. Term used by Christian writers in the Middle Ages to describe Arab Muslims, Persians, and Turks. Possibly from the Arabic *sharqiy* meaning 'easterner' [etymonline.com].
3. Mentioned by Bruce Lee in his 'Jeet Kune Do'.

8. CULTURAL AND RELIGIOUS NUANCE

1. According to Biblical prophecy, the place of the 'final battle' between good and evil. The word Armageddon is derived from the Hebrew 'Har Megiddo'.
2. Diogenes of Sinope [404-323 BC] an odd character, famous for carrying a sleeping tub around with him.
3. Attributed to the Chinese philosopher Lao Tzu.
4. Quintus Horatius Flaccus [65-8 BC] the leading Roman lyric poet during the time of Augustus.
5. Organisation that records and measures anti-Muslim incidents in the UK and supports its victims.
6. His Turkish great-grandfather Ali Kamel.
7. The Greek Stoic philosopher [50-135 CE] best known for his works 'Enchiridion' and 'Discourses', foundational works in Stoic philosophy.
8. Emperor of the Ming Dynasty [1328-1398 CE]. Famously wrote a hundred-word eulogy in praise of The Prophet: https://en.wikipedia.org/wiki/The_Hundred-word_Eulogy

9. THE ALGORITHM OF CHAOS

1. Muhammad Ibn Musa al-Khwarizmi [780-850 CE], the Persian polymath produced major works in mathematics, geography, and astronomy. Often described as the Father of Algebra. The word algorithm is derived from his name.
2. The group known in the West as the *Kharijites* (Arabic: Renegades) appeared during the first century of Islam [7th Century CE]. They introduced radical, extreme beliefs and rebelled against the fourth Caliph Ali (the cousin and son-in-law of the Prophet). Many modern-day extremist groups share beliefs with the Kharijites. Islamic scholars throughout the ages have warned against the group.
3. King Lear Act 3, Scene 2

ACKNOWLEDGMENTS

'Whoever does not thank the people, does not thank God.'

— PROPHET MUHAMMAD (ﷺ)

I first started writing this book in early 2011. Once I'd sketched Chapter 1, I faithfully filed the manuscript away with the others in a deeply nested folder structure on my ThinkPad. Over the following years, family commitments, an active social portfolio, and a constant stream of IT projects didn't leave much time (or cerebral capacity) to continue with the book. Well, that's my miserable excuse.

Deep into the second 2020 COVID lockdown, once I'd become a little bored with my newly acquired hobbies (including iPad drawing), I flicked through my portfolio of unfinished manuscripts. *Well, if there's any chance of finishing one of these in a reasonable timeframe, it's this one*, I thought. With that, the creative juices started to flow, and neurons sparked once more.

Around the same time, several distinct events also converged. First, I casually picked up *Boy* from the coffee table (my son's copy, I think) and read about Roald Dahl's regimented writing routine described at the back of the book. I needed something similar, but swapped his pencils, sharpener, and gin, for Microsoft Word, Excel, and PG Tips.

Second, I found a useful article stressing the motivational and psychological importance of 'completing a piece of writing'. This is presumably why people seldom complete an 80,000-word book off the bat. I wrote a couple of 1000-word articles on LinkedIn, which proved surprisingly motivational. Finally, my sister mentioned on the family WhatsApp group, that she was attending a creative writing course and penning her own experiences.

By the start of 2021, I set myself the goal of completing the book before the end of the year. I added an hour's worth of writing to my daily regime, and by September 2021, I'd completed the first draft (though, in my mind, I'd 'finished'). I sent the manuscript to John, my editor, who suggested a 'few improvements'. Roll on another five months, and I finished, again.

Some snippets the reader may or may not find interesting:

1. For a few moments, at least, I considered sending the manuscript to a traditional publisher. However, their position: 'If we're interested, we may get back to you in about six months – and by the way – you'll lose rights to the content' soured the option a little. Aliksir (Elixir) Press was born shortly after.

2. Excel helped me track the number of words written each day. Though, of course, it quickly became a distraction as I fiddled with the hundreds of ways displaying two simple columns of data.

3. I used Vellum on the Mac to format the book (superb software, but quite costly).

4. The title and subtitle morphed at least 20 times.

5. A graphic designer based in Macedonia created the initial book cover (yes, I scoured the world to find the right people). However, I quickly realised the benefit of learning Photoshop for myself; otherwise, I'd forever ask for minor revisions. In the end, I became reasonably adept with GNU Image Manipulation Programme (GIMP) – a free, slightly esoteric, Photoshop variant.

6. The final word count: 84,500. More words than I expected or planned, particularly after snipping several sections.

7. I'll leave it there, as I can't exceed 313 pages.

Clearly, it's not possible to write such a book in isolation, and there are many people I could mention at this point. However, in the interests of limited time and space, I would like to especially thank:

-My parents for their ongoing enthusiasm and support (they are eagerly awaiting the Urdu translation).

-My wife and children: Maryam, Saalihah, Dawud and Asma, who reviewed the book and suffered innumerable 'don't worry, I've nearly finished' comments.

-My brothers and sisters: Tasneem, Amjad, Sajad, Amer, Uzma and Atique, for their unwavering support, encouragement, and the usual robust Rana-sibling critique.

-John Seymour (of WriteNow), who provided valuable advice throughout, and diligently checked the final manuscript.

-The countless colleagues, friends, and preacher community, who all provided input, knowingly or unknowingly.

Everything happens in its correct time and place. This book wouldn't have been quite the same back in 2011.

ABOUT THE AUTHOR

Asif Rana is an IT Consultant by trade, and has worked with some of the largest and most celebrated global organisations (some not so celebrated). He's also started more than half a dozen books, though never quite reached Chapter Two.

He holds a Bachelor's degree in Pure Mathematics and Master's degree in Artificial Intelligence from Imperial College, London (neither were particularly useful while completing this book). He lives in the South of England with his wife and four, trying children.

When not writing or buried in some recondite IT project, he enjoys keeping fit, still convinced a sub 20-minute 5K is within reach.

Asif is a reluctant social media user, mostly restricting activities to LinkedIn for professional related matters (https://www.linkedin.com/in/asifrana) and Twitter to complain about train companies.

If you would like to report typos/errors, express disagreement, have a chat, or generally provide feedback, email: asif@aliksirpress.com

Printed in Great Britain
by Amazon